DAILY LIFE DURING

THE CALIFORNIA GOLD RUSH

D0075358

DAILY LIFE DURING

THE CALIFORNIA GOLD RUSH

THOMAS MAXWELL-LONG

The Greenwood Press Daily Life Through History Series

 GREENWOOD

AN IMPRINT OF ABC-CLIO, LLC
Santa Barbara, California • Denver, Colorado • Oxford, England

Library of Congress Cataloging-in-Publication Data

Maxwell-Long, Thomas.
  Daily life during the California Gold Rush / Thomas Maxwell-Long.
    pages cm. — (Greenwood Press daily life through history series)
  Includes bibliographical references and index.
  ISBN 978-0-313-36309-2 (hbk. : alk. paper) —
ISBN 978-0-313-36310-8 (ebook)   1. California—Gold discoveries
2. California—Gold discoveries—Social aspects.   3. Gold mines and mining—California—Social aspects.   4. California—History—1846–1850—Social aspects.   I. Title.
  F865.M39   2014
  979.4′04—dc23   2014017769

ISBN: 978-0-313-36309-2
EISBN: 978-0-313-36310-8

18 17 16 15 14   1 2 3 4 5

This book is also available on the World Wide Web as an eBook.
Visit www.abc-clio.com for details.

Greenwood
An Imprint of ABC-CLIO, LLC

ABC-CLIO, LLC
130 Cremona Drive, P.O. Box 1911
Santa Barbara, California 93116-1911

This book is printed on acid-free paper ⊗

Manufactured in the United States of America

CONTENTS

PREFACE

Gold is a chemical element represented by Au on the Periodic Table of Elements and has the atomic number 79. Since the beginning of time, gold has been known around the world as one of the most sought after precious metals. Most gold is under ground. In California, however, due to its unique physical geography, hundreds of tons of pure, placer gold were in its rivers and streams before the Gold Rush. Gold is found as nuggets, grains, alluvial deposits, and veins in rocks. Gold is one of the softest of the shiny metals and therefore one of the most malleable. While not a metal of particular value as a conventional tool, in the age of computer technology gold has found its way into the high-tech world as a useable metal in the construction of circuit boards and recovery chips. Additionally, gold is an effective metal for medical procedures, in particular dental work, and radioactive gold isotopes are also utilized in some cancer procedures. However, when most people think of gold, the two most common uses come to mind: jewelry and financial exchange. Archaeologists have uncovered gold adornments, artisan works, and gold currency from Ancient Egypt that may date back to 3000 BC.

While a very malleable metal, gold is also durable in the recycling process. According to a *National Geographic* article "The Real Price of Gold" published in January 2009, roughly 161,000 tons of gold have been unearthed, used, and reused on countless occasions since the beginning of time. In effect, gold excavated nearly 5,000 years ago could conceivably have been recycled and used in hundreds of ways and now may actually be found in the wedding rings of contemporary Americans. It is impossible to know where, in fact, the gold we use today originally came from, and for what uses it may have served before ending up inside our mouths as dental work. Gold today is also recognized as one of the most stable commodities traded globally. One other common thread that has connected gold with the vast majority of societies throughout history is the aggressive manner by which it has been collected. Societies have not just waged war over gold; some societies have actually faced annihilation because of gold. Such was the case in the Americas. This is due to the value that humans have placed upon this shiny metal, and its relative scarcity on the earth.

No other so-called gold rush has ever demonstrated this better than the California Gold Rush. When examined in its historical context, the California Gold Rush brought about such dramatic changes in the population of territory, the environmental impacts from mining and population growth, national and international politics, as well as economics that it ranks as one of the most significant events in the history of the United States. The social implications, internal to California, include the most efficient series of genocides against Indigenous societies in the nation's history as well. In fact, during its statehood infancy, California passed a series of bond initiatives and requested further funding from the U.S. Congress to pay ad hoc militias to hunt and kill Indians: men, women, and children. In contemporary geopolitics, these would be considered clear-cut cases of crimes against humanity, although in 1907, Congress issued military medals for those who participated in these and other "Indian Campaigns"; the militia who participated in the California Indian Wars far exceeded any other campaign in medals issued.

The environmental impact from the California Gold Rush is shown by changes wrought upon the land from the massive open pit mines that dot not only California but the entire West. There are continuing issues with arsenic, used in gold mining to separate the precious commodity from materials not so precious, and still lingering in so very much of the groundwater throughout the gold regions. The mass clear cuttings that took place throughout the state that helped sustain a housing boom that lasted for decades as well as the deforestation that took place so that one could "get at the diggings" much easier has left its mark. One need only drive down the highways and county roads in Northern California along the coastline and into the central valleys to see the absence of old growth Redwood forests. The impact made by the growth and development of the "roads" to California may be the greatest examples of man changing the environment to make transit more accessible. The most obvious carved out paths after the wagon train routes were the Transcontinental Railroad, the Panama Canal, and all of the highways that followed in their wake as the Eastern United States did all that it could to connect with the Golden State. The progression of people into the West did not end exclusively in California. The wagons, trains, horses, ships, and later cars all helped "fill in" the West that was east of the Golden State, a process that continues to the present day.

While many, even today, think of the golden-haired surfer as the quintessential Californian, the truth has been, and continues to be, very far from this image. The Gold Rush catapulted California into being one of the most ethnically diverse geographic regions in the world. And this beacon to emigrants and immigrants continues to foster the continued diversification of a state that has no single ethnic group that can claim majority status. Though the growth of the ethnic diversity of California came with many substantial bumps in the road, beginning with the wars wrought upon the California Indians and continuing through the racist anti-Asian legislation and laws, the Golden State has survived many periods in its history that were less than egalitarian. Perhaps the most lasting impact of the Gold Rush, and one that for several junctures in California history seemed to ring true, was the perception of California as a "Golden State."

In this work, the historical California is examined not only during the height of the Gold Rush years, 1849–1855, but also the pre–Gold Rush era and then through the close of the 19th century. In this manner, the reader will be able to fully understand the impact of this remarkable and unprecedented historical event. The changes that were wrought by the California Gold Rush can really only be understood in the context of what California was like previously and then the remarkable changes that followed.

Central throughout this book is how the daily lives of the historical actors in the pre– through post–California Gold Rush played out. In the wake of the rush for riches, Californians had access to remarkable economic opportunities that simply have not existed at any other place and time. A good number of the Argonauts who came for the gold found wealth in other areas, ranging from real estate to politics and agriculture to the hospitality industries—broadly defined. In the process, California "grew up" and it did so quickly; many might say a bit too fast—whether seen through its near instant statehood and a highly flawed first form of state governance, including its first state constitution, or in the arena of law enforcement or lack thereof. Gold Rush California, despite all of its remarkable trying times, remained a beacon to the world, a symbol of great possibilities, and with just enough stories of triumph to make the perception of the so-called California Dream seem plausible.

ACKNOWLEDGMENTS

There are many people to whom I owe a great debt of thanks in putting together this book. My former professor, still my mentor as well as my friend, Gordon Morris Bakken, who suggested me as a possible author and then provided some very sage advice, really beginning back in his fantastic graduate seminars in American History, American Legal History, Environmental History, American Military History, History of the American West, and California History. There is a very lengthy list of historians that lay claim to being one of Gordon's students and graduate students. As we can all attest to, Gordon not only focused on grooming top-notch historians, he also taught his students how to find their own muse and succeed. Gordon assigned a healthy and brilliant selection of readings in all of his seminars, and over the course of teaching us about history, he also showed us such a fine variance of works that we all came to understand that there were remarkably broad manners by which people reconstruct the past. Of course, this also broadened our own understanding of historical possibilities. While so many folks remember grad school as a "grind," and granted, some professors essentially made the experience something along those lines, Gordon Bakken made it exciting. I find myself among those who are most fortunate to be in this select group of historians and I am now, and will always be, most grateful to Dr. Bakken.

At my university, Dean Jamal Nassar has provided me with a remarkable amount of support and to list each individual example would be an essay unto itself. Dean Nassar is a man with great vision and remarkable dedication to his students, staff, and faculty, and on several occasions he assisted me in the acquisition of grants that permitted me to dedicate significant time to conduct research for and then compose this book. Additionally, Pedro Santoni (author and editor of the *Daily Life in the Mexican Revolution*), who served as my department chair for the first five years of my tenure, was always available when I needed advice, and he wrote many a letter of support for the numerous grant proposals that I composed over the years. The outstanding support that Pedro provided made the process of research and composition much easier.

My editor, Michael Millman, is not only a man of great talent but also one who possesses remarkable fortitude of character and who is as responsible for the completion of this work as anyone else. Michael always provided exceptional support and very strong prodding along the way.

My spouse, Roberta, is the most remarkable and inspirational person I have ever known. I dedicate this work to her and to our wonderful son, Alexander. Together, they provide me with all the love and happiness that anyone could hope for.

CHRONOLOGY

40,000 years ago	First Native Americans emerge in California.
20,000 years ago	Native Americans occupy and utilize all of California.
10,000 years age	Last Ice Age ends and Holocene begins.
	Megafauna, such as the Smilodon, short-faced bear, dire wolf, American lion and the mastodon, head toward extinction.
1500	Estimated Native American Population of California reaches 1.5–2 million.
1542	The first European explorer of California Juan Rodriguez Cabrillo, a Portuguese captain sailing for Spain, goes ashore in Southern California.
1579	English privateer Sir Francis Drake makes an emergency landing along what is contemporary Marin County, 20 miles north of San Francisco.
1595	Portuguese captain Sebastian Rodriguez Cermeno, sailing for Spanish interests, crashes along the same northern California Coastline as where Drake landed. After receiving considerable aid from the Coast Miwok, Cermeno and his entire crew walk to Acapulco, a trek that takes a year.
1602	Spaniard Sebastián Vizcaíno explored Central California's coastline with his northern most landing in Monterey Bay.

1769	Spanish colonization of (Alta) California begins with Gaspar de Portola serving as both military leader and governor. Franciscan priest Junipero Serra serves as first president of the Roman Catholic Missions in California. First mission, Presidio and Pueblo, is established in San Diego.
1770	Mission San Carlos Borromeo de Carmelo founded.
1771	Mission San Antonio de Padua and Mission San Gabriel founded.
1772	Mission San Luis Obispo de Tolosa founded.
1776	Mission San Francisco de Asís (Mission Dolores) and Mission San Juan Capistrano founded.
1777	Mission Santa Clara de Asis founded.
1782	Mission San Buenaventura founded.
1786	Mission Santa Barbara founded.
1787	Mission La Purisima Concepcion founded.
1791	Mission Santa Cruz and Mission Nuestra Senora de la Soledad founded.
1797	Mission San Jose, Mission San Juan Bautista, Mission San Miguel Arcangel and Mission San Fernando Rey de Espana founded.
1798	Mission San Luis Rey de Francia founded.
1804	Mission Santa Ines founded.
1810	Mexico declares its independence from Spain.
1812	Russian's found Fort Ross.
1817	Mission San Rafael Arcangel founded.
1821	Spain recognizes Mexican Independence.
1823	Mission San Francisco Solano founded.
1833	Missions secularized by Mexican government.
1834–1848	Mexican Rancho Period.
1840	Clear Lake Indian Massacre led by Salvador Vallejo against Pomo and Wappo Indians.
1843	Sutter's Fort is built.
March 1846	Sacramento River Massacre led by John C. Fremont against Yana Indians.
December 1846	Temecula Massacre of Luiseno Indians.
1846–1848	Mexican–American War.
1847	Yerba Buena renamed San Francisco.

January 13, 1847	Treaty of Cahuenga ends Mexican–American War in California.
1848	Congress authorizes funds for Pacific Mail Steamship Company.
January 24, 1848	James Marshall discovers gold at Sutter's Mill.
February 2, 1848	Treaty of Guadalupe Hidalgo ends Mexican–American War.
March 1848	Sam Brannan begins to draw attention to the gold fields
August 19, 1848	The *New York Herald* announces the news of the gold discovery.
December 5, 1848	President James Polk informs Congress of the gold in California and the Gold Rush begins.
December 31, 1848	Nearly 7,000 gold seekers arrive in California.
January 1– December 31, 1849	An estimated 100,000 gold seekers arrive in California.
1850	Squatters' Riot in Sacramento on John Sutter's land.
1850–1851	Mariposa Indian War.
1850–1859	California militia and expeditions against the Indians.
April 22, 1850	The Act for the Government and Protection of Indians is enacted.
May 10, 1850	Bloody Island Massacre led by Nathaniel Lyon against Pomo Indians in Clear Lake.
September 9, 1850	California is admitted as a Free Soil state via the Compromise of 1850.
1851	First San Francisco Vigilance Committee is formed.
1852	Foreign Miners Tax is imposed.
1853	California Academy of Sciences established; hydraulic mining becomes common throughout California; Levi Strauss opens his first store in San Francisco.
September 1853	Sebastian Indian Reservation established—first Indian Reservation in California history.
June 24, 1854	Fort Tejon established next to Sebastian Indian Reservation to ensure that Indians remained on the reservation.
1855	Gold Rush concludes; gold recovery continues and geographically expands across California.

1856	Second San Francisco Vigilance Committee formed.
February 26, 1860	Wiyot Indian Massacre in Humboldt County, documented by Bret Harte.
1861	Civil War begins and California enters as a Union state.
1861–1865	Owens Valley Indian Wars.
1862	Congress enacts Morrill Land Grant Act providing for Land Grant Colleges, the Homestead Act providing land grants encouraging westward settlement, and the Pacific Railroad Act for the development and construction of a Transcontinental Railroad system
1865	Civil War ends; Mark Twain publishes "The Celebrated Jumping Frogs of Calaveras County."
1869	Transcontinental Railroad opens.
1870	San Francisco's Golden Gate Park established.
October 24, 1871	Chinese Massacre in Los Angeles.
1872	General Mining Act passed by Congress.
1872–1973	Modoc War, California last designated Indian War.
1876	Jack London born in San Francisco.
1877	California Workingmen's Party founded.
1879	California passes Second State Constitution.
1882	Congress passes Chinese Exclusion Act.
1890	First time California's population exceeds 1 million in U.S. Census (1,213,398).
1906	The Great San Francisco Earthquake.
1970	California passes New York as the most populous state.

1

CALIFORNIA BEFORE THE GOLD RUSH

PHYSICAL GEOGRAPHY OF CALIFORNIA

The physical diversity of California includes an eastern mountain range, the Sierra Nevada, a lowland central valley that extends from Mexico to Oregon, the Coastal Range mountains, much lower in elevation than their neighbors to the East, periodic deserts that run from the southernmost border to the northernmost, active volcanic regions such as Calistoga, and inactive volcanoes such as Mount Shasta. Northern California receives significantly more precipitation than the arid south. Snowfall is common from November through March on all mountain tops exceeding 10,000 feet, even on the peaks that tower above the Southern California desert communities in the Coachella Valley. California's active tectonic activity is well known, and its most famous fault line is the San Andreas, which runs 800 miles, north–south, and is actually the plate tectonic boundary between the oceanic Pacific Plate and the North American Plate. While gold has eventually been found in many regions throughout California, the easy-to-find surface gold, in particular in the beds of rivers and streams, was located along the western slopes of the Sierra Nevada. This is where the California Gold Rush began.

Why the gold existed, and continues to exist, in California is simply due to its geographic location and geologic forces. Tectonic plate movement and volcanic eruptions resulted in California rising from under the ocean to the surface. Somewhere in the range of 450 million years to 150 million years ago, the continual collision of the Pacific and North American plates resulted in enough action to form the land of California. The magma cooled and became the granite and also quartz that dominate the Sierra Nevada, the latter of which contained the larger, more significant veins of gold. Water erosion over the next 100 million years broke down the integrity of the rock and exposed the gold. As gold is denser than the other alluvial materials, it is not washed away as easily, which resulted in high concentrations in the river and stream beds. Since California is highly active geologically, this process has continued, literally uninterrupted, over these many tens of millions of years, thus producing the incredible yield of gold that has long since been the envy of the world.

CALIFORNIANS BEFORE THE GOLD RUSH

The first inhabitants of California comprised over 500 independent, sovereign nations of Native Americans. While no one knows for any certainty when California Indians began to populate the region, in particular due to their common burial practice of cremation, physical evidence suggests that they had first discovered California at least 15,000 years ago. For many generations, the common belief among scholars has been that during the last ice age, which ended somewhere around 10,000 years ago, peoples from Asia migrated across the land bridge that at that time connected Alaska with Russia. Other theories include migrations across the Pacific Ocean, essentially island hopping. Indeed, some California Indian creation stories contain a migration from across the sea, while others specifically refer to being created on terra firma, with exact, known locations, either on their traditional lands or from a distant point from which a migration took place. Regardless, the right of first discovery, which had been falsely invoked by Europeans when they invaded the Americas, was without exception the natural right of California Indians.

California Indian population prior to European invasion was for many years estimated at 300,000. However, contemporary scholars suggest, based on natural resources, climate, and Native American oral traditions, that upward of 500,000 or more indigenous people may have occupied this vast land of over 163,000 square miles prior to the European invasion. Additionally, as California

Indian Nations collectively held thousands of villages at the start of the European invasion, many of which had populations in excess of 1,000 individuals, simple arithmetic shatters the 300,000 mark. Contemporarily, California Indian Nations are reconstructing their ancestral maps through oral tradition, European and U.S. surveys, cartography records, and archaeological evidence, which continue to demonstrate the high population density of their ancestors, in their respective nations.

One question that non-Indians typically have in relation to this new paradigm of pre-Contact California Indian Nation population levels is how did those people in such semiarid regions sustain such a great number of lives. The answer is simple. Over the course of thousands of years, the peoples who made up the California Indian Nations developed keen, sophisticated understandings and approaches to environmental land management. Fire ecology controlled problematic insects and aided in soil enrichment; advanced horticulture practices ensured bountiful harvests; multiple and not necessarily linear uses for natural resources were utilized throughout California. All of these and other innovations contributed to sustaining life with relative ease, and of course, the incredible abundance of natural resources and a temperate climate played a significant role. However, one must also remember that not all of California enjoys the same temperate climate as San Diego. Indeed, snow is common in much of Northern California, in particular in the Sierra Nevada, as emigrants such as the Donner Party would realize. And Mark Twain has famously been known for having stated, "The coldest winter of my life was the summer I spent in San Francisco." While the quote is believed to have been falsely attributed to Twain, it is nonetheless recognized as an accurate statement by those who have experienced San Francisco in that season.

The reason why non-Indians today ask such a question is the false manner by which California Indians have been portrayed by the Europeans who invaded the land in the 18th century, by the United States as it sought justification for the "legalized" mass extermination of California Indians, and well into the 19th and 20th centuries by so-called academic and scholars, who, by dint of their training, in a social Darwinist fashion, sought to "study" the "exotic" and "primitive" others as specimens in a lab. Luckily, this mode of inquiry is as antiquated as the kerosene lamp.

The cultures and customs of Native American nations in California were influenced by their natural environment, as is the case with all societies around the globe and throughout time. Thus, the

Luiseno of Southern California whose lands stretched from the beaches of San Diego County to the interior deserts of Riverside County were as different from the Hoopa of Northern California, who lived along the coastline of Humboldt County and through the vast lands covered with Redwoods that once stretched into Trinity County, as were the Fins from the Greeks.

The language variation in Indian California was one of the most complex of any region of comparable size anywhere in the world. Indeed, California Indian linguists suggest that the number of languages most probably exceeded over 100. While cognates in these different languages did exist, as they often do with bordering societies, significant overlap was a rarity. Language, being the base of any culture, dictates that cultural variation must have been in as great a range as well.

The concept that the pre-Contact California Indians were primitive societies is a misnomer. While it is true that they used predominantly stone and wood tools as opposed to metal, in the 17th and 18th centuries, they were not "stone-age" cave dwellers, who were limited in their communication skills, artisan crafts, and without any system of cross-national commerce. For example, their vast trade networks that extended for over a thousand miles beyond their respective lands indicates a complex economic structure based not strictly on survival but also on regional artisan expertise and conspicuous consumption. Additionally, the long-held fallacy that California Indians strictly adhered to a life of peace and simple happiness, were without any knowledge of war (California Indians Nations have had their own respective histories of failed diplomacy), and had a diet primarily of roots, berries, and whatever fell from the trees is truly a form of soft racism—lower expectations of those who are deemed to be lesser inclined intellectually. This false representation of their intellectual capacities and unproductive use of the land and its resources justified the taking of their lands first by the Spanish and later the Americans. First, the Spanish declared the right of "discovery" gave them title to the land, and their justification for colonization was associated with protecting Divine interests; they declared their duty to convert the Indians into Catholicism and bring them into Hispanic culture and, in the process, "civilize" them. Today no one doubts the less noble, economic designs of the Spanish as being at the core of their motivation behind the colonization of the Americas. Later, when the Americans poured into the state and onto Indian lands, their planned and implemented attempts at genocide left no doubt of their intention to utterly remove Native Americans. Thus, it was in the attempt to put the evils of the past to rest, to cleanse the conscience, that the lie of the primitive "digger" was carried for so long, as it is much easier to justify for one's children the extermination of a lesser being than of ones co-equal.

DAILY LIFE OF CALIFORNIA INDIANS

Rather than attempt to compose a history of the daily lives and cultures of such an incredible range of pre-Contact Indian Nations, which would require more than one shelf of books, the following select examples are aimed at shedding some light on just a few.

One set of great overarching similarities that all California Indian societies shared was connected to spirituality, kinship, and ceremony. California Indian spirituality should not be confused as analogous with the majority of contemporary religions today and their roles in American society. For example, there was no separation of "church and state," nor was there any separation between spirituality and any aspect of life itself for California Indians. Spirituality was the fiber that was woven through every aspect of existence. Life, death, and nature were all bound together, utterly inseparable components of the greater understanding of existence, and at the core of spirituality itself. The concept of kinship was well defined in every California Indian Nation. Leadership, marriage, and land and resource ownership were defined components of kinship. As Europeans from Russia, Spain, and other nations noted, California Indians appeared to have ceremony rituals for virtually everything. While such a statement that was slightly hyperbolic, at least in comparison to their own Euro-Christian culture, California Indians did have longer, more extensive, and more complex ceremonies. Indeed, marriage and burial ceremonies often took place over the span of days as opposed to hours.

The material cultures of California Indians was influenced by the physical geography of their respective nations, as were all societies in the pre-industrial 18th century, before modern technology freed man from such limitations. Therefore, northwestern Indian nations such as the Hoopa and Wiyot were adept at utilizing Redwoods for home building and watercraft construction. And, as no California Indian society had knowledge of metal tools, creative solutions were required in their lumber industry. For example, when accessing trees that had not fallen as a resource, these northern societies used fire at the base of the mighty Redwoods to fell the trees. However, it should be noted that most California Indians historically did not cut down healthy living trees. Obsidian blades, arrowheads, and tools were common throughout Indigenous California. Though certainly not as durable as forged steel, obsidian is a highly effective material to construct sharp, serrated blades, which can be used for purposes ranging from the carving out of canoes to the cleaning and dressing of game.

A ubiquitous culinary set throughout California was the pestle and mortar. Most commonly made of bedrock and granite, the pestle and mortar was used for crushing, grinding, and blending materials. Due to their exceptionally durable nature, pestles and mortars had the potential to last not only for generations but also millennia as archeological sites continue to yield examples of these tools believed to be more than a thousand years old.

One of the most commonly traded artisan wares in California was the woven basket, which was made in a remarkable variety of sizes, forms, functions, and designs. Basket weaving was a highly respected and lucrative profession. Made from a variety of natural regional materials, such as sedge and willow, California Indian baskets continue to be one of the most actively sought-after California Indian artisan works today and are recognized for their artistic beauty, functionality, and durability. Basket types and uses ranged from a seed beater, a shallow, round-handled basket used for the removal and collection of seeds; storage baskets, typically large, and, as the name indicates, for storage of items, including foodstuffs; gift baskets, which were almost always the most elaborate in their design; serving baskets were typically shallow and broad and at times had intricate designs patterns; cooking baskets that would hold heated rocks as their heat source; water baskets, which were made of a double weave that would yield a leak-proof effect; basket cradle and caps, for the transportation and care of infants.

Jewelry and body adornments were common throughout California Indian societies. Shell beads were highly favored for necklaces, and given the expansive choices that the Pacific Ocean yields, colors and textures were diverse. While no California Indians wore feathers in the form of the famous Sioux war bonnets, many did fashion and create a wide range of elaborate feathered head and body adornments.

The ubiquitous bow and arrow was widely used by California Indians, as was the side bow, or atlatl, which delivered an arrow through a reflex action. Arrowheads were typically napped out of obsidian or flint, shafts were made from lightweight wood, such as willow, and feathers were commonly used for the fletching. Sketchings of California Indians during the late 18th and early 19th centuries reveal the similarities throughout California in the design of these weapons and hunting tools.

Home construction varied throughout California for Native Americans, reflective of the wide variety of climates. Northern California Indians, such as the Yurok and Hoopa, crafted wood plank homes that were most resilient and offered protection from cold in winter. In the much warmer Southern California region, Indians such as the Luiseno and Kumeyaay, built their homes, known as "kicha" by the Luiseno, and "ewaa" by the Kumeyaay, out of lighter wood materials and grasses that were efficient at keeping their residents cool during the long, hot summers.

FOOD

Hunting and gathering was a significant component in the daily lives of all California Indians. In the northeast, the Modoc, Atsugewi, and others enjoyed a well-balanced diet, nutrient and protein rich, which included salmon, a variety of berries, venison, grains, and rabbit. The outstanding obsidian from this once highly active volcanic region was a valuable trade commodity as well given its popularity for use as arrowheads. San Francisco Bay Area Indian Nations, such as the Miwok, Wappo, and Maidu, enjoyed an abundance of not only fish, including the salmon, but also the acorn, which could be harvested and stored in granaries. The acorn, the fruit of the Oak trees, has a special significance for many California Indians as a dietary staple. Inedible in the raw, if properly prepared through a soaking, leaching, drying and milling, a carbohydrate-rich porridge is the final product. Acorns are an exceptionally nutritious food, and with over a dozen varieties of Oak indigenous to California, Indians were able to effectively farm a crop that would provide them with a nutrition source that would not only simply sustain life but also promote great health. The nutritional value of some acorns includes a fat content in excess of 15 percent, vitamins A and C, complex carbohydrates in the range of 50 to 60 percent, and over 5 percent protein.

GEOGRAPHY OF CALIFORNIA INDIAN NATIONS

Some California Indian Nations were quite expansive, and in some cases, their territories were literally larger than the contemporary state of Connecticut. In Southern California, the Cahuilla, Kumeyaay, Serrano, Luiseno, Chemehuevi, and Chumash were examples of large, powerful, and ancient nations. Central California was home to the Yokuts, Paiute, and Ohlone. Northern California, which also had a greater number of smaller nations such as the Wappo, Cahto, and Wiyot, was home to the Miwoks, Pomo, Maidu, Wintu, Modoc, and Shasta. The first Indian Nations to be affected by the Gold Rush were the Yosemite Miwok, Washoe, Paiute, and Nisenan. Their lands held the easy–to-find surface, placer gold, though in time all California Indians were impacted by the California Gold Rush. These independent sovereign Indian nations typically shared the common political practice of permitting a significant amount of independence for their respective villages, which closely resembles the contemporary concept of home rule.

SPANISH INVASION OF THE AMERICAS

All would change for the California Indians once the Europeans arrived and began to colonize. The first such European Empire to do so, not just in California, but throughout the Americas was the Spanish. Their colonization of the New World began in earnest in 1492, when Christopher Columbus set sail from Europe and led three vessels, *Santa Maria, Pinta,* and *Nina,* in a quest to expand Spanish trade with China and India. Columbus, not knowing that the New World stood between Europe and Asia as he headed west, came upon the Caribbean islands and landed at one of the Bahaman islands, which he subsequently named San Salvador. Columbus made three more round-trip journeys between the Americas and Europe, and in his fourth and final expedition, he made contact with mainlanders from Central America. Throughout Columbus's colonization efforts, he exploited the indigenous populations, holding them in a state of virtual slavery when possible, forcing them to build Spanish settlement pueblos and collect natural resources, which included the mining of gold and other precious metals. Though his tales of gold routinely exceeded the reality that he knew, Columbus was able to procure enough of the shiny yellow metal to greatly expand the coffers of the Spanish crown and to whet their appetite for even more riches. Thus, the Spanish colonization of the Americas was a most aggressive campaign of conquest, the likes of which the world had never witnessed before or after.

Influenced by Columbus's wild tales of fantastically wealthy Indian nations, some of which he claimed lived in virtual golden cities, in 1519 the Spanish sent Hernan Cortez, a highly experienced

Conquistador, into what today is Mexico. Cortez and his men briefly warred against and then formed an alliance with the Tlaxcalteca, an independent nation that was fearful of being conquered by the most powerful Central American nation, the Mexica, commonly referred to today as the Aztec. In this alliance, the Spanish and the Tlaxcalteca conspired to launch an attack against the Mexica, beginning first with Cholula one of the towns under Mexica control. Cortez and his Tlaxcalteca allies massacred thousands of Cholulans, and the conquest of Central America began. Cortez plundered as much of the vast Mexica holdings of gold as he could, which impressed the Spanish Crown, and encouraged the next significant movement of Conquistadores into the New World.

In 1533, Francisco Pizarro entered the vast Incan Empire of South America and followed the same violent, destructive pattern of colonization that won Cortez kudos from Spain. Pizarro too experienced great success in his efforts, and as the Incan gold flowed into Spanish hands, more tales and fantasies of golden cities began to circulate throughout Europe. Francisco Vazquez de Coronado began his quest in 1540 to find the Seven Cities of Cibola, which, according to legend, were filled with gold. Coronado never found these fabled cities in his exploration of the Southwestern deserts of today's New Mexico and through the Plains states and into Kansas.

The Spanish also began to formulate plans to conquer and colonize California in the late 1530s. California at that time was considered a formidably difficult and far-flung region. Travel on land was hindered by the rocks and desert of Baja California as well as the great distance from Mexico City to Alta California. As the great Gold Rush historian J. S. Holliday noted, Alta California was the "Siberia" of the Spanish Empire in the New World. Regardless, New Spain's viceroy Antonio de Mendoza ordered Juan Rodriguez Cabrillo to explore the vast coastline in search of riches and Indians. Cabrillo's first mainland anchoring took place in what today is San Diego. Cabrillo explored as far north as Sonoma County. While heading back south, Cabrillo docked at Santa Catalina Island, where he injured himself, developed gangrene, and eventually died on January 3, 1543. While Cabrillo's official reports were lost, his adjutants apparently did not inspire the Spanish to colonize California, which they claimed were virtually devoid of wealth and inhabited only with poor Indians, unlike the famed Mexica or Inca. For the next 226 years, Spain ignored this northern region, though they continued to claim it fell under Spanish rule at least on paper.

SPANISH INVASION OF CALIFORNIA

In 1769, Spain set out in earnest to expand its empire beyond a mere parchment document of proclamation with the establishment of its California mission system. Two years prior, King Charles III had expelled the Jesuits from the Spanish Empire because he considered them subversive due to their independent thinking. The Jesuits had been the Roman Catholic order of priests who had developed and managed the Baja California missions, which King Charles also believed to be severely mismanaged. Charles selected the Franciscan order as the Jesuit replacement, and this decision proved fortuitous.

One of the prime motivations for this expansion into Alta California, generations after the first and last abandoned Spanish expansion into the region, was the aggressive growth of Russian economic outposts that had been cascading southward from their original point of entry and colonization in North America, Alaska. While the Spanish did not have the best military intelligence on the development of the Russians in North America, they did have knowledge of the Russian intent to construct fortified trading posts along the Pacific coastline, with southernmost locations in Alta California. It would be this aspect of the Russian expansion plan that gave Spain pause.

Russia in the last quarter of the 18th century was an empire on the move. Since the dawn of the Romanov era in 1613, Russia desired to extend its reach in a manner similar to Spain, England, and France. By the time of Catherine the Great, 1762–1796, Russia had moved from a second-tier European power to nearly on par with its continental neighboring empires as it opened fortified trading posts and small villages and established spheres of influence beyond its borders and in North America. Russia, however, would only extend its trading posts as far south as Fort Ross, about 50 miles north of San Francisco. Established under the watchful eye of Ivan Kuskov in 1812, Fort Ross was more an economic outpost than a formal Russian attempt at colonization. Kuskov and his men negotiated regular trade with the local band of Pomo Indians, the Kashaya. Kuskov himself developed a deep interest in the Kashaya as well as other surrounding Indian societies while he conducted his formal census of the Indian villages, a task that had both economic and militaristic significance. In the process of his ongoing interactions with the tribes, Kuskov recorded both populations and sites of the Indian villages in roughly a 50-mile radius of Fort Ross.

Although the primary objective was economic, with a focus on the fur trade, Russian settlement did expand slightly. The Russian settlement, known as the Russian Colony, reached out in the range of 30 miles from the fort, and even took in the Farallon Islands, located in the Pacific, nearly 30 miles from contemporary San Francisco. The Farallon station provided the Russians with an abundant supply of seal furs. In just under five years, the economy of Fort Ross had changed dramatically. The prodigious Russian fur trappers nearly eradicated the local animal populations, and rather than relocate to a new location, they shifted their economy to agriculture, both subsistence and trade oriented.

By the late 1830s, Fort Ross and its surrounding Russian settlements began to decline drastically. In 1841, both the fort and the colony formally folded. While the Russians did attempt to grow their enterprise in California, they clearly recognized Spanish hegemony over the region as evidenced by the repeated gifts of homage, which continued for a generation into the 19th century. Although the Russians never proved as ambitious or successful as the Spanish in their American endeavors, they nonetheless were a significant catalyst behind the development of the California mission system.

THE FOUNDING OF THE CALIFORNIA MISSIONS

The two men who were the architects for the Spanish takeover of California, Father Junipero Serra and Gaspar de Portola, were well chosen. The Crown named Serra "president of the missions" and Portola the "governor" of both Alta and Baja California. Junipero Serra was born in Majorca, Spain, in 1713, entered the Franciscan Order in 1740, and moved to Mexico in 1749. Serra proved most talented in all things logistical, and his ascendancy within the Franciscan Order was a surprise to none. In 1768 he was given charge of the Baja California missions, wherein he began to design a new plan for missionization, which would become the blueprint for what would transpire in Alta California in the following year. Gaspar de Portola was born into lesser Spanish nobility in Catalonia, Spain, in 1716. Portola entered the Spanish military as a junior officer in 1734, and he consistently demonstrated his leadership skills and military acumen, which led to a series of promotions early on. Portola was the senior officer in Baja California who was subsequently given the charge of expelling all Jesuits, an assignment that he carried out with great fluidity. In response to his demonstrated military and political skills, Gaspar de Portola was given the charge of military governorship of Baja and Alta California.

In 1769, Visitador of New Spain, José de Gálvez, officially sent Serra and Portola expedition into Alta California to found the mission in San Diego and the presidio in Monterey, thus began the Spanish colonization and missionization of Alta California. As virtually all Franciscans in Baja were needed for the expansion to the north, the Dominican Order was given the charge of administrating the Baja missions.

Beginning with the establishment of Mission San Diego de Alcala in 1769 and ending with Mission San Francisco de Solano in 1823, Spain founded 21 missions in California that extended from San Diego in the south to San Francisco de Solano in Sonoma to the north. The design of the California mission system had the specific aims of establishing missions, presidios, and pueblos in areas throughout California that had significant Indian populations, access to freshwater and also the sea, a physical location in the low country that allowed easy transportation, and an abundance of natural resources. The end objective of the Spanish was that once the Native Americans had become "civilized" in each successive mission, the entire facility would be turned over to the Indians, though still be retained as a part of the Spanish Empire. However, not one mission was ever released from the grip of the Spanish.

The California missions were established in the following order:

1. San Diego de Alcala–1769
2. San Carlos Borromeo de Carmelo–1770
3. San Antonio de Padua–1771
4. San Gabriel Arcángel–1771
5. San Luis Obispo de Tolosa–1772
6. San Francisco de Asís–1776
7. San Juan Capistrano–1776
8. Santa Clara de Asís–1777
9. San Buenaventura–1782
10. Santa Barbara–1786
11. La Purísima Concepción–1787
12. Santa Cruz–1791
13. Nuestra Senora de la Soledad–1791
14. San Jose–1797
15. San Juan Bautista–1797
16. San Miguel Arcangel–1797

17. San Fernando Rey de Espana–1797
18. San Luis Rey de Francia–1798
19. Santa Ines–1804
20. San Rafael Arcangel–1817
21. San Francisco Solano–1823

While the Spanish colonization model of California was not completely reflective of the brutal massacres and reigns of terror that had taken place in Mexico and in South America, it was nonetheless brutal and oppressive. As the Spanish established each mission, presidio, and pueblo, they forced California Indians who resided in each respective location to perform the labor of constructing the infrastructure and buildings under Spanish supervision. The most common form of productivity encouragement was negative reinforcement through physical and psychological punishment. Physical punishment came in three forms: corporal, extreme, and capital. Corporal punishments, beatings, were the most common form of attempted behavior modification. If an Indian were not working as diligently as the Spanish supervisor might believe necessary, it was not uncommon for the Spaniard to club or whip the Indian. When an Indian would refuse to submit or would blatantly break the orders or laws of a Spaniard, extreme punishment—severe bodily harm that resulted in broken bones, damaged appendages, or permanent impairments—were carried out. Just as in the case of the corporal punishments, extreme punishments were facilitated in public as a form of intimidation. Capital punishment was the last resort. The Spanish did not want to kill the California Indians; rather, they wanted to subjugate them to utilize their labor. However, if Indians were considered a threat, or deemed unwilling to surrender their sovereignty and accept Spanish hegemony, or if they fought back against the Spanish, a death sentence was the typical course of retribution carried out by the Spanish. It is also important to note that it was the duty of the Spanish military to carry out the punishment. Spanish soldiers also routinely raped Indian women and in this process spread venereal diseases in addition to the adverse psychological effects suffered by the Indians.

Other aspects of the forced subjugation of the Indians were the conversion to Roman Catholicism, the adoption of the Spanish language, and the attempted eradication of indigenous spirituality and culture by the Spanish. Daily life in the missions for the Indians was highly regimented and tightly controlled by the Spanish. Indian men and women were at first forcibly separated from each other, even if they were husband and wife. Children were separated from the adults, regardless of familial ties. In this manner, Indian families were fragmented. Understandably, California Indians were not receptive to the attempts the Spanish made to shatter their society and lives.

The regimented work schedule for the Mission Indians began before sunrise and continued until the sunset. Indians were responsible for all the labor that took place in the missions, presidios, and pueblos. Meals were brief affairs and offered only enough nutrition as to sustain life and permit labor. Indians had to ask permission from their Spanish overseer to relieve themselves and were typically physically held in check by group shackle systems. When foreigners visited the Colonial Alta California, they overwhelmingly noted the hostile fashion by which the Spanish ruled the Indians.

Throughout the missionization period, California Indians rebelled against the Spanish invasion and occupation. One of the earliest of the significant Indian rebellions took place only five days after the establishment of the first mission in San Diego and then again in 1775 at the very same mission. This 1775 attack by Indians was in response to the growing level of physical and mental abuse set forth by the Spanish. On November 5, 1775, a large force of Kumeyaay Indians surrounded the San Diego mission, executed the priest, Padre Jayme, and burned down the mission. Specific reason behind this rebellion, as collected during the extensive, brutal interrogations by the Spanish that followed, pointed to the decimating impact of the diseases the Spanish introduced, the coercive tactics implemented in the conversion process, and the general mistreatment of the Indians by the Spanish. Occurring just six years after the establishment of the San Diego mission, the 1775 rebellion was a sign of things to come as rebellions continued to be commonplace throughout the Spanish occupation. The last mission rebellions occurred in 1824, when Chumash Indians attacked and destroyed the Santa Barbara and Santa Ynez missions. The constant rebellions reflected the weak hold that Spain actually had on this region, and, more significantly, the refusal of the Indians to surrender their sovereignty. Throughout the missionization process, Indians continued to speak their respective languages in private and continued with their indigenous spiritual beliefs and practices out of the view of the Spanish. In essence, they continued being who they were and not simply Spanish peons. However, the inescapable truth is the concentration camp atmosphere of the California missions. The forced labor, the squalid living conditions for the

Indians, and the intrusive Spanish practice of introducing destructive flora and fauna that devastated indigenous plants and animals were a combined destructive force that was felt well beyond the walls of the missions. Ultimately, by the close of the mission era in 1836, over 100,000 California Indians lost their lives through disease, starvation, or murder at the hands of the Spanish.

MEXICAN CALIFORNIA

Beginning in 1810, Mexico began its war of independence from Spain. Following the U.S. Declaration of Independence in 1776, colonies throughout the Americas began to witness the seeds of rebellion being planted. After the successful establishment of the United States of America with a fully operational federal government in 1789, the fervor for independence grew throughout Latin America. After a long, protracted war that resulted in the death of over 15,000 colonials and nearly 10,000 regular Spanish soldiers, Mexico gained its independence, and Agustin Iturbide raised the Mexican flag and became the fledgling nation's Constitutional Emperor.

Alta California was not a significant concern of the Mexican government, following much in the fashion of Spain. Due to its relative far distance from central Mexico, low population, and thus weak productive economy, Alta California did not become a beacon for mass Mexican settlement and was widely ignored by Mexico City. The missions, though still in existence, did not receive the support that they had from Spain and thus began a period of significant decline.

As a device to encourage population growth and economic expansion, Mexico aggressively expanded its system of Ranchos. Vast tracts of lands, some of which were literally hundreds of thousands of acres, were granted or purchased by men of Spanish and other European descent. The regions most sought after were those with freshwater, closest to the sea, and with large labor forces, overwhelmingly California Indians. While ranchos did exist in Spanish California, the Mexican government vastly expanded this land system, in the hope of developing an agricultural empire in its northernmost coastal and semi-coastal region. While the Spanish Crown granted less than 40 ranchos, the Mexican government permitted over 800.

The process by which one could acquire a rancho did, at times, involve a bit of backroom politics; however, the legitimate process was most accessible. First, one needed to submit an application that stated what religion one practiced, their traditional occupation or skills, the size of one's family—children were also a part of the labor and management of the rancho—and a map of the proposed rancho. Second, the local government bureaucrat would check on the availability of the tract, with a brief inquiry into the applicant himself. Third, the applicant either was granted the land or refused. Fourth, if granted the land, a local judge or mayor signed the title of land over to the new ranchero. An important distinction between the Spanish and Mexican eras was that in the Spanish era, the land was still a possession of the Crown, while in the Mexican period ranchos were privately held by the rancheros.

In 1833, the important Secularization Act was passed in Mexico. By the late 1820s, it had become apparent that the Mexican government was not pleased with the influence that the Roman Catholic Church held in Alta California, although the economic maturity and strength of the missions must have also caught the attention of Mexican officials and individuals who looked upon the successful mission farms and artisan works with wanton eyes. Secularization of some missions had routinely taken place throughout the Spanish Empire, though the new design set forth by Mexico of blanket secularization was a much more aggressive campaign. In 1825, Mexico sent Jose Maria Echeandia to survey the economic possibilities of such a bold move, and over the next five years, Echeandia delighted his superiors with his suggestions for taking over the missions and turning them into pueblos, which would in turn be conduits for tax revenues. After a good deal of political bickering, the Mexican Congress passed the Secularization Act of 1833, and thus the legal transfer of Church property over to the State, and then private citizens, began to take place.

The impact of the Mission Secularization Act on the Mission Indians of California was also significant. During the early Mexican period, the relationship between the Indians and their respective mission had greatly diverged from that of the first, formative years. With generations of Indians being born at and around the mission, the Spanish brutality waned for the most part and a gradual melding of cultures took place. By 1833, many more California Mission Indians called the mission home than had in 1790. Now, in the wake of secularization, the Indians were overwhelmingly evicted from their mission homes and literally rendered homeless. Part of the intent by the Mexicans in this eviction process was to further encourage the "homeless" Indians to work for the rancheros, which many did. In fact, the vast majority of the Mexican cowboys in these regions, known as "vaqueros," were actually California Indians.

The economy of Mexican California expanded considerably beyond the plateau reached by the Spanish. Unencumbered by the rule of a virtual foreign crown and not tethered to the Roman Catholic Church, Mexican California witnessed an expansion of its agriculture and shipping industries. And although Spanish California did not fully adhere to the Spanish Crown's ban on international trade, Mexican California was in comparison an open, free-market economy. Major industries also included the hide and tallow, which was responsible for mass trade with China and the United States. During this period, the most significant ports of trade in Alta California were Monterey and Yerba Buena (later named San Francisco). The ships that came into these ports also purchased freshwater, food stuffs, and hardware needed for repair and maintenance practices. Consequently, career opportunities in these areas expanded.

Americans, more so than any other nationality, expanded their trade with Mexican California. Within a year of Mexican independence, the Boston shipping magnate Bryant and Sturgis had even bested the total trade value that this growing community had with Great Britain. The one issue that plagued Mexican California was the lack of specie or currency. This limitation forced international trade with Alta California to be almost completely reliant upon a primitive barter system. Regardless, business people, artisans, and laborers all benefited from a system that encouraged hard work, ingenuity, and the exploitation of the natural resources, which had gone virtually untapped by early Western 19th-century standards.

Traders and sailors also took notice of the yet untapped economic possibilities in Alta California, in particular the fur trades, resulting in a minor, though significant, influx of immigrants. The Russians and the Spanish had not come close to tapping the vast supply of fur-bearing animals throughout California as they typically kept their activities local. Americans entered California from its Northeastern flank; a region virtually ignored by the Russian and Spanish. Conflict with local Indian societies, such as the Modoc, resulted when Americans fur trappers encroached on Indian land. Typically, these fur trappers would set out traps by the dozens, at times losing track of where they had actually laid them out. Many valuable furs went uncollected. Also, when short on provisions, trappers would steal food from the Indians, including hunting without permission on their lands.

Migration into Mexican Alta California by Europeans and Americans never reached a flood; however, immigration numbers did consistently increase, encouraged by the prospect of owning land, the abundance of natural resources, the potential in agriculture and animal husbandry, and certainly the temperate climate played a significant role. With dreams of economic success and upward mobility, people from countries such as Ireland, Switzerland, England, and the United States embarked upon the long journey to the exotic California in search of a better life from the 1820s forward. Slight urbanization did take place, though the hub of the population growth in Mexican Alta California was centered in the ranchos, which were increasingly self-sufficient communities by themselves, although their respective economies were tied to networks of trade and commerce.

The journey to Alta California from the Midwest or Eastern United States was typically over land. These emigrants would have to cross anywhere from 1,500 to 2,500 miles to reach their final destinations, most of which would not be on roads but merely trails, which were nothing more than routes drawn out on maps. Once the emigrants reached the Mississippi River, the journey, if they were lucky, would take another three months and require them to cross a series of mountains and deserts. Immigrants from Europe would overwhelmingly come by sea, which required them to navigate the Atlantic around the southernmost point of South America, Tierra del Fuego, and then hug the coastline for thousands of miles as they headed north to California. Food and water routinely ran out, requiring dockings, which only extended the already long trip. Morale typically ran low, and frustrations high, on what could turn out to be a five-month trip. These exceptionally trying circumstances kept the population of migrants into California relatively low during the Mexican period. Additionally, as most migrants would have to spend almost their entire fortune to make the trek, hesitation was abundant.

Mexico also had a significant challenge in maintaining control over those who entered Alta California. Outlaw trappers and roadside bandits took advantage of the sparse law and policing that took place in Alta California. Men such as Jedediah Smith, a trapper and fur trader by profession, used the vast lands of California to their advantage as they formed parties that profited and then refused to comply with Mexican tax laws and trade regulations, knowing that they could easily avoid arrest. Ultimately, Smith was banned from California after his second trip led to significant legal problems, and rather than face authorities, Jedediah Smith decided to leave and never return. While Jedediah Smith may have come to represent the ills associated with a significant foreign population for Mexico, others such as Jasper O'Farrell were welcome additions to the growing society.

Born in 1817 in Ireland, Jasper O'Farrell migrated into Mexican California by way of Chile in 1842. Upon entering Alta California, O'Farrell found gainful employment with Mexico as a surveyor and cartographer. With his services in need, due to the confusion born out of a series of land transfers and establishments of ranchos, O'Farrell set to work and mapped out the complex properties of what is contemporary Sonoma and Marin counties. With a growing reputation, O'Farrell found enough work to afford him great social and economic advancement. Also, O'Farrell's indifference to politics made it easy for him to transition into life at the very start of the U.S. occupation of Alta California. In 1847, Jasper O'Farrell was given the charge of a full survey and map making of Yerba Buena. O'Farrell's map was an obvious improvement upon the previous Spanish–Mexican version. Eventually, O'Farrell became one of U.S. California's leading citizens, a significant landholder and even state senator, representing Sonoma County. Others who migrated into Alta California fancied the idea of creating for themselves anywhere from a quasi-sovereign fiefdom to an independent republic. Such was the case with Johann Augustus Sutter and Lansford Hastings.

Johan Sutter, or John Augustus Sutter as he came to refer to himself once in the Americas and as he is commonly remembered today, desired to create an economic empire based in agriculture and millworks along the American River east of Sacramento and west of Lake Tahoe. The fertile soil, abundant sunshine, and ample labor force of Yosemite Miwok and eastern Maidu Indians was a strong enticement that led Sutter to file for a rancho with the Mexican government. In June 1840, Sutter began operations on his nearly 50,000-acre rancho, which he named New Helvetia, in homage to his homeland. Sutter established a millwork, extensive agricultural enterprises, including attempts at growing cotton, which were quite unsuccessful, within the first two years of operation. Sutter proved most prodigious in two areas of endeavor, amassing debt and political intrigue. While the debt was connected with his purely economic ambitions, the political issues that he found himself drawn to were due to his desire to establish his own empire. Sutter reasoned that if he could manage to develop a militia of significant size and strength, he might be able to successfully negotiate a governorship for himself with Mexico at the minimum, though as his diaries indicate, following in the tradition of the declaration of independence made by the Texas Republic, he desired most to be the emperor of New Helvetia. It was a dream that he would never realize. Sutter's economic ambitions also never materialized any great success. By 1848, John Sutter was in debt not only to traditional creditors; rather, most of his labor force was significantly behind in collecting their wages from him. Furthermore, James Marshall, his foreman and ostensibly business partner, began to press Sutter for a quite nearly a controlling share, though when the historic discovery of gold on Sutter's land took place, the events of change that swept through would forever alter the business plans of both Sutter and Marshall. In the process of laying the bulwark for the mill, James Marshall and his workers came across gold particles and even gold nuggets. Marshall brought the discovery to the attention of Sutter, and the two men conspired to keep the discovery a secret, which they did for nearly one year. Remarkably, Sutter never recognized the economic and political potential that the abundant gold deposit on his land represented; instead, he viewed it as an economic hindrance.

Lansford Hastings was more direct in his ambitions of establishing a California empire with himself as its emperor. Beginning in the early 1840s, Hastings began to recruit European Americans to move into Mexican California. Hastings utilized the promise of land via the rancho system, exaggerated stories regarding the wealth of the society and its climate and natural resources, and with promises that slavery would always be a significant part of the California economy. Hastings was a Southerner who would later after the Civil War attempt to establish colonies of former Confederates in South America; he was unsuccessful in that particular enterprise.

Hastings understood the great deterrence that the difficult trek to California played in his difficulty to recruit emigrants, which he believed could reach such significant numbers that would then facilitate a conflict-free transfer of California over to him from Mexico. As ridiculous as his political scheme was Lansford Hastings's bizarre solution. He composed a book, *Hastings' Guide to Emigrant California*, in which he promised offered a short cut, later known as "Hastings Cutoff." Though rather than being a short cut, it was actually longer by nearly 500 miles than the traditional overland route and also led those who were unfortunate enough to take this path, through the Great Salt Desert and a nearly impossible series of mountain crossings through the formidable Sierra Nevada. Hasting himself had never taken the routes he proposed to emigrants. Ultimately, those who followed Hastings path found nothing but great hardship, with nearly 100 dying en route, including the historically tragic Donner Party. Before Hastings ever had a chance to plant the seeds of revolution in California, other events began in 1846 and swept through Alta California, as the United States and Mexico became embroiled in a war that would forever change the course of history and lead directly to the Gold Rush.

THE DONNER TRAGEDY

Migration into Mexican California by Americans accelerated in 1846. Influenced by the clamor in Washington, D.C., by innumerable politicians for the Western border of the United States to reach the Pacific and propelled forward by the formal declaration of war between the United States and Mexico, many an emigrant recognized the potential opportunities in California and began to plan their migration. In early 1846, George Donner, his wife, children, and brother, Jacob, decided to leave behind their middleclass life in Springfield, Illinois, and move into Mexican Alta California. The Donners were joined in this venture by another successful, middle-class family, the Reeds, led by husband and father James Reed. On April 14, 1846, the Donner–Reed Party departed Missouri for California with their combined six wagons for the first leg in the cross-county trek, Independence, Missouri, generally considered the official departure point for emigrants heading out for California and Oregon. On May 10, the party arrived in Independence, where they camped and discussed the trip with other Argonauts who had gone and returned as well as with other greenhorns, such as themselves. The Donners and Reeds took on extra provisions and in the process received advice from many other travelers that they were taking on too much weight for their animals to manage. One week after they departed Independence, the Donner–Reed Party met up with a much larger party, led by Col. William Henry Russell; 10 days later, a second party, the Murphy family, joined the Donner–Reed–Russell train.

On June 16, Tamsen Donner recorded that the party was 200 miles from Fort Laramie, enjoyed dining on buffalo steaks that they had cooked over a kindling of buffalo chips, and in her opinion, the hardest part of the journey was at the start. June and July were the halcyon days of the journey, and as the month of July ended, James Reed coerced his party to take the allegedly shorter path mapped out by Lansford Hastings, his so-called Hastings Cutoff that would soon land the emigrants in the Great Salt Desert, which would ravage their livestock, and became one of the first of many hardships they would endure before being stranded in the Sierra Nevada. On October 6, as the party moved along the Humboldt River, James Reed became embroiled in a fight with one of his hired drivers, John Snyder, whom Reed then stabbed to death, which resulted in James Reed being banished from the party. In Reed's absence, the group voted George Donner as their new captain in place of the banished Reed.

At the end of October 1846, the Donner Party had worked their way to the very gates of California; however, as they reached Truckee Lake (now Donner Lake), it began to snow. The flurries quickly turned into a blizzard, which trapped the party high in the mountains, only 100 miles from Sutter's Fort. Over the next five months, members of the party would live and die in their encampments. A few rescue parties, led by none other than James Reed, from Sutter's Fort led out several members in successive intervals; however, rescue efforts were severely hampered not only by the weather but also by the fact that so many of Sutter's men joined in the Mexican–American war effort on the side of the United States and thus could not attend to the needs of the stranded emigrants, who, to preserve their lives, resorted to cannibalism, first on their deceased colleagues and then on the ones who were the weakest.

Word of the cannibalism shot through the newspapers and filled the pages of dime novellas. By the time all of the survivors made their way out of the mountains, it was late April 1847. Of the 87 original emigrants, only 46 survived. Their gruesome ordeal played a significant role in curbing the flow of migrants into California. However, once the discovery of gold was made known, the trail filled with emigrants in search of their fortune.

MEXICAN–AMERICAN WAR

Nearly in a comical fashion, U.S. commodore Thomas ap Catesby Jones was mistakenly under the impression that war between the United States and Mexico had broken out before it had, and on October 19, 1842, he seized the port of Monterey. Jones had previously developed a naval career of significant distinction, beginning with his outstanding strategies that blocked the British from entering New Orleans in a timely fashion in 1812, which aided the American cause led by Andrew Jackson. Jones also represented the United

States in establishing a treaty with King Kamehameha III of the Sandwich Islands in 1826, though it was his accidental takeover of Monterey during his command of the Pacific Squadron that is best remembered for in California history.

Beginning in June 1845, the most significant expedition since Lewis and Clark departed St. Louis for the West. Leading the contingent of over 50 men was none other than the famed explorer John C. Fremont, known throughout the United States simply as "Pathfinder." With the legendary Kit Carson as his primary guide, Fremont and his collection of cartographers, riflemen, and adventurers combed a path to the Sacramento Valley. Arriving in the early spring of 1846, Fremont and Carson beat the drums of revolution as they promised that the United States was actively planning to liberate Alta California from Mexico to anyone who would bend their ear. Fremont was one of the first U.S. military leaders on hand in Alta California during the Bear Flag Rebellion.

BEAR FLAG REBELLION

Before the United States and Mexico engaged in a formal war, a few dozen U.S. immigrants in the greater Sonoma region in Northern California took it upon themselves to capture Alta California from Mexico and establish an independent republic. In early spring of 1846, rumors began to circulate around Alta California that Mexico intended to either expel or imprison all residents who were not official Mexican citizens. The rumors were inspired by the growing gossip that the United States and Mexico were headed for war and in preparation Mexico would attempt to secure the interior by removing all noncitizens. Several Anglo-American residents of Alta California began to develop a strategy that would afford them the opportunity to arrest power from Mexico prior to what most had come to conclude was inevitable, the Mexican–American War, and thus give the United States a distinct naval advantage in this westernmost and northernmost Pacific Mexican territory. Leading the eventual Bear Flag Rebellion was William Brown Ide, who immigrated into Alta California a year earlier from Missouri with his wife. The rebels fashioned a flag to represent their newly established republic that included the lone star, the words "California Republic," and the silhouette of a bear, the latter of which would anchor the moniker given to the 1846 insurrection activists, "Bear Flaggers" and their cause, the "Bear Flag Rebellion" also referred to as the "Bear Flag Revolt."

On June 14, 1846, the Ide-led Bear Flaggers, unaware that war between the United States and Mexico had been officially declared in Washington, D.C., a month earlier, captured Mexico's Northern California commandant general, Mariano Guadalupe Vallejo, and held him prisoner in his own military barracks before moving him to Sutter's Fort. News quickly spread throughout the area of the rebellion, including that the Bear Flaggers were quite intoxicated during their attack on Vallejo, who ironically supported U.S. annexation of Alta California. John C. Fremont officially took charge of California from California Republic president William B. Ide on behalf of the United States on June 23, 1846.

Relative to the other regions during the war, California witnessed very few battles. The war was in the favor of the more industrialized and technologically and economically advanced United States from its inception. Additionally, the Mexican army, still in its infancy, had a significant problem with desertion, which further exacerbated its military capabilities. By the end of 1847, the Unites States had accepted the surrender of numerous Mexican military leaders and occupied or outright controlled all major ports and most major cities, including Mexico City. Mexican surrender was at that point inevitable. Additionally, the internal political divisions further undermined any chances Mexico might have to force out any of U.S. military personnel.

The U.S. War Department, Congress, and President Polk began to weigh out the options for peace. At the heart of the matter was the issue of Mexican land that would be transferred over to the United States. Clearly, the intention of securing the continental nation, which was one of the catalysts for going to war in the first place, guaranteed that great portions of west would fall under the American flag. Ultimately, Mexico ceded over 50 percent of its territory, which in the process transferred over 500,000 square miles to the United States, as both sides signed the Treaty of Guadalupe Hidalgo on February 2, 1848, outside of Mexico City. The treaty also called for the United States making a onetime payment of $18,500,000 to Mexico, which was less than 50 percent of what the United States had offered its neighbor for the lands it took by conquest prior to the outbreak of war. In addition to the entire state of California, the lands transferred over to the United States included all of Nevada and Utah and sections of Arizona, New Mexico, Wyoming, and Colorado.

One of the provisions of the Treaty of Guadalupe Hidalgo guaranteed all Mexican citizens who continued to live in what was now a part of the United States the right to citizenship. However, once the flood of Anglo-Americans began during the Gold Rush and continued thereafter, the Spanish-speaking Californios would find that equal access to and protection under the law was, at times, beyond their grasp. The groups who would witness the greatest injustice were California Indian Nations. While under the Spanish and Mexican flag, the California Indians faced extreme injustices; however, once California became a part of the United States, these indigenous societies would find themselves literally being hunted into near extinction.

As California transitioned into a U.S. territory following the conclusion of the Mexican–American War, it was a land that in comparison to the eastern seaboard sparsely populated and overflowing with natural resources and riches beyond its bountiful supply of gold, although very little was known of the fantastic yield of natural wealth. In 1843, John C. Fremont published "Exploring Expedition to the Rocky Mountains," a colorful account of the expedition that he led through the Rockies the year before sparked the imagination of many a reader about the wonders of the West. Fremont's words of praise for the untouched lands, beautiful vistas, and economic potential would later pale in comparison to California, which President Theodore Roosevelt would later call the "Garden of the Lord" and the "West of the West." Fremont himself, upon seeing several regions of California during the war, was in awe of its abundance, beauty, and potential. However, Fremont could not have predicted what discovery lay ahead, when on January 24, 1848, James Marshall saw a shiny, yellow rock in the South Fork of the American River, and life in California would never be the same again.

THE DISCOVERY OF GOLD

In the late spring of 1847, John Sutter recognized the growing need for both lumber and flour in California. Sutter believed that the opportunity to meet the demand for these two products was greatest chance for the wealth and power that he had been seeking his entire adult life. Sutter and his men mapped out the greater American River in search of the best location to establish a flour mill and sawmill that could be powered by the constant flow of water and also be built with local materials and on firm ground. Eventually, Sutter settled on a site just a few miles from his fort. Sutter reached out to James Marshall to serve as the manager of the sawmill. For the next seven months, dozens of Mormon and Native

American laborers diligently excavated stones and fell area trees from which they carved out finished planks with whipsaws, while simultaneously building the mill. Additionally, the workers were charged with digging a canal that would serve as a diversion from the American River, bringing water necessary for power, directly to the sawmill. Hampered by heavy rainfall, John Sutter did not get his wish that his mill be operational by the Christmas of 1847. Precipitation would continue to hamper the construction efforts of the workers throughout January, which ironically led directly to James Marshall's discovery of gold on January 24. While inspecting the mill structure for damages at dawn, a quick sparkle of light in the water running by the mill caught Marshall's attention. He reached down and recovered the small nugget. Marshall held it in his hand and inspected what he believed was gold. His near disbelief led him to look away from the nugget and back into the water, where he, to his amazement, saw several more flakes and nuggets. After recovering a handful of gold, a nearly frenetic Marshall presented his find to his workers, who actually refused to believe that the shiny metallic pebbles were actually gold. Incredibly, Marshall was unable to persuade any of his men that he had actually discovered gold on that historic day.

The following morning, James Marshall went right back to his hunt for gold, effectively becoming the fine gold miner in California history. By midday, Marshall recovered a handful of small nuggets, pebbles, grains, and flakes, and once again he presented his findings to his employees, who once again demonstrated their skepticism. Indeed, the discovery of gold right there at the mill that they had been building for several months seemed incomprehensible. Why had they not come across any hint of gold while digging out the bypass? The answer was simple: Once the water began to flow and thus wash away the lighter sediment, the gold began to be exposed. After a few months of this process, a considerable amount of this fine, placer gold was exposed on the bed of the recently dug waterway. Marshall insisted that what he found could not be anything but gold, and he and his workers agreed to performs a series of rudimentary tests to verify the authenticity of what at least appeared to be gold. The men took a pinch of the grains and pounded them out with a hammer. Rather than shatter, the shiny metal objects flattened out. After a few more rudimentary tests, their disbelief vanished, and in an instant the workers abandoned their tasks associated with the mill and began to comb through the frigid water for gold. Marshall joined them in their quest, and the first squadron of California gold miners was born.

After a few days of gold recovery fever, James Marshall met John Sutter back at the fort and revealed to his employer what he and his workers had been finding around the mill. Neither man had any previous experience in gold mining, nor was either particularly well versed on how one might actually verify if, in fact, the yellow, metallic grains were gold beyond the elementary tests that Marshall and his workers had already conducted. Sutter did have a set of encyclopedia in his library, which served as the only source of information available, though it did not offer any significant insight on how they might test the material to verify if it was actually gold. Falling back on the one quality of gold as a metal that they were aware of—its malleable nature—the two men pounded out the pieces as flat as they could. Following several minutes of this near charade, Sutter accepted the reality that Marshall had discovered gold. The two men went back to the mill, looked for, and discovered more and more small grains and flakes of gold. Sutter's workers eagerly showed him their own personal collections, adding further encouragement to an already excited John Sutter.

However, one concern quickly came upon John Sutter as he looked his men's faces—keeping them on the job would be a difficult task when they could amass far greater wealth from simply collecting gold than working at the mill. For the time being, Sutter and Marshall accommodated the men to the best of their abilities by permitting a liberal amount of downtime for gold recovery, and for the next two weeks, the men continued to work on the mill, though as each day passed, fewer hours were spent in construction as the amount and frequency of gold discovery grew.

The sawmill workers, Sutter, and Marshall were able to keep the gold discovery somewhat under wraps until the early part of March, when Sutter's other employees from the flour mill and fort heard the news, which led them to become gold miners, at least on a part-time basis. On March 11, Sutter's sawmill became operational, and a jubilant Marshall reported that the saw was in perfect operating form. Plank after plank was cut to near perfection. But, just as Sutter had envisioned, gold was by far too great a competitor for his mill, and within one month, he had nary a worker. While his men kept their word and stayed with Sutter until the construction of the sawmill was completed, the siren call of the gold was inescapable. Indeed, many of the men had collected pounds of gold by the time the sawmill was operational. And, with each passing day, they continued to pull more and more from the gravel. Encouraged even further with the first big strike just over a week earlier at a bend in the South Fork, which quickly became known as Mormon Island, it became apparent that any chance of keeping his workers or keeping a lid on the news was forever gone.

John Sutter understood that the land on which he had been operating would quickly be filled with fortune seekers. His hold on the land was tenuous at best. Having first been given title during the Mexican period, the borders of Sutter's rancho lay in a state of confusion, as did the other ranchos. Sutter first approached the Nisenan Indians, the Yalesummy, and arranged an ad hoc agreement from them that permitted Sutter to work the lands surrounding his mills. Sutter eagerly wrote to Col. Richard Barnes Mason, military governor of California, that he had reached an agreement with the Indians to lease their lands. Sutter made no mention of the gold in his letter; however, word had already reached Mason, having come from none other than Sutter's own men. While Governor Mason made no mention of the gold in his response to Sutter, Mason did make it abundantly clear that he would under no circumstances honor Sutter's agreement with the Yalesummy because official policy in his administration was that Indians had no legal right to any lands. Consequently, all Indian lands were deemed public lands. Sutter therefore had no legal rights to lease the lands from the Indians, nor was he afforded the opportunity to negotiate for the land with Governor Mason.

On March 15, 1848, news of the gold discovery was finally reported on by the first English language newspaper in California, the *Californian*, and the paper's rival, *The California Star*, owned by Sam Brannan, at first railed against the reports of gold along the American River. On the surface it seemed ironic that Sam Brannan, who would soon become the biggest booster of gold mining in California, was refuting the fact that gold, more and more each day, was being plucked from the beds of the American and its tributaries. But Brannan had his own plans for striking it rich, and he needed some time to implement his schemes. For now, Sam Brannan attempted to put the Gold Rush on hold.

2

LIFE IN TRANSITION: THE CALL OF THE CALIFORNIA GOLD RUSH

SETTING THE STAGE FOR THE GOLD RUSH

Before the world, or even those in California who did not work at Sutter's mills, learned of the vast deposits of gold within the borders of the new U.S. territory, California was a sparsely populated region with its economy based heavily on agriculture. The biggest city was Monterey, with its greater metropolitan region containing a population of over 1,000. Located in the southeast corner of the Monterey Bay, the town developed because of its central coastal location and exceptionally fertile lands that went for over a hundred miles north, south, and east. The original inhabitants, the Rumsen Band of Ohlone Indians, had made this region their home for thousands of years. The Rumsen enjoyed a diverse, nutritious diet that contained grains, fish, fowl, and local game. The Rumsen also practiced fire agriculture, which not only afforded them exceptional harvests of grains and acorns but also played a significant role in maintaining a rich and balanced soil. Father Serra and Gaspar de Portola arrived to establish the mission and presidio in 1770, and from 1777 to 1849, Monterey served as the capital for both the Spanish and Mexican governments.

To the north, the hamlet of San Francisco, formerly known as Yorba Buena, was a quiet port town in comparison to Monterey. In 1846 there were no more than 200 residents, though by the following year, the population had more than doubled. In that same year, San Francisco welcomed its first weekly English language newspaper, the *California Star*, published by Sam Brannan. As one might expect, the economy of San Francisco was utterly dependent upon the shipping industry, though the military presence, which continued to grow following the conclusion of the Mexican–American War, brought in additional opportunities. Saloons, lodging halls, and brothels were the most common commercial enterprises after shipping. The great scarcity of women afforded ladies the opportunity to earn exceptional wages in these service industries, a trend that would continue throughout the Gold Rush. While San Francisco appeared to be a town with potential, none could have predicted that its population would increase exponentially over the next five years. And, just as dramatically was the population explosion would be the cost of living in San Francisco. By 1850, inflationary prices on everything from real estate to food would drive the cost of living to such exorbitant prices that San Francisco was the most expensive U.S. city to live in by the end of the first year of the Gold Rush.

The population in what would soon be known collectively as the gold fields was almost completely composed of Native Americans societies. The Mexican rancho system of vast land grants, with economies heavily focused on agriculture or animal husbandry, widely ignored the western foothills regions of the Sierra Nevada. The very few who attempted to carve out a living in what was considered at best a secondary option were those who were late arrivers in Mexican Alta California, such as John Sutter.

However, population growth had been a reality in the region precisely because of the European colonization from San Diego to Sonoma, as many Native Americans who fled the brutal expansion and subjugation fled to their neighboring Indian societies in these interior regions.

By the early 1840s, the relationships between those of European and California Indian descent had evolved into a more shared economy in the traditionally Native American lands, where whites had developed their own settlements from the Spanish era forward. While conflict between these divergent societies continued, a negotiated existence continued to slowly emerge. In particular, the ranchos needed skilled and unskilled labor to run the day-to-day operations across these vast estates. A genuine scarcity of European workers led to a heavy reliance on Indians; consequently, the white–Indian relations softened. However, after just one of the Gold Rush, a complete reversal would take place as the Indian societies that had experienced the least amount of encroachment or contact with the Europeans resided throughout what would become Gold Rush California.

PUBLICIZING THE GOLD RUSH

Samuel Brannan was born on March 2, 1819, in Maine. Brannan entered the printing trade in his youth and also joined the fledgling Church of Jesus Christ of Latter-day Saints, commonly known as Mormons. After rising within the church ranks, Brannan led a community of over 200 Mormons into San Francisco, then still known as Yerba Buena, in 1846. Brannan successfully established the second English language newspaper in California, the *California Star*. Not content with the simple life, Brannan expanded his interests into the retail sale of dry goods in 1847, when he opened his store at John Sutter's Fort in Sacramento, then referred to as New Helvetia. Brannan's timing at opening this store at this particular location is one of the greatest strokes of luck in modern economic history. However, his keen understanding of monopoly was what earned him the distinction of being the first Gold Rush millionaire. After discarding his original goal and charge of establishing a Mormon colony, Sam Brannan focused exclusively on making as much money as possible and the potential fortune that could be made by fleecing a flood of gold miners was too incredible an opportunity to ignore.

Sam Brannan first became aware of the gold being discovered at Sutter's Mill and other points along the American River, when Sutter's workers paid for the wares at Brannan's store in gold nuggets. Brannan's strategy to capitalize on this mineral find proved genius. Rather than impetuously getting the word out that gold was in abundance, Brannan first purchased all of the tools necessary to pan and dig for gold, as well as live in the gold fields, throughout all of Northern California. After successfully securing the monopoly on all of these items, Brannan then walked the streets of San Francisco with specimens of the gold that he received in payment from Sutter's workers, proclaiming, with some hyperbole that later proved rather conservative when the massive strikes began, about the abundance of gold and, just as importantly, where the precious metal was located, what the tools were that one needed, and where, of course, they could be purchased. One of the immediate effects of Sam Brannan's provocative advocacy that produced a small rush to the gold fields was the difficulty the U.S. Army and Navy had at controlling the desertion of its military personnel.

After first refuting his rival newspaper's claim that gold had been discovered in and along the American River, Sam Brannan began in earnest to first verify just how much gold had been discovered, if miners were still collecting gold and from which locations. At the opening moments of gold discovery, in addition to owning the *California Star*, Brannan also operated a hotel and dry goods store in San Francisco. In his first expansion out of San Francisco, Brannan leased a storefront at Sutter's Fort and then proceeded to begin operations of a third store in the vicinity of Sutter's sawmill and a fourth just a few miles southwest of Sutter's Fort at the Sacramento River docks, the busiest station on that river. Believing that an incredible economic opportunity was just coming to the surface, Brannan risked everything that he had with his unheard-of business expansions. However, owning the most read English language newspaper in Northern California afforded Brannan a distinct business advantage.

On March 25, 1848, Brannan's *California Star* issued its first reports of the discovery of gold. However, the weak response in San Francisco, one filled with doubt, was not the reaction that Brannan had sought. Perhaps Brannan had simply misjudged the public. Not one to be dissuaded easily, the following week the *California Star* issued a special print. Dr. Victor J. Fourgeaud, a physician and surgeon of prominence in San Francisco, penned what would become the first California booster literature. Victor Fourgeaud was born to parents of French descent in Charlestown, South Carolina, in 1816. At the age of 10, his parents sent him to France for his schooling, and upon his return in his late teens, he entered the Medical College of South Carolina, and at the age of 21, Victor Fourgeaud was conferred the degree of M.D. After three years of postgraduate study in France, he returned to the United States and settled in one of the French enclaves in St. Louis, Missouri. Hearing the call to go even further into the West, the young doctor relocated to the then hamlet of San Francisco, where he became one of the leading figures. It was not a surprise that Sam Brannan approached this gentleman and community pillar to author the article that celebrated California's splendor and, of course, its gold.

As word of the gold in California began to spread, concerns arose in both the nation's capital as well as the small emerging towns of San Francisco, Sacramento, and Monterey about securing the land and recovering the gold and keeping the wealth in American hands. The obvious solution was to flood the region with U.S. emigrants from the East as quickly as possible. At the conclusion of the Mexican–American War on February 2, 1848, the population of California was yet only in the tens of thousands, the vast majority of which were California Indians and Californios, the former Mexican citizens of Alta California. While the threat of Mexico attempting to retake California was never a concern, this far-flung land, over 1,000 miles from the previous western most settlements in Texas, was open to foreign opportunists who might recover the gold and bring it back to their native lands. To witness a vast depletion of natural wealth was not in the best interests of the new U.S. territory or the federal government. Not surprisingly, men acting in the interests of both California and Washington, D.C., emerged as gold field boosters. While Sam Brannan was the voice in the West calling for fortune seekers, none other than President James K. Polk was responsible for promoting the discovery of gold in the East.

James K. Polk was born on November 2, 1795, in North Carolina. At the age of 30, James Polk was elected on the Democratic Party ticket to Congress as a representative. After 10 highly years in the House of Representatives, James Polk was elected Speaker of the House, and while serving in this capacity, Speaker Polk loyally and dutifully served his president, Andrew Jackson. While Andrew Jackson is generally recognized as the first "commoner" president, James K. Polk carries the distinction of being the second commoner to occupy the White House, when he was elected in one of the closest races in history in 1844. Polk's opponent, Henry Clay (W-KY), was one of the most celebrated members of Congress and known as the "Great Compromiser" and "Great Pacifier" for his roles in preventing Southern succession. Clay was also one of the "Great Triumvirate" members of the Senate, the others being Daniel Webster and John C. Calhoun. While Polk was certainly a respected member of the House, signified by his ascendancy to Speaker, Henry Clay was favored by many to win. However, Polk had something in his favor that Mr. Clay did not, the endorsement of Andrew Jackson, the most famous man in the United States in 1844. Additionally, Andrew Jackson was known as "Old Hickory" due to his celebrated strength of character and will; James Polk cleverly played on this character trait of his mentor and championed his own nickname of "Young Hickory" with fervor.

James Polk also ran on the political platform of "Manifest Destiny," a political and economic theory that the United States had the divine right to occupy the central zone of North America from the Atlantic to the Pacific, and to allow its people the uninterrupted opportunity to expand anywhere on this vast land between the two oceans. Polk preached annexation of Texas and blustered war with Mexico rhetoric until achieving both. Following the successful conclusion the Mexican–American War, Polk fervently believed that to secure the vast land now under the U.S. flag, settlement in the West was a necessity. After hearing about the discovery of gold in California, Polk withheld from making any public pronouncements until his State of the Union Address on December 5, 1848, when he made announcement of the "abundance of gold" in the new western territory, which helped launch tens of thousands of fortune seekers into Northern California from all corners of the earth.

The combined efforts of President Polk and Sam Brannan helped launch one of the greatest mass migrations to that point in history. While his word did not reach as many as President Polk, Sam Brannan's impact as the first local Gold Rush booster and advocate is monumental in its own right. Within a few months, the newspapers of the nation would join Brannan in publicizing the Gold Rush with daily stories, advice columns, and serials; often the line between fact and fiction was blurred. Dime novels about life in the gold fields and the long journey to California soon became popular. America quickly developed an obsession with the Gold Rush as the biggest story of the day.

By late 1849, the steady growth of newspaper reports of gold strikes in California fueled an expansion of gold seekers. While many of the newspaper accounts in the Midwest and East were merely the outgrowth of the imagination of ambitious newspaper men, there were enough verified accounts that arrived via mail from actual gold miners to friends and family that word-of-mouth advertising became a literal siren's call as the stories, combined with an ever increasing number of photographs, were disseminated through the villages, towns, and cities. The exceptional ease by which the miners recovered the surface gold during from 1848 through the first few months of 1849 became the national story. The fact that the vast majority of California land had yet to be explored by men with picks, shovels, and pans only enhanced the dream of striking it rich.

GETTING TO CALIFORNIA

Following quickly on the heels of President Polk's announcement, transportation companies formed and existing ones expanded their offerings to include the gold fields of California. There were two choices for Americans in the East and Midwest: over the land or by sea. Overwhelmingly, those Argonauts who lived west of Ohio chose the land route, while many from the East predominantly preferred the sea route. The major land route used, the California Trail, stretched for 2,000 miles from the Missouri River into the West. The sea route, if one were to sail completely around the southern tip of South America, was in excess of 18,000 miles. Both options were fraught with their own set of unique challenges; however, both held in common the scarcity of fresh water.

In addition to the physical challenges associated with making the long trek to California's gold fields, potential 49ers were subjected to a range of hucksters who made promises that were well beyond what reality would permit. Taking advantage of the general lack of knowledge concerning the trip out to California that most urbanites in the Midwest and East possessed, confidence men routinely offered transportation services that guaranteed record paces across the Great Plains, over the Rocky Mountains and through the Sierra Nevada range that simply defied reason. These false promises of making it through in as little time as a month at times included guidance to the premiere diggings. While such shady con artists were able to fleece would-be miners in the first part of 1849 with ease, as newspaper reports of crossing the Overland Trail and life in the gold fields became more abundant with each passing month, a more informed emigrant was much less apt to fall victim.

In 1849, about 100,000 people rushed into California, with about equal numbers by land as by sea, and about 60,000 to 65,000 of these fortune-seeking 49ers were Americans, with the rest being foreigners. Those individuals who came from abroad hailed from Chile, Mexico, Ireland, France, England, and China, to name just a few. While no exact documentation exists on all those brave souls who made the long journey from points around the world, dozens of nations contributed gold seekers. Early on, when gold was still relatively easy to find, these international miners experienced little discrimination, though by 1850, when much of the surface gold had already been gathered up, nativism quickly sprang up.

GOING BY SEA

Advancements in clipper ship technology permitted those going by sea to experience a three- to four-month trip from New York to San Francisco. Limited space aboard the vessels prohibited the emigrants from bringing many of the necessary tools for mining and any significant creature comforts with them. Typically, the fortune seekers brought one or two change of clothes, a blanket, and a mining pan; all other necessities would then have to be purchased in California, which were guaranteed to be at an incredibly inflated price. For example, a pickax would be in excess of 10 times the cost in California as what a storekeeper would charge in Ohio in 1849. Since most of the emigrants in the first year of the Gold Rush had little to no accurate understanding of the nearly incomprehensible inflation in California, financial ruin came quickly if one did not find a few ounces of gold in the first few weeks in the gold fields. Ticket prices ranged from $100 for a small bunk in steerage to over $500 for a small cabin, which were sizeable financial investments for the mid-19th century.

Food provisions for the travelers on the high seas were less than gourmet. Dry biscuits, jerked meats, and stale, foul water were commonplace. The lack of fresh fruits and vegetables lowered the immune systems of emigrants and resulted in sicknesses that ranged from influenza to cholera, and dysentery was also a common threat to one's life. If a lack of nutrition was not enough, shipwrecks occurred on a regular basis, in particular when traversing the dangerous southern Atlantic passage, the Strait of Magellan. This subpolar waterway was first navigated by a European in 1520, when Ferdinand Magellan, a Portuguese sea captain who sailed for Spain, successfully navigated this narrow route, which runs over 300 nautical miles and tapers to just over one nautical mile at its most constricted point. Virtually impassible in the South American winter due to glacial expansion in the mid-19th century, the summer months were a key period to move from ocean to ocean. Glaciers and icebergs were not the only threats in addition to a very unpredictable weather pattern as the entire pass is riddled with rock outcrops, thousands of which are barely visible above the surface and many thousands more laying just below the ever-changing surface level due to tidal activity. The only other route in the southern hemisphere of significance was the so-called Drakes Passage, named for the 16th-century English captain Sir Francis Drake. This passage, while hundreds of miles wide, is in the open seas and is completely unprotected from the incredible tempests that dominate the weather cycles at the bottom of the earth. Consequently, avoiding Drakes Passage was a central navigational tenet during the Gold Rush.

When daily life on the high seas was not a harrowing experience, it was filled with boredom. There were none of the contemporary activities associated with cruise vessels; additionally, there was nowhere near the amount of physical space that modern ships afford. The size of the ships ranged from 150 to 250 feet in length, and those around 200 feet were the most common size. In addition to 80 to 100 passengers, the ships carried a few dozen seamen and provisions. All of these elements took up considerable space, and while freedom to move about the vessels was not prohibited beyond the work spaces and captains chambers, it was certainly impeded and minimal. The most common complaints logged by the sailors and emigrants included the foul odors associated with people who rarely were able to fully bathe over the course of a few months, which were further enhanced by the common diseases and sicknesses that plagued the ships, and the extreme lack of potable water and edible food. Culminated with the inability for anyone to genuinely stretch their legs, let alone have even a moment of privacy, these tightly packed ships afforded all aboard a most hellish experience, in particular if one were caught in the windless doldrums, which added anywhere from a few days to a few weeks to an already unpleasant journey.

Enterprising shipping entrepreneurs soon looked for viable shortcuts. The Isthmus of Panama quickly became a popular third choice. Companies such as the California Steam Navigation Company began an operation that boarded gold seekers on the Atlantic Ocean through the Gulf of Mexico and then led the emigrants across 75 to 100 miles of land followed by freighting them north on the Pacific to Monterey or San Francisco. One of the greatest problems associated with the Central American crossover was negotiating the jungles, which were difficult to trudge through due to not only their thick vegetation, high rainfall, and other physical impediments but also the lingering threat of typhoid, which overwhelmingly culminated in death. But for those who managed to make it through the jungles, once aboard a steamship the gold fields were less than a month's travel away.

By early June 1849, the Pacific Mail Steamship Company set a regular schedule of picking up gold-seeking passengers who bravely negotiated their way through the Panamanian jungles. Originally the steamer lines had been established in 1847 to serve as U.S. government–subsidized mail carriers, though their daily routines were inexorably changed with the discovery of gold. The three Pacific

Mail Steamship vessels—the *Oregon, California*, and *Panama*—were not as beholden to the whims of nature as the sailing vessels and in comparison to the clippers, these steam-driven behemoths maintained a considerably more reliable schedule than their clipper counterparts.

The SS *California* was first launched in May 1847. Designed to accommodate 60 in her saloon and over 100 in steerage, the *California* became the first steamship to arrive in San Francisco in February 1849. On this maiden voyage, the *California* delivered nearly 200 eager 49ers. The *Oregon* and *Panama* arrived soon after, both with a passenger count that reached their full capacity. As the number of miners continued to soar over the next two years, the three Pacific Mail Steamship vessels began to take on a passenger count well beyond the ships' manageable capacity. In 1852, the *California* was reported to have taken over 500 passengers in one of its runs from Panama to San Francisco. The weight pushed the steam engine beyond its ability to make forward progress, which compelled the captain to call for a level of steam pressure that resulted in a boiler fracture. Luckily on this eventful day, the Pacific was calm and the *California* lumbered slowly into the San Francisco Bay under the weak power of sail. Breakdowns of this nature became commonplace as captains found it nearly impossible to turn away eager miners willing to pay premium prices, upward of $250 and endure remarkably unpleasant accommodations to reach the gold fields of California.

CROSSING PANAMA

The miners who traversed Panama traveled thousands of miles less than their counterparts who rounded South America. Those who made took this cutoff in early 1849 were fortunate enough to find an accommodating Panama City, once they successfully found their way out of the untamed jungles, where cholera and dysentery trimmed the number of successful Argonauts. By early 1850, the Panamanian experience dramatically changed as the number of emigrants soared from a few hundred to several thousand making their way for the Pacific shoreline. This incredible spike in prospectors quickly became a blight for the Panamanians as their numbers far exceeded potential accommodations in Panama City. Additionally, steamship companies had not foreseen the rapid explosion of passengers. Consequently, there simply were not enough ships available to transport the would-be passengers. Thousands of miners camped out on the beaches, waiting for their chance to board a vessel. At times the wait exceeded a month. As stories of gold strikes continued to pour through the rumor mill, tensions and alcohol intake increased. Violence became routine as the sense of being stranded in a foreign land was exacerbated by the anxiety that all of the gold might run out before one had the chance to strike it rich.

Movement across Panama became much easier and safer in 1855 following the completion of a railroad that ran from the Atlantic to the Pacific. In one of the great historic strokes of luck, William Henry Aspinwall, who also founded the Pacific Mail Steamship Company, assembled a cadre of investors, raised over $1 million, and established the Panama Railroad Company in 1848. The construction of a railway across Panama had been bantered about since 1827, after Columbia, then known as the Republic of New Granada, gained its independence from Spain. French engineers had designed plans for a railway, and in 1838, their first attempts fell apart due to poor funding as well as poor construction planning. When Aspinwall established his company, his initial intention was for the railway to primarily serve as the intermediary carrier of mail and freight from his Atlantic vessels to his Pacific vessels. The discovery of gold prompted an unforeseen expansion of his business that compelled completion of the rail lines.

With the incredible economic potential beckoning, Aspinwall contracted G. W. Hughes of the U.S. Topographical Corps to survey the best possible routes to lay track. Hughes, accompanied by a small army of engineers and surveyors, presented Aspinwall and his fellow investors with his findings and recommendations after months of difficult and dangerous traverses through the jungles. According to Hughes, the construction of a railway was most feasible. On April 15, 1850, the Panama Railway Company had a formal agreement with New Granada, which carried two generous codicils. First, the construction of the railway had to be completed in no more than six years. Second, the Panama Railway Company was granted exclusive operating rights to the line for up to 49 years—a coincidental number given the impact the 49ers and subsequent gold seekers had on its success once completed.

In 1850, construction began in earnest on what would become the first transcontinental railway. Aspinwall, recognizing the historical significance of the project, began to bill his ambitious undertaking as the first inter-oceanic railway. While miniscule in comparison to the later built U.S. Transcontinental Railroad, which stretched a few thousand miles as opposed to just over 47 miles, the Panama Railway did effectively connect the Atlantic and the Pacific Oceans.

The route of the railway carved through the treacherous jungles and dismal swampland that dominate the Isthmus of Panama. The workers, just like the Argonauts, were constantly plagued by mosquitoes, and the constant threat of diseases such as cholera, dysentery, and yellow fever made an already unbearable working condition potentially lethal. All construction practices began at first light of day and did not end until sunset. For nearly five years, thousands of workers worked on constructing the rail line, and on January, 28, 1855, the Atlantic and Pacific Oceans were connected by a railroad. Station houses were laid in four-mile intervals. By the time the line opened for business, the overall cost for its construction had skyrocketed past the original estimate of $1 million to well over $6 million. In the first year, a one-way first class ticket cost $25, and a second-class ride was $10. In the first 12 years of operation, the Panama Railway successfully transported over $700 million in gold. While the completion of the U.S. Transcontinental Rail Road would devastate it, the Panama Railway's historic significance in the California Gold Rush cannot be swept aside. Of particular note, it became the only transporter of gold that never reported any loss of specie, a remarkable feat in itself.

GOING BY LAND

In the popular mythology of the day, the most harrowing aspect of travel through the West was the threat of an attack by Native Americans. However, reality presented a much different experience. While it was true that conflict existed between the vast Native American nations and the non-Indians who crossed through their sovereign lands, it was an incredibly rare occurrence that Indians attacked any Argonauts. In fact, many Native Americans recognized the economic potential in conducting business with the gold seekers. The most common forms of business conducted between the Native Americans and the emigrant was the sale of food and water. Nearly as frequent as the purchase of provisions by the emigrants was their contracting Native Americans to serve as guides. Some Indian nations charged tolls for crossing over their lands. Emigrant–Indian relations began to deteriorate in the Plains as more and more of the Argonauts poured through Indian lands, hunting indiscriminately and leaving waste in their wake.

The inflationary prices that began in 1849 extended beyond shipping and were evident in the cost of all material goods sold in California. By the early 1850s, ocean shipping became such a lucrative and expansive industry due to the inflationary Gold Rush prices of all commodities that many former passenger ships began to carry strictly cargo into San Francisco. Human passengers were simply not as profitable for the ocean vessels, and consequently, the cost of a ticket became prohibitive. Thus, untold thousands were compelled to take trek across the continent, significantly adding to the numbers of what was the most traveled path.

The most frequently chosen land route over the course of the Gold Rush was the conjoined California–Oregon trail, also known as the Overland Trail. This route began at the Missouri River in various jump-off points, crossed the Great Plains, and moved into the Rocky Mountains, branched off at Fort Hall in Idaho, with one route heading south into California and the other, much less traveled path, heading into Oregon Territory. Before the Gold Rush, less than 3,000 hearty individuals had ever used the trail, which predominantly served as a pathway for the U.S. military. During this pre–Gold Rush era, the Overland Trail was little more than, and sometimes only, a line drawn on a map. At various points, markers, most often natural terrain features, guided travelers along. The trail itself had previously gained some notoriety connected to two distinct historical events: first, being the route of choice for Americans who migrated into Mexican California and who served in Captain John C. Fremont's California Battalion in the Mexican–American War, and secondly as the first leg of the tragic Donner Party, before they made the fateful decision to follow Lansford Hastings's *Emigrant Guide to Oregon and California*, which took them through the so-called Hastings Cutoff across the Great Salt Desert followed by a series of nearly impassible mountains that stalled their progress and left the emigrants stranded high in the Sierra Nevada just in time of one of the heaviest snowfalls in recorded history. However, by spring 1849, tens of thousands of people were on the California Trail, creating an endless stream of wagon trains, ox-pulled carts, men on horseback, mules, and even men on foot.

The two most prominent southern routes that began in Texas were the Upper Emigrant Road anchored in the port town of Galveston and the Lower Emigrant Road, which started in Port Lavaca, south of Galveston. Eventually these two routes merged in El Paso and hugged the shoreline of the Gila River before crossing into California at Yuma, wherein the route divided into two, with a southern run to San Diego and a northern route to Los Angeles. In these two, sleepy port towns, emigrants would catch any ship available that would take them to San Francisco. This southern route had one distinct advantage over its northern counterparts, a very temperate winter. However, during the agonizing summer, when daily temperatures average for weeks and months around the century mark, it was nearly impossible for greenhorns to survive.

A popular central route, the Gregg-Marcy, departed Fort Smith Arkansas and headed due west to Santa Fe and Albuquerque, before taking a sharp southern turn where it joined up with the Gila River Trail. There was a good reason for the sharp turn south, which added a few hundred miles to the trek. First, the arid Southwest had few water resources; thus emigrants literally had to hug the shoreline of the Rio Grande, which runs north–south, and then the Gila River, which runs east–west, to survive. The Santa Fe Trail, which began in Independence, Missouri, and followed the Arkansas River to Bent's Fort in Colorado before heading south to join the Gila River Trail, was the second most popular route after the Oregon–California Trail coming out of the Midwest.

Water may have been the most sought-after commodity on the trail, though at times this most desirable asset became the emigrants' greatest adversary. In addition to the challenges associated with crossing the great rivers, the powerful storms that routinely blast through the Plains and Rockies during the spring presented considerable obstacles for the emigrants. Heavy rains for several days would turn the grassy plains into a soft mud. The heavy wagons with weights exceeding a few tons would see their narrow wheels sink down not inches, but rather feet into the saturated soils. Animals, in particular massive oxen, would routinely get stuck in the mud. Flash floods would create impassible torrents out of dry washes. While lightening posed a threat, it was rare that a bolt actually hit an emigrant. However, the spring storms in these regions also brought large hail, capable of shredding canvas.

While there were several routes and modes of locomotion employed in getting the gold fields, there was one thread of continuity that ran through the minds of the emigrants: get to the gold fields as fast as possible. Not surprisingly, the creative minds of ambitious individuals, who dreamed of making their fortune not in the act of gold mining, but in transportation, produced some memorable failures from the earliest moments of the Gold Rush. One of the most colorful of the fanciful speculations was developed by Rufus

Porter, the founding publisher of *New York Mechanic* and *Scientific American*. Porter was both a highly talented inventor and magazine editor, who was also a true pioneer in theoretical aerial dynamics. Porter was also prone to exaggeration, a not too uncommon trait during the Gold Rush. In early 1849, Porter published that he was making "active progress" in the building of a revolutionary "aerial transport" that could carry between 50 and 100 passengers at an average speed in the range of 60 to 100 miles per hour. His design was virtual dirigible hotel that was, in essence, jet propelled. Porter received more scoffs of doubt than support for his airship. Undeterred by his critics, Porter guaranteed that his aircraft would be able to transport passengers from New York City to the California gold fields and return to New York in seven days. While Porter was able to convince many a speculator to purchase their tickets in advance of the completion of his airship for $50 a head, instead of paying the gate price of $200, the aerial transport never came to fruition. Alas, the overland crossing would be limited to ground transportation, which relied on either human or animal-powered locomotion—that is to say, by foot.

The covered wagon, commonly referred to as "Prairie Schooners," became a nearly ubiquitous site on the trail. While in the urban environment one of these large wagons could be easily pulled by one or two horses, depending on the burden inside the wagon, when crossing the unimproved trails across the plains, let alone the mountain passes, the much more powerful oxen were the preferred method of muscle power. Directing oxen also differed in technique than horses or mules required. Rather than sitting atop the buckboard behind the beasts, the teamster would walk alongside the lead ox. As these wagons had little to no shock absorption capabilities, many emigrants whose health and physical strength permitted did in fact choose to walk rather than ride inside during what was an overwhelming a bumpy, and at times bone jarring, ride. However, small children and the elderly were the most frequent passengers. Often, these wagons were little more than covered carts. Bowed wooden frame slats provided the skeleton for the heavy cloths that provided minimal protection from the elements. The primary services that these wagons afforded beyond transporting those who could not walk or ride a horse was a relatively safe place to sleep at night and the vessel that carried the supplies.

Of all the wagon designs, the Conestoga was one of the most sought after. The original design of the Conestoga harkened back nearly a century before the Gold Rush. By 1849, these wagons were being built over 20 feet long and were capable of hauling over 8 tons. The unique design of the Conestoga, its trademark hull that curved upward on both ends, permitted easier movement up and down sloping terrain. A curve design was also incorporated into the canopy, which provided cover from the elements beyond the base frame of the wagon. These rugged wagons, along with other designs, also utilized ironclad wooden wheels, which did not make for a more comfortable ride but did significantly add to their durability; wheels were one of the most common appendages to break during the great trek to California.

As more and more well-to-do emigrants took to the trail, the fancier and larger the wagons became, and the presence of more than one wagon per family was also a more common occurrence. These middle- to upper-class adventurers were certainly motivated by the prospect of striking it rich, though they often appeared nearly as eager to leave their traditional, mundane lives behind, if only temporarily, and find adventure on the trails, though not without substantial creature comforts. Remarkably, some of these gentleman emigrants would bring dozens of heads of oxen, several horses, mules, and milk cows that were managed by small units of farm hands. Inside of their luxury wagons, it was not uncommon to find feather beds, stoves, small collections of books, enough kitchen utensils to outfit a small eatery, and a relative gourmet expanse of foods. However, given the rough terrain that these folks would face once past the Plains, lightening one's load became commonplace. Additionally, the conspicuous consumption of this gentry class captured the attention of thieves and bandits as they stood out quite prominently from their less well-heeled colleagues.

Although water was scarcer on the Overland Trail than any emigrant could have cared for, when gold seekers were forced to cross rivers without the aid of a ferry barge it would become necessary to ford the wagons across. To prevent the wagon from taking on water, tar pitch was commonly applied to holes and seams whenever possible. Animals were led across at the shallowest points to minimize the chance of drowning. One of the most widely recorded river crossings was the Northern Platte.

The most common threat that emigrants faced in their great trek across the arid plains and west was running out of water, the most essential substance for all known life forms. Not always able to travel along a river, and given the intensity of the summer heat in the West and Southwest, the Argonauts may have consistently attempted to ration water, though at times that approach was simply not practical. Additionally, the livestock needed to be hydrated as well. Abundant stories of people slaughtering their dehydrated animals became a part of the growing mythology of life on the trail. While there is no doubt that extreme cases such as that occurred, more common were the stories of water being sold to thirsty emigrants at exorbitant prices. Also important to note, water was not a prized commodity at the most frequented forts along the California–Oregon Trail, as Kearney and Laramie were located along the Platte. However, if emigrants took the southern cutoff at the South Pass west of Fort Laramie, which took them to Fort Bridger and Salt Lake City, water brokering was big business in this arid stretch of nearly 400 miles.

FORMATION OF COMPANIES

Similar to the migrants who ventured into Mexican Alta California during the early through mid-1840s, many emigrants pooled their resources and entered into cooperative enterprises, known as joint-stock companies. Early on in the Gold Rush the joint-stock companies proved popular. The security they provided, both psychological and genuine, typically extended beyond the trek and into the gold fields. The population of the companies ranged from a dozen to a few hundred in size. The agreed-upon laws within the companies directly influenced the overall law and order atmosphere on the trail. Most associations restricted vice activities such as gambling, alcohol consumption, and even foul language in some instances. The reasoning behind such a rigid social structure was that on the frontier, far from so-called civilization, man needed significant guidelines that would prevent conflicts within the party that could prove disastrous. Punishments for transgressions were included in the agreed-upon constitutions and ranged from fines to banishment from the party and the forfeiture of one's capital investment in the company. Decision making was overwhelmingly done by a vote of all adults rather than by a committee or single decider. The most common indiscretion was the consumption of alcohol.

The companies quite often were formed not simply for the trek but also were designed to work collectively in the mining camps. The greater purchasing power of the companies, as opposed to the average, solitary miner, permitted them to take on more mining claims, establish actual cooperative mining camps, and, in the process, bring an atmosphere of normality.

STOPS ALONG THE TRAIL

In addition to the fast growth of the Native American entrepreneurs who developed commerce and trade with the emigrants, military outposts located along the routes witnessed a significant increase of traders in and around their installations. Along the Oregon–California Trail, one of the first significant trading outposts frequented by the Argonauts was Fort Kearney, also the first such military fort built to actually protect the Americans along the Overland Trail. Construction on Fort Kearney began in earnest in 1842 as the U.S. sentiment of Manifest Destiny escalated. Located in the contemporary state of Nebraska, the military installation, originally christened Fort Childs, was strategically located along the Platte River by Lt. Daniel Phineas Woodbury, as graduate of West Point. Woodbury, who originally served as an artillery officer, made a name for himself as an engineer during his service in the construction of a western segment of the Cumberland Road in the early 1840s. Woodbury's original construction of Fort Childs was not heavily fortified, due in no small measure to the general lack of building supplies and manpower. The fort was renamed Fort Kearney, in honor of General Stephen Watts Kearney, a hero of the Mexican–American War, who died prematurely after contracting Yellow Fever in 1858. Kearney also played a prominent role in the conquest of Mexican California, and in a twist of historical coincidence, the fort bearing his name would subsequently play a significant role in the California Gold Rush.

By 1849, Fort Kearney began as a literal frontier boom town as emigrant numbers increased with each passing day; consequently, what began as a single adobe structure grew to a small collection of such structures within a year. From the onset, the constant flow of emigrants guaranteed that Fort Kearney would serve predominantly as a trading post. Roughly 350 miles from start of the trail in Independence, Missouri, Fort Kearney, emigrants came upon this welcomed site after having spent between 25 and 30 days on the trail; a good daily pace was considered 15 miles. Still relatively fresh on the trail, emigrants tended to purchase more than what they needed with virtually every commodity. Hence, the economy of Fort Kearney was particularly strong. Additionally, the heavy mail volume of letters composed by gold seekers during the first leg of their journey led to a greater apportionment of carriers and ultimately the establishment of a Central Overland California and Pikes Peak Express Company Pony Express station at Fort Kearney in 1850.

The next significant outpost for emigrants along the Oregon–California Trail was Fort Laramie, located in contemporary Wyoming along the Platte River. Arguably the most significant outpost, Fort Laramie was the anchor for the economy on the trail. While the Fort Kearney to Fort Laramie leg was a slightly shorter in distance than the segment from Independence to Fort Kearney, it was typically a more arduous trek, and it also marked the entry into the Rocky Mountains in the West. Originally Laramie was named Fort William, after William Sublette who built it as an unfortified outpost during the fur trade in 1834 with the ambition to trade with Sioux Indians. Sublette's ambition of establishing a lucrative industry in this remote location relied heavily on his ability to supply the Native Americans with alcohol and tobacco in exchange for buffalo hides. As more and more non-Native Americans went into the buffalo hide business, the price for each unit dropped significantly, and by 1840, Sublette was no longer able to sustain his business enterprise; in the following year, the robust American Fur Company took over the fort, and rather than operate out of the small wooden structure erected by Sublette, the corporation built an adobe. The fur trade continued its decline through the 1840s, which led the American Fur Company to sell the fort to the U.S. Army in 1849. Changing the name to Fort Laramie, the charge given to the army was to provide support for the emigrants.

From its earliest moments, Fort Laramie was a serious military installation and home to the 6th Infantry. The economy of the fort had been transformed from its previous heavy reliance on the fur trade, and by 1850 it enjoyed a very diverse array of businesses. From being a mail route station to housing dry goods shops, Fort Laramie welcomed its guests, and given its relatively high level of creature comforts compared to the trail, emigrants would set up their encampments for a few days, allowing their livestock the opportunity to feed and rest while necessary repairs were made to their wagons. A great deal of useful information about what laid ahead on the trail was also disseminated at Fort Laramie that proved most beneficial. Also, all the emigrants knew fully well that once they departed Fort Laramie, the most difficult terrain laid ahead. Prostitution around Fort Laramie also grew as the numbers of emigrants increased. While never on the same scale as the brothels in the Gold Rush boom towns or San Francisco, this vice, along with the sale of alcohol, became two of the most profitable enterprises at the fort.

Fort Laramie also, by dint of its geographic location, became the focus of the Sioux Nations, which began to resent the further encroachment of white settlement on and passage through their lands. One of the most significant altercations between the Sioux and the whites and military personnel at Fort Laramie occurred in 1854. Over 3,000 and perhaps as many as 4,500 Oglala and Brule Sioux had built their villages around Fort Laramie, following the terms of the 1851 treaty between the Sioux and the United States, which guaranteed American emigrants a right of passage through their lands and also protected the integrity of the Indian villages and also a significant toll payment made to the Indians for the passage rights. In August 1854, a dairy cow belonging to an emigrant wandered into the Indian camp and was slaughtered. Brule Lakota Chief Conquering Bear attempted to pay for the lost cow by offering the owner of the cow any of his horses. The owner refused the exchange and demanded a cash settlement. Lt. John L. Grattan heightened the tensions when he led a detachment into the Lakota camp in search of the alleged cow-killer. When Conquering Bear refused to turn over the person responsible, High Forehead, Lt. Grattan, returned to Fort Laramie, though the next day Grattan assembled a well-armed cadre of 30 men and two units of artillery. After a long session of failed negotiations, in part due to a poor translator in service to the fort, Grattan assembled his men and prepared to exit when one of his soldiers shot Conquering Bear in the back, mortally wounding him. Completely surrounded by over a thousand Sioux warriors, Grattan and his soldiers were annihilated. Only the translator, who was married to a Sioux woman, was spared. The event, commonly known as the Grattan Massacre, fueled anti-Indian sentiment in the United States as news accounts of the event portrayed the Native Americans in an exceptionally poor light. While the incident at Fort Laramie was by no means the first conflict between the Native Americans and the United States in the West, it did significantly influence the course of history. The United States ramped up its efforts at placing the Native Americans on reservations, which were placed under the supervision of the military.

The next stop along the trail came after the split at the South Pass, where those heading into Oregon veered north and those en route to the California Gold Rush proceeded south toward Salt Lake City, stopping first at Fort Bridger. Unlike Fort Laramie, Fort Bridger was at best a ramshackle outpost that had virtually no hint of civilization as conceived by the emigrants. Heavily populated with Native Americans and trappers who lived in common in and around the premises, Fort Bridger was built by Jim Bridger, a trapper who conceived of a trading empire with the Indians, though one component of his strategy was in violation of federal law. Jim Bridger traded alcohol and munitions with the Indians in exchange for pelts. Mormon movement into Utah led them directly through Fort Bridger in 1847, and the conflict of lifestyles between Brigham Young and his followers with Jim Bridger led to a series of legal battles, though ultimately the Mormons purchased Fort Bridger in 1855. However, during the flood of Gold Rush migration, Jim Bridger controlled the fort bearing his surname.

Many of the emigrants who passed through Fort Bridger noted the high prices for goods relative to the costs at Fort Laramie and Fort Kearney. There was also a genuine lack of quality as well as a very high rate of fraud. In the end, the exceptionally poor physical environment encouraged the briefest of encampments, effectively saving the emigrants both time and money as they did not find Fort Bridger hospitable.

After rounding the growing Mormon settlement of Salt Lake City, emigrants again headed north, avoiding the Great Salt Desert to the south of Salt Lake City, which was nearly impassible in its own right, though due east of the desert lay a series of rugged Sierra Nevada, the same ones that destroyed the Donner Party just a few years earlier. After passing Salt Lake, the California Trail then hugged the shoreline of the Humboldt River, which is the longest river to run through this region, known as the Great Basin. Explored and mapped by John C. Fremont, this became one of the final legs of the California Trail as well as one of the easiest.

The southern route from Independence, Missouri, known as the Santa Fe Trail, was considerably less popular than its northern rival. William Becknell established the trail in 1821 as a trade route with Mexico. The Santa Fe Trail cut through the growing empire of the Comanche, who permitted a right of way through their land for a toll, before it joined with the Gila River Trail, which ran from El Paso, through Tucson and into Yuma. The greatest impediment that discouraged emigrants from using this southern route was the intense summer heat, with average temperatures cresting 100 degrees Fahrenheit from early June through September. Additionally, upon arrival into California, at its southernmost point, the journey to the gold fields was far from complete. Emigrants could not simply head due north from Yuma as they would have to cross nearly 450 miles of desert, including both the Mojave and Death Valley. Instead, they continued west to either San Diego or Los Angeles, both sleepy hamlets at the time, wherein they would board ships that would take them to the ever-growing port city of San Francisco in the north. From San Francisco, they would then head toward Sacramento, their last stop before moving out to their respective mining claim sites.

FROM ALL AROUND THE WORLD

The trek to California's gold fields became worldwide news in 1849, and, consequently, the tales of abundant, free gold, just waiting to be picked up, became a beacon for fortune seekers from Europe, Asia, and South America. From Asia, the Chinese were by far the greatest in number. At the start of 1849, there were less than 100 Chinese living in California. Within the next decade, their population in the Golden State would crest over 10,000. Known in their homeland as "Gold Mountain Men," these brave travelers came across the Pacific Ocean and entered California through its great western gateway, San Francisco. More than most of the other miners, the Chinese then walked from the port town to the gold fields, carrying their basic tools with them in a pack. From South America, the Chileans, many of whom were already experienced miners, far outnumbered all others. As Chile is on the west coast of South America, their trek was much shorter than the Americans who came by sea. There were even tales of Chileans who walked from their homeland to California. Mexican migration into California grew considerably in 1849. Mexico's relative close proximity to the gold fields, as it shares the entire southern border of the state, afforded Mexican gold miners a distinct advantage; rather than being months away from the gold, most could make the trip in a matter of weeks. From Europe, the Irish and the Italians became the most common entrants into California, and within a matter of just a few years, these two ethnic groups would come to play a central role in California's political and economic makeup. In addition to the free gold, California's laissez-faire culture was quite an incentive. However, this seemingly open society would radically change as 1849 came to an end, and those who felt the sharp changes the most were the foreigners, in particular the non-white immigrants.

CHANGES ON THE LAND ALONG THE TRAIL

The environmental impact of the constant flow of traffic along the trail was recognizable within months. Items no longer needed, wanted, or functional were simply discarded en route. While some "recycling" did take place as emigrants scavenged the droppings, much was left behind to later be recovered by archaeologists, anthropologists, historians, and treasure seekers. Humans were not the only scavengers along the trail. As people discarded unwanted or inedible foods or leftovers, scavengers in the animal world ranging from the coyote to the crow found sustenance. As emigrants would note, the crow became one of the constant companions along the route.

Emigrants also brought with them a variety of domesticated animals. Most common were the horse, milk cows, donkeys, jackasses, oxen, dogs, and cats. While these animals provided the locomotion power, food, protection, and companionship, they also impacted the manner and speed of movement. Animals, unlike most modern machinery, cannot operate uninterrupted for stretches of several hours. Rather, animals must be rested and fed routinely. Some, such as the dairy cows, had other points of care to consider if they were to be productive in supplying milk, which became a staple food product on the trail, they need to consume grasses for a few hours each day and must also sleep for several hours per each 24-hour cycle, with the nighttime serving this obvious necessity. While slumber typically was not an encumbering problem, grazing was an issue, as literally hundreds of thousands of cows, ox, and other domesticated herbivores with voracious appetites fueled by long, grueling walks consumed vast quantities of grasses and other forms of vegetation, leaving great swaths of land barren as though consumed by a plight of locusts. As these animals consistently fanned out in search of fresh fields, the wake of environmental destruction also reached a broader range. Although the manure they left behind proved environmentally beneficial for the most part, the foods they consumed impacted the indigenous animal kingdom. In particular, the migration and feeding patterns of the Bison stand out as one of the most affected, which also led to increased tensions between the Indians and non-Native Americans.

THE DIET ALONG THE TRAIL

The emigrants on the overland trails fared much better nutritionally than their counterparts on the high seas. Wagons could carry considerably more food and meal preparation amenities than one could bring on a ship. Additionally, depending on the geographical location, wild game was a fine supplement. For those who had the economic means and could afford one or more dairy cows, milk, cream, and cheese supplied ample protein and enhanced the emigrant's immunity. The cream of the milk contains a high level of fat and protein and was a staple at breakfast for those with a dairy cow in tote. Typically, the first and last activity of the day was the milking of the cows. The cream is then separated from the milk and placed in a butter churn. Cheese making, though much less common, did take place. The great threat to the well-being of the cows took place when crossing great stretches of land that lacked the necessary grasses and clover for grazing. In these extreme cases, dairy cows not only would lose their ability to lactate; rather, they faced potential starvation resulting in death. While a dead dairy cow's meat could be harvested, with no means of preservation beyond salt or jerking, a great deal of the meat would have to be sold, used for barter, or simply lost. Indeed, the milk was a much more precious dietary component, and the cow's health was of a significant concern for its owner.

Emigrants were strongly influenced by storekeepers and travel advice publications on what food products and their respective quantities that they should stock up on before departure. At least 200 pounds of flour per person was standard. Flour could be turned into johnnycake or biscuits and added to soups or stews as a thickening agent. Second to flour, rice was a popular starch and following rice was barley. Sugar and salt were not simply for seasoning; they also served as a preservation agent of wild berries and meats. Emigrant provisions of 30 pounds of each were quite common. Any meats brought on the trip were salt and or sugar cured. Not surprisingly, bacon was one of the favored meat products along with pork and beef jerky. A typical planned ration of such meats was 20 pounds. Dried fruits and dried beans were quite popular. Beans could be used in stews or as a separate meal component, and they provided iron, protein, and dietary fiber. Virtually every fruit grown was sold in dried form to emigrants; some of the more common included apples and peaches. By far the most popular beverages on the trail were coffee and whiskey. Coffee was made by bringing a pot of water to a boil, tossing in a handful of grounds, and, after a few minutes of boil, taking the pot off the fire to allow for a settling of the grounds to the bottom. This morning brew was certainly a far cry in flavor and composition from contemporary coffee. The preferred whiskey came in at around 90 percent alcohol or 180 proof, and was commonly referred to as rotgut. Far too potent and harsh to be consumed straight, this beverage was commonly added to either water or coffee. Whiskey was also used for medicinal purposes, including sterilization.

Typically, the greenhorn emigrants packed too many frivolous items if they were traveling by wagon, and as they came to understand the virtue in traveling light and which provisions served their interests the best, they tried to sell or barter away any excesses. Failing to secure remuneration for these unwanted items led many to simply cast them aside. When emigrants discarded items along the sides of the trail to lighten the load on their beasts of burden, coffee and whiskey were always the least likely to be tossed aside. One of the most commonly discarded items, due to their weight, were the stoves that many gold seekers packed. The culinary utensils were just the bare essentials. One cup or mug per person, a tin plate, a frying pan, kettle, coffee pot, and a knife and fork were enough, and tens of thousands of utensils littered the routes and continue to be recovered today.

Women, when a part of an emigrant family or a company, typically held the responsibility of the food preparation and cleanup, though if children were in the party and of a reasonable age were often given the charge of cleanup as well as the milking of cows. If no women or children were present, or if a man were traveling alone, he would then have no choice but to take on all roles.

Hunting wild game took place whenever the possibility presented itself. In this regard, emigrants proved most pragmatic about extending their diet. Deer and antelope were sought after perhaps more than any other animal. Easy to dress and providers of some of the sweetest meat, when emigrants spotted these either of these two animals, the formation of a hunting party soon followed. Bison was also a popular food source and much easier to fell than the antelope or deer. Young bison were preferred over adults for their flavor. Given the large size of bison, the parts left behind encouraged scavengers such as crows, buzzards, and coyotes to follow the wagon trains. The bison at times also presented another unique challenge for the emigrants. Some emigrants encountered herds that stretched for a dozen miles deep and over a mile in width. The large buffalo herds were prone to scaring the domestic animals, and only the most impetuous emigrant would ever attempt to cut through a herd, which was almost always a tragic decision. Buffalo chips (manure) were also commonly used as fuel in place of wood along the trail.

Some of the most abundant game animals were rodents; rabbits, prairie dogs, and squirrels. Not particularly a tasty meat when grilled, prairie dogs and squirrels were most commonly tossed into a stew pot. Wild rabbit, on the other hand, though tougher than one that had been farm raised, was nonetheless a tastier morsel and was consequently one of the more prized small game animals. Fowl was popular, though more difficult to bag. Prairie and sage hens were not only the easiest birds to shoot; they were also one of the tastiest. Birds of prey were known to be shot, prepared, and consumed. However, scavengers such as crows and vultures were only choked down when one's survival depended on it. Another meat, similar in taste and composition to the domestic chicken, was rattlesnake. While one might feel apathetic about consuming their first rattlesnake, if cooked over an open flame or in a stew, this tasty morsel tended to become a favorite. Not only are rattlesnakes easy to prepare, most emigrants were enthusiastic about killing these dangerous vipers. If provisions were running low, and there was not much promise in finding game, the domestic animals could be slaughtered. However, emigrants understood the greater implication of consuming the animals that provided the muscle behind their locomotion across the continent.

The two big meals of the day were breakfast and the evening dinner. Breakfast preparation began before the sun came up and the ubiquitous presence of coffee being brewed filled the air with its enticing aroma. Johnnycake, biscuits, beans, and cured meat was the common menu, though when a shortage of supplies occurred, which was commonplace, anything edible sufficed. Dinner was typically more than just the biggest meal of the day. It was a social event along the trail as emigrants would discuss the day's events and plan for the next day's travel. The conversation, typically well lubricated, was filled with chatter about striking it rich and, not surprisingly, getting to the gold as fast as possible.

LAW AND ORDER ON THE TRAIL

The absence of any organized or official peace officers in the vast unorganized territory that the emigrants moved through required self-reliance. The letters and journals of the emigrants indicate that their long migrations were predominantly free of criminal threats. The most common crimes committed were larceny, spousal abuse, robbery, and assault. Murder and manslaughter did occur, though quite infrequently.

One of the contributing reasons behind the lack of criminal activity was the fact that everyone carried at least one weapon and most brought a few. The knowledge that virtually all were capable of self-preservation, and also revenge, proved a strong deterrence. The most preferred collection of weaponry included a handgun, a long rifle, and an assortment of knives. What is most apparent is that the majority of emigrants understood that they would have to periodically use their guns not only for hunting but also for personal protection from belligerents, land pirates, and aggressive wild animals. One of the realities that they had overwhelmingly not given much thought to or prepared for were the accidents that resulted from a lack of experience with fire arms of large, razor-sharp knives used for dressing downed game. As many of the Argonauts were greenhorns, accidents when hunting, conducting target practice, or even in the cleaning or carrying of guns resulted in tragic situations. Due to the difficult nature of providing a sterile environment on the trail, first aid was often inadequate, and the onset of infection, followed by death, was feared and for good reason.

While not a prevalent feature of life on trial, crimes were committed. Theft on the trail was a serious offense, in particular if the item commandeered was an ox, horse, or cow. The lives of the travelers depended on these particular beasts, and the theft of one was viewed as a life-threatening criminal act. The most common forms of punishment for this crime were banishment, if one were in a party, and death, if one were not.

Violence within the party was never tolerated. If a member were consistently belligerent, a party would typically vote to banish the troublemaking member. Banishment, if done in one of the more precarious locations, such as in the arid zones of the Great Plains and Utah, or in the deserts that dominated the southern routes that cut through Texas and into Mexico, was tantamount to a death sentence. If murder had been committed, punishments included whippings, banishment, and death. Additionally, one consistent feature in the meting out of justice was its swiftness as the call of the gold beckoned, and no one wanted to spend any more time en route than necessary.

END OF THE JOURNEY

The primary goal of all who made the journey was virtually the same: get to California and strike it rich. Not all that attempted to get to California made it to their perceived promised land. As many as a thousand fortune seekers along the sea route died before ever reaching their destination. While shipwrecks occurred, the primary culprit was disease; most common was dysentery. Those unfortunate souls who traveled by land but who passed away en route and never reached the famed gold filled rivers, streams, and creeks were often victims of cholera. Violence claimed hundreds of lives, though when compared to the great number of emigrants, over 100,000, and given the incredible stress that these Argonauts were under, death delivered by the hand or action of another was rare. Some emigrants decided along the way to turn back and head for home. This was more common for those on land. Physically more demanding, many pioneers concluded after the first 300 miles along the trail that the next 1,200 miles, which included mountains, deserts, and possible altercations with Native Americans, was simply beyond their desire. However, the vast majority of those who embarked upon this fanciful journey did make it to California, though for most, the reality did not reflect what their imagination had conceived of.

3

THE GOLDEN YEARS OF THE RUSH, 1848–1850: ECONOMIC EXPANSION, POPULATION EXPLOSION, AND RUSH TO STATEHOOD

The physical appearance of life in the gold fields went through a series of evolutionary changes after 1848 that no one could have foreseen. In the first year, when John Sutter's workers made up the majority of the gold miners along the American River, life was exciting for these few, lucky individuals, though it was peaceful as well. By the spring of 1849, mining camps had come and gone, and in the process, the future state of California had its first ghost towns. Additionally, the numbers of miners had increased from several hundred to several thousands, with the majority of these hearty individuals still hugging the American River and its tributaries. At the start of 1849, the majority of the miners were from relatively local points of origin and primarily from California. By the midpoint in that same year, California had been transformed into a polyglot society, and along the way, the population of those directly connected with the Gold Rush reached over 50,000. Throughout 1849, the diggings were productive, sparsely populated and plentiful. Miners were able to locate "color" with relative ease. By early 1850, that reality was seemingly lost to history. While an incredible amount of gold was recovered in 1850, the laborious effort needed to fill one's sack had increased tenfold. Society itself grew more complex in the diggings, boom towns, and cities. Indeed, anyone who bore witness to California before and during these years witnessed a social and physical transformation, the likes of which the world had not seen before or since. The changes wrought out in California also propelled the territory into statehood and in the process pushed the United States closer to being a truly continental nation and also to the brink of civil war.

TOOLS OF THE TRADE

Of all the tools utilized in the California Gold Rush, none is more common than the stamp iron pan. These flat-bottomed pans, typically measuring between 18 and 24 inches at the base with a rising side between 3 and 5 inches, were the first and most prevalent tool throughout the period. Miners would scoop up stream or riverbed pebbles, usually a handful at a time, and, in a swirling motion, use the water to separate the particles. Since gold was the heaviest, the slight angle at which the miners held the pan while putting it through the motions would result in a settlement of the gold toward the most elevated part of the base as the alluvial was washed down. Additionally, the bright yellow color and shimmer of the gold distinguished it from all other materials. As the miners swirled away with the pans, they would pluck the gold dust, gold pebbles, or gold nuggets out and carefully store them in a secured manner. Pans were also used in so-called dry diggings, which took place away from a waterway on dry land. With nearly the exact principal method, miners would sift through the earthen materials in their quest for "color," simply without the aid that water provided.

As miners were completely dependent upon the light of day, speed and focus were of the utmost concern when one was panning for gold. Careless movements could lose precious flakes or pebbles of gold, and if one spent too much time per pan at sorting and sifting, then significant amounts of materials were not examined through the course of the back-breaking day. Most efficient miners were able to work through 40 to 50 pans per day. It was incredibly difficult and redundant work. Hands took a beating, as did the backs of the miners. Depending on the season and elevation, if a miner were working in a river or stream, hypothermia was a constant threat. Exposure to the elements and the repetitive motions associated with panning took their toll on the miners, and at the end of each exhausting day, whiskey was one of the most welcomed elixirs. While innovations in mining came rather quickly during the Gold Rush, the pan never vanished, though its role certainly diminished as it was relegated from its central role as a tool of choice to a strictly supporting role of fine sifting.

Picks and shovels afforded the miner the ability to remove pounds of earth at a time and also break up larger rocks in the quest to find out what was beneath them. After a miner would clean out the surface gold within his claim, the next step was to dig down as far as possible in order to extract any underground gold. The larger nuggets tended to be the ones that the miners had to dig for and in their earnest manner the dirt would literally start flying when the shovels and picks were employed. The physical terrain was much more dramatically impacted with this invasive mining method. Gold seekers at the small rivers and creeks would note in their journals how in the matter of just one day, 10 dedicated miners could remove all vestiges of nature. It was a common sight in the dry diggings to witness a miner dig down between four and six feet in just one day's work. When one would strike a few ounces or an even a pound or two, the diggings of those around the lucky miner would only accelerate.

GOLD MINE CLAIMS

The image of the California Gold Rush miner of a solitary individual stooped over in a shallow creek, swirling a pan, sifting carefully through the gravel and debris in search of gold is one of the most lasting images and common understandings that contemporary society has of the 49er. However, the mining practices were actually quite varied, as was the physical environment where the laborious quest for color took place, and consequently, there were several different topographical classifications of the mines.

At the start of the great discovery in 1848, the two most common types of mining practices were focused on recovering placer gold and gold veins in quartz. The placer gold was found as grains, pebbles, and nuggets that were typically free of foreign material and found either on or close to the surface of the bed of streams, creeks, or rivers, strewn by nature among the gravel or covered by sand or mud. The surface gold was by far the easiest to recover, though very rarely did a miner come across a unit any larger than a few ounces. Miners quickly discovered that deposits of placer gold on the surface or in shallow mines also suggested that more gold lay underneath in the vicinity. It was not uncommon to find miners using their shovels and picks to dig down to depths as great as 20 feet as they slowly and carefully processed each square inch of earthen materials in search of color. These deep mines were primarily located in the adjacent flatlands, though as the miners fanned out in all directions from the running water, diggings covered the hills and even sprang up in the mountains.

Ancient river claims, essentially dry river beds, also proved on many occasions to contain significant gold deposits in their beds and in shallow levels beneath the surface. These dry creeks and rivers with the nearly concrete-like beds proved quite difficult to penetrate for the miners. Unlike the functioning riparian mines or even the hillsides covered with vegetation, mining in the ancient river mines was an incredibly slow process. Hours of pick axing was required to break the sunbaked surface. Shoveling a depth of 20 feet in this harsh environment took three to four times the effort and time, as did digging in the grass- and flora-covered locations. While the miners were not encumbered by a flowing water stream that might prevent them from penetrating very far beneath the surface, these extinct rivers proved a great challenge to the miners.

Sandy or gravel bars exposed during a period of relatively low water levels in creeks, streams, and rivers along virtually every major Gold Rush waterway were popular mining claims that yielded thousands upon thousands of rich deposits. While miners could not dig very deep in the bars, as they would invariably fill with water from their neighboring flow, the relative ease to spot the glistening color was but one of the engaging features that this form of dry claim offered. Miners could pan while standing on dry land and still utilize the flowing water as an effective agent of debris removal. So popular was this mode of mining from the onset of the Gold Rush that it led to dramatic environmental changes throughout the gold fields. Miners very often diverted the flow of creeks, streams, and rivers to establish a bar claim. Once the bed was exposed and the water flow diverted by several yards from the claim site, diggings could proceed to significant depths. This form of claim also led directly to another form of mining, sluicing, and long toms.

Sluice claims became ubiquitous by mid-1849 throughout the gold fields. Miners would comb the water beds with their pans in search of a placer deposit. Once one was located, the sluice boxes were brought in. Sluice mining had not been invented during the California Gold Rush. Archaeological evidence suggests that this form of gold mining took place as early as 1st century BC throughout the Roman Empire. Sluicing is a very effective placer gold recovery form of mining. Water flow from any significant creek or greater is diverted to flow over a sluice box; short boxes are known as long toms, and shovel loads of gravel and earth are then deposited directly on the apparatus. A series of barriers trap the gold, while the lighter materials are then washed out at the end of the sluice. This type of mining was most common with the mining companies as it required the labor of three to four individuals. One to two miners shovel in the earth, one constantly removes the heavier debris that is not washed out of the long tom, and one is needed to continually shovel away the tailings in order to preserve an uninterrupted flow of water. The gold is then removed from the traps. A four-man team such as this could, over the course of an eight-hour day, move through eight cubic yards of earth. By late 1849, sluice boxes joined together stretching out to lengths of 40 to 50 feet could be seen along most waterways. Teams of miners worked these large-scale operations that separated tons of debris. Rocking the sluice boxes also aided in separating the gold from the unwanted tailings.

reproduire dignement.
Une servante française m'accompagna dans la chambre

Je pris bientôt congé de mes hôtes charmants et je gagnai ma chambre. Les chiens, me reconnaissant déjà pour

Chinois lavant les sables aurifères du rocker. — Dessin de Chassevent d'après une gravure californienne.

un ami de la maison, m'accompagnèrent poliment jusque sur le seuil. Au moment de me coucher, je m'aperçus que ma porte, qui donnait en pleine campagne, n'avait ni clef ni serrure. Je me rappelai que la fenêtre

calme et de sécurité que je rencontrais en Californie, mais je me plaisais encore à reconnaître dans mes nouveaux hôtes, si accueillants, une image de Philémon et Baucis, sauf l'âge et moins la pauvreté, sauf aussi votre

While more efficient and less back breaking than just a pan, the labor-intensive rocker, as depicted here, was nonetheless a very labor-intensive form of mining. (G. Chassevent, *Chinois lavant les sables auriferes du rocker*, 1862. Steel engraving, 4.75 × 6.25 in. Collection of the Oakland Museum of California, Oakland Museum of California Donors Acquisition Fund.)

Quartz gold was a different matter altogether. Gold veins, literally encased in hard rock, such as quartz, required a considerable amount of effort to recover during the both the location and separation processes. These considerably more labor-intensive efforts had the potential to reward the diligent miner with a remarkable yield that went beyond a few ounces and into the range of a few pounds. One of the first finds of quartz gold in California occurred in 1850 in Nevada County. This first find, located near Wolf Creek, led to a flood of gold seekers, who fanned out across the county in search of quartz laden with gold veins. The output of quartz gold was so significant that a new industry formed within a few months that focused specifically on gold extraction from quartz. Gold Hill is commemorated as California Historical Site number 297 and the official historical marker states: "The discovery was made on Gold Hill by George Knight in October 1850. The occurrence of gold-bearing quartz was undoubtedly noted here and elsewhere about the same time or even earlier, but this discovery created the great excitement that started the development of quartz mining into a great industry. The Gold Hill Mine is credited with a total production of $4,000,000 between 1850 and 1857." Gold Hill ran dry in the mid-1860s, though not before giving birth to the city of Grass Valley.

BOUNDARIES AND UNDERSTANDINGS

The pans, picks, and shovels also served as boundary markers for the miner's claim. During the early stage of the Gold Rush, 1848–1849, there were very few quarrels associated with claim infringement. The physical area of the claims was usually in the range of 8 to 12 feet squared, and it was rare for anyone to have more than two productive claims at any given time. The communities of miners self-regulated the understanding that claims could not be left to go fallow. Thus, if a miner physically left his claim for a few days, the gentlemen's agreement to respect his property disintegrated as others would start to work the abandoned spot. Also important to note, the miners virtually never had an understanding that they held title to the land where they worked their claim. Rather, their intention was to work that spot until it was barren and then move on. Throughout the gold fields, miners resented and, in most cases, prevented slaves from digging and panning for a master. Additionally, the Spanish-Mexican system of Indian peonage was looked upon with distain and strongly influenced the anti-foreigner sentiment that began to brood in late 1849. The miners saw themselves as independent business operators and refused to see their social status diminished by working alongside black slaves or Indian peons.

Each mining district from 1848 to 1849 tended to compose its own constitutions to maintain decorum, which in turn permitted the miners to focus on getting gold and not on politics or policing. Punishments for infringements nearly mirrored the wagon train parties from the Overland Trail. Speed and efficiency marked how justice was meted out, and while leniency occurred most often for a minor offence, a second offense was often reconciled with a hanging. The common lenient punishments for acts of theft or encroachment on a claim, which were the most common crimes, were a beating or banishment. Crimes such as assault routinely resulted in a severe beating, at times including a branding or the loss of a digit and were concluded with banishment. Murderers overwhelmingly found themselves dangling at the end of a rope. The swift and stern nature of the justice at the mining camps played a significant role in maintaining order, as did the commonly held belief that there was enough gold to go around. Though once the easy gold began to vanish, the harmonious settings did as well, and the law of the gun soon replaced the association agreements as the peacekeeping agent.

GEOGRAPHY OF THE GOLD FIELDS

Throughout 1848, miners from around California tried their luck along the American River and as the weeks and months passed, both the experienced miner and newcomers began to fan out in the foothills of the Sierra Nevada Mountains. No longer tied to just the American River, miners were pulling gold from along the Feather, Consumes, Stanislaus, Tuolumne, Bear, and Yuba rivers, as well as a growing number of tributaries, creeks, and streams. Gold was being discovered seemingly everywhere along the western flank of the Sierras from Mount Lassen in the north to Kings River in the south. There were several great strikes that occurred before the massive influx of Argonauts, which no doubt played a significant role in the sirens' call to the gold fields.

MORMON ISLAND

The first significant strike of gold that occurred after the original January 24, 1848, discovery at Sutter's Mill occurred just a stone's through from that location at what has become known as Mormon Island, and it quickly spread north, south, and east. Mormon Island itself, just southwest along the American River from Sutter's Mill, was actually a sandbar and not an island. Mormon men, who had previously made their way into California as part of the Mormon Battalion during the Mexican–American War, had planned on migrating into the Utah territory to join up with Brigham Young. However, Young sent word that they were to remain in California, find gainful employment, and send back money that would be used for the development of the Mormon community in Salt Lake City. These Mormon men found work under Sutter and Marshall and were at the original gold discovery. As Marshall and Sutter permitted their employees to gather gold during their downtime, the Mormon men began to migrate along the American River in search of more surface gold as well as under rocks and in the crevices along the river banks. As Sutter could not keep up with the salary demands of the Mormons, which reached $10 per day, a fantastic sum at the time, the men parted ways with Sutter and Marshall and mined full time in less than three weeks after the original discovery. In February, the Mormon miners made found a significant yield at the sand bar, which became the subject of much discussion throughout the growing Mormon community, and by early March, the once lonely sandbar became inhabited full time by at least 150 miners. By June, the number of full-time resident miners swelled to over 500, and Mormon Island was on its way to becoming an incredible strike as an estimated $100,000 of gold in 1848 prices was recovered in the first three months. Mormon Island would eventually become of the greatest strikes in Gold Rush history as millions of dollars of color would be plucked from this spot, which did not go dry until 1855.

The Mormons working the site did not limit their mining tactics to panning; rather, they quickly brought in long toms and set up diversion irrigation to both harness the water flow to use as a separating agent and dry out segments of the riverbed to dig it out and uncover more gold. As more and more people came to Mormon Island, entrepreneurially minded individuals, intent on striking it rich, but not by breaking their backs in mining, opened up hotels and shops. By 1852, there were over 2,000 people living and working at Mormon Island, which by then proudly boasted of being an actual town, complete with four hotels and over 10 shops and stores as well as a post office. At its peak in 1854, Mormon Island had a population of nearly 3,000, though the gold ran out and so did the people. In 1856, the nearly abandoned community suffered a nearly all-consuming fire, and the remains of the structures simply became ruins. California had its first, authentic, full-fledged ghost town. In 1955, the former mining town was completely razed as the Folsom Dam was erected and Mormon Island was now under Lake Folsom. The only remnant of the town that still exists is the relocated cemetery.

JOHN BIDWELL AND BIDWELL'S BAR

On the Fourth of July in 1848, John Bidwell was moving along the middle fork of the Feather River, a couple of hundred miles northwest of Sutter's Mill, when he noticed several well-formed gold nuggets glistening in the shallows of the clear, flowing water. He reached down and began picking up one after another. Some were simply small flakes, while others were nuggets that weighed a few ounces. A former employee of John Sutter, John Bidwell had just struck it rich. Originally born in upstate New York in 1819, John Bidwell moved with his family into Pennsylvania when he was ten and then to Ohio two years later, where the family settled down. After completing his high school studies at Kingsville Academy, John Bidwell began his first career as educator, eventually becoming the principal at Kingsville. In 1840, John Bidwell became bored with what he perceived to be a mundane life. As his restlessness grew, he decided to head west into Alta California of the young nation of Mexico, not only for adventure but also for the chance at striking it rich as a land baron. Bidwell joined John Bartleson and together the two men formed the Bartleson-Bidwell Party, which in May 1841 became the first wagon train to make for California from Missouri. With nearly 70 members, the Bartleson-Bidwell Party successfully arrived at their destination near present-day Mount Diablo in Contra Costa County in Northern California as the summer came to a close.

In his first position in California, Bidwell served as John Sutter's business manager, though in 1845 he decided to try his own hand as an independent rancher and acquired the 8,700-acre Rancho Colus from the legendary Alta California governor Pio Pico. When the Mexican–American War broke out, John Bidwell joined the U.S. Army and was quickly promoted to the rank of major. Bidwell was known for his diligence, intelligence, courage, excellent ability to perform as a scout, and natural leadership—qualities that would serve him well in the Gold Rush and throughout his life. While he proved successful before 1848, his discovery of gold would catapult him forward.

John Bidwell had come to an area later known as Bidwell's Bar to trade with the Colusa Indians. Though unlike many of the whites who traded with the Native Americans, Bidwell was not interested in the fur trade; rather, he had learned that the Colusa Indians had been actively engaged in trading gold for food and dry goods. Bidwell took advantage of the situation and reasoned that the gold the Indians used in trade must be relatively close to their dwellings. Thus, when he came upon gold in the Feather River, it was strictly not by accident. Bidwell's claim quickly made him rich, and in the process, literally thousands of miners poured into the area within the first two years of the Gold Rush. In 1850, Bidwell's Bar had morphed into a town, at least in terms of population. Though, unlike Mormon Island, it did not evolve into a cosmopolitan community. Instead, Bidwell's Bar became plagued with riffraff, and the crime rate seemed to grow in lock step with the population expansion. Conventional hotels and shops did not materialize as most miners felt living under the stars or in tents was an adequate lifestyle. After all, no one dreamed about making the diggings at Bidwell's Bar their homestead. The only vestige of permanent settlement was the bridge built over the Feather River in 1852. Homes constructed with stone and wood planks did emerge by 1853 as the diggings continued to be strong and the gold continued to be abundant throughout 1855, though the prodigious miners cleaned the region of color by the following year and by 1857, California had yet another ghost town.

After the demise of Bidwell's Bar, John Bidwell continued his political career, which he had embarked upon in 1849 after striking it rich in the prior year. Bidwell eventually became a congressman. In 1875, Bidwell unsuccessfully ran for the California governorship, and in 1892 he was the Prohibition Party candidate for U.S. president. Bidwell received nearly 300,000 votes, though never came close to living in the White House. In 1900, John Bidwell died a very wealthy man and one of the most significant pioneers of California. He published his autobiography *Echoes of the Past about California and In Camp and Cabin* that same year, and it remains in print today and is widely considered a classic account of life in the California Gold Rush era.

MURPHYS

Brothers Daniel and John Murphy and their impoverished families migrated into Alta California in 1844 seeking a hospitable environment to practice Catholicism and their own land, and in less than five years, they would become two of the richest men in the California Gold Rush. The men had crossed the continent in the Stephens-Townsend-Murphy Party, which had been the first wagon train to successfully negotiate what later came to be known as Donner Pass. Originating from Council Bluffs, Iowa, the party was led by the famed mountain man Caleb Greenwood, who successfully guided them at the age of 80 to Sutter's Fort. Another future notable who accompanied the Murphy clans was Dr. John Townsend, who was the first licensed physician in California. The Murphy men first entered into the dry goods business soon after their arrival, though when the rumors reached their ears of gold being discovered by Sutter's men in the spring of 1848, the two men

Murphy's Camp was one of the most successful and well-known mining ventures in the early part of the California Gold Rush. So much so that many an immigrant and emigrant spoke of the example of Murphy's Camp as the compelling force behind their decision to head for California. (Isaac W. Baker, *Murphy's Camp*, July 1853. Quarter plate daguerreotype, 2.635 × 3.5 in. Collection of the Oakland Museum of California, gift of an anonymous donor.)

decided to try their luck in mining. Heading southeast from Sutter's Mill in Coloma, they came upon the Stanislaus River, where they would find nearly over $1 million in gold within one year. News of the success the two brothers were having brought in hundreds upon hundreds of miners and the region, which had been virtually unoccupied just two years prior, became one of the most densely populated mining camps along the Sierras. Frustrated by the rapid population growth, which severely hampered their ability to mine, in particular when the mining claims were limited to less than 10 square feet in 1849, Daniel and John Murphy decided to go another direction than panning for gold in the cultivation of their wealth; they returned to their earlier practice as store merchants. As the diggings continued to fan out along the Stanislaus River, the population of miners grew at a nearly exponential rate, and consequently, the Murphy's general store experienced a growth in its customer base that increased the wealth of the two men nearly tenfold by 1850. While the gold eventually dried up, Murphy's did not vanish as a town, as did most other mining camp boom towns, and remarkably, the townsfolk rebuilt their beloved residence after three successive fires completely destroyed the village in the second half of the 19th century.

SPENDING THE GOLD

By the end of 1849 California's population had swelled to over 100,000 residents, the vast majority of which were lured in by the promise of striking it rich in gold. While the intent of most of these immigrants and emigrants was to hit the gold fields, some also came in search of riches that they could make off of the miners or in relation to the enormous population growth itself as this young, growing territory was in need of the creature comforts associated with American life in the East, Midwest, or South.

Miners were quite often willing to spend the gold as fast as they plucked it out of the earth. While bank deposits of gold were made, the majority of the gold on deposit came from those who procured the gold from the miner. This zealous spending not only led to a rapidly expanding, diverse economy but also inflation at levels never before witnessed. The price of property in San Francisco also skyrocketed. Homes that had sold for under $100 in 1848 were fetching over $10,000 by 1850. Property in San Francisco had reached such a premium that many took to living aboard ships in the harbor. Additionally, ships served as jails as the number of convicts grew.

The cost of all goods and services reached new inflationary heights annually from 1850 to 1855. The wages that laborers demanded consistently reached new heights, as did the challenge of keeping a business staffed for prolonged periods as the gold fields proved a difficult competitor for employers.

ARTISTS IN THE FIELDS

Gold Rush era California became a major draw for the newly emerging field of Daguerreian photography. Overwhelmingly, the miners understood that they were participants in a historic event as evidenced by the content of their journals, letters, and also the vast number of photographic portraits that they commissioned and posed for. In 1839, Louis Daguerre, a Parisian, had perfected a new form of permanent imagery that was secured on a copper plate, which he patented and named "daguerreotype." The French government purchased the patent and then opened the process to the general public and in doing so had literally launched a new profession. Over the next decade, daguerreotype photography had spread across the Atlantic, and by the time of the Gold Rush, processes and techniques had improved, consequently so did the quality of the images as well as the artistry involved in their creation.

The dramatic and diverse landscapes of California offered photographers incredible backdrops as well as primary targets for them to aim their cameras at. The miners, being a highly varied and dramatic lot themselves, understandably had become much sought-after entities. Whether in formal, studio pose, or at their diggings, the miners became a popular muse for photographers. The growth of the mining camps, towns, and cities became popular subjects, as did the businesses and the people on the streets. In effect, the rapidly evolving society of California provided photographers with an exceptional range of materials from which they recorded for posterity the rapidly evolving society.

The market for photography expanded as fast as did the population of California. As the interest in the Gold Rush was national and international, newspapers and popular magazines purchased and published daguerreotypes of the remarkable vistas and the miners. Photographers also directly marketed their service to the miners, in particular when one came upon a strike of significance. Miners would pay in upward of $20 for their portraits, though photographers were also known to charge less than $1 for their services.

While most of the photographers of Gold Rush California were men, there are records of women who captured the still image as a profession. The first known female photographer was Julia Shannon, who advertised her work in the *Alta California*. Shannon, whose studio was in San Francisco, also took advantage of the scarcity of women in California by accentuating her femininity as her advertisements coaxed men into having their picture taken by a lady. One of the most prolific female photographers, as well as one of the most talented of either gender, was Julia Randolph. Over the course of her long career, which spanned from the dawn of the 1850s and well into the 1880s, Randolph had studios in Nevada City, Sacramento, and San Francisco. While it is rare to come across a Julia Shannon image, there is an abundance of Julia Randolph images that have survived into the 21st century.

In addition to the photographers, sketch artists and fine artists found their muse in the California Gold Rush as well as in the journey to California. A. D. O. Browere's works included *The Lone Prospector* (1853), the growing waterfront town of *Stockton* (1856) and the journey through the jungles of Central America that thousands of 49ers traversed with his *Crossing the Isthmus* (ca. 1860). George Henry Burgess found his muse in the mining camps and the big city as evidenced by two of his celebrated works *View of San Francisco* (1850) and *Artist's Gold Mining Camp* (1854). Harrison Eastman's *Saint Francis Hotel, Corner of Clay and Dupont Streets* (1849) recorded for posterity a San Francisco that was just emerging from its time as a quaint hamlet and transforming into a bustling center of commerce, shipping, and entertainment. Frances Samuel Marryat captured the tragic fire of 1850 that consumed San Francisco with his work *San Francisco Fire of 17 September 1850* (1850)—the second major fire in San Francisco of that same year. William McIlvaine's *Panning Gold, California* (1849) presents the backbreaking labor of panning in the rivers and streams in a most romantic fashion and is one of the earliest known paintings on the subject of the California Gold Rush. William Smith Jewett's *Portrait of General John A. Sutter* (1856) is one of the most iconic images of John Sutter during the Gold Rush.

Merchants and salesmen combed through the gold fields attempting to sell the gold miners everything that they needed. It was not uncommon to see a wagon loaded with foodstuffs, tools, clothing, canvas, and liquor being pulled along by 20 mules and two horses as it entered a camp that would later depart empty, except for the driver and his plunder of gold and sufficient cadre of guns, and

SAN FRANCISCO IN 1850

San Francisco went from being a small, sleepy hamlet and port to a boom town over the course of just one year. The city by the bay, for decades built of wood, suffered from crime and fire and seemingly had to be rebuilt every few years. Some of the most common businesses in early San Francisco, as evidenced by this 1850 rendering, were saloons, hotels, and dry goods stores, all of which fed off the Gold Rush frenzy. (Unknown artist, *San Francisco in 1850* [Niantic Hotel], 1939. Work on paper, 10 × 12.75 in. Collection of the Oakland Museum of California, Museum Purchase.)

pulled along by only the two horses, with all the mules being sold, along with the other goods, to the miners. Most of these itinerant salespeople were independent, though all of the significant merchants employed mining camp delivery wagons.

WOMEN IN THE GOLD FIELDS

According to the 1850 census, there were nearly 87,000 men and slightly over 8,000 women in California, not including California Indians and many of the transients from abroad. That highly skewed gender imbalance gave women an exceptional advantage in the California society and economy that they would never have realized in states such as New York or Pennsylvania. While not afforded the right to vote in the first state constitution, women's rights were strong as what they brought to the burgeoning California Gold Rush society was well respected and much needed, in the gold fields and in the towns and cities.

In 1850, the female presence was less than half of what it would be the following year as the flood of male fortune seekers who went to work in the diggings on a more regular, though still rare, occasion, brought a wife along. In the gold fields, women could be seen working alongside with men, panning and sorting out the gold from the debris. Additionally, women helped construct the shacks, tend to the livestock in tote, as well as perform the majority of the domestic work, which often became a significant source of income for the family as the scarcity of women in the gold fields presented an entrepreneurial opportunity. Single male miners very frequently paid the women in their respective camps to provide them with meals as well as laundry services, which in turn permitted the miners to focus more of their attention on gold retrieval. If in a productive mining camp, a woman could make several hundreds of dollars per month if she only had a dozen clients. Meals could fetch between $2 and $5 and the cost of laundering a single item was typically $1, with payment being made in gold.

Successful and visionary women developed quickly parlayed their domestic services businesses into boarding homes for the miners. In the boarding homes, the miners were fed one or two full meals a day, had access to the luxury of warm baths, slept in cots or atop simply mattresses, and took advantage of laundry services. Compared to living under the stars or in canvas tents, the boarding home experience was considerably more desirable. The cost of a stay at boarding homes ranged from $5 to $10 a day, and, like the general cost of everything during the Gold Rush, reflected the inflationary prices of the period and the willingness of the prospectors to spend gold quite nearly as quick as the recovered the precious yellow flakes and nuggets.

Brothels in the gold field regions provided another economic opportunity for women, albeit a considerably more dangerous profession than domestic services or boarding home management. However, the potential income was considerable, and thus prostitution proved alluring for many ladies. The typical boom town brothel employed between 5 and 10 women, and it typically offered the patron not only carnal services but also, at times, musical and theatrical entertainment, as well as beverages and limited food services. Many also provided men with bathing and hygienic services, which must have been nearly as welcomed by the women who serviced the prospectors. The atmosphere in these frontier brothels did resemble their urban counterparts, though typically they were much smaller in their physical size and they often lacked having many private rooms for the women to entertain their clientele. While management typically retained the lion's share of the revenue, the prostitutes could easily realize hundreds of dollars a month income, which depended heavily on the luck of the miners at their claims. As the mining towns came and went, so too followed the brothels.

The real threats to the safety and health of the women were tied to their clients. Violence did occur and was often linked to alcohol consumption by the patrons, though the greatest threats to the health and well-being of the women were connected to communicable diseases. Two of the most common were syphilis, a sexually transmitted disease, and tuberculosis, an airborne virus. With no medical treatment available at the time that could cure these horrific diseases, if one became afflicted, it was a death sentence. Birth control methods, such as condoms, douching, and intrauterine devices, were available, though not utilized in all instances. Unwanted pregnancies were also a significant problem given the lack of modern birth control methods. When the unwanted outcome of the sexual encounter was not given up for adoption, infanticide and abortion were the most typical responses. For obvious reasons, abortion was a harrowing experience and was most problematic for the pregnant woman when the abortion was done through the ingesting of a potion. Typically a tea derived from plants or herbs such as lavender and thyme was ingested in large quantities and rarely produced the intended outcome. Instances of consuming toxins such as turpentine were not unheard of and routinely led to the death of not only the fetus but also the mother. Surgical procedures were incredibly crude by contemporary standards, and the risk of a fatal infection or death from bleeding was genuine.

Property laws in California afforded women significant legal rights that nearly were without equal in the rest of the United States. For example, women were able to acquire real estate distinct from their husband, if they were married, and were not in need of a man to purchase land or, for that matter, file a mining claim. The first California State Constitution recognized in Article XI, Section 14: "All property, both real and personal, of the wife, owned or claimed by marriage, and that acquired afterwards by gift, devise, or descent, shall be her separate property; and laws shall be passed more

clearly defining the rights of the wife, in relation as well to her separate property as to that held in common with her husband. Laws
shall also be passed providing for the registration of the wife's separate property." The liberal real estate laws in relation to women's
rights were developed, in part, because of the practical intent of the
men to encourage female migration into the region.

PREACHING IN THE GOLD FIELDS

Organized churches came quickly to Gold Rush California. Some
of the more common Protestant faiths were the Church of Christ,
Methodist, and Baptist, which joined an already strong Roman
Catholic presence that harkened back to the Spanish missionization era of the late 18th century. Catholicism had long been the
dominant faith in the region, though as emigrants began to pour
into California from the Midwest, South, and East, they brought
with them their own denominations, which resulted in a significant
influx of Protestantism. Along the Overland Trail, the moral and
legal codes established by the soon-to-be prospectors reflected their
Christian beliefs, which resulted in many a wagon train parked on
the Sabbath. When no minister was present on the trail, which was
most often, elders led the parties on reading the scriptures. While
the itinerant lifestyle was not particularly conducive to preaching,
the boom towns of the gold fields and the rapidly growing towns
were quite the opposite, and preachers became attracted to Gold
Rush California, and consequently, congregations began to form.

Prospectors and the growing number of local merchants longed
for stability and success, and also some resemblance to a normal,
structured life. Ministers and their burgeoning Sunday services
helped provide this sense of community, and their sermons helped
the miners through the dry times that were often and at times
lengthy. Settlements grew from the rapidly expanding congregations, which typically began with just a minister reading the scriptures aloud from his Bible reading in the great outdoors. Successful
preachers in the gold fields followed the boom, bust, and migratory
cycles of the miners. One of the first, highly successful gold field
preachers was Thomas Thompson.

Thomas Thompson had taken the Overland Trail into California in 1848. A native of Kentucky, Thompson moved with his family into Missouri during his childhood. Though raised a Baptist,
Thompson in adulthood converted to the Church of Christ, and in
the early 1830s, he went into the ministry. While crossing the Great

Plains, Thompson practiced his profession, and upon his arrival at the gold fields of Coloma, he found men obsessed with gold mining and understandably so, as he arrived when the prospectors were still just plucking flakes and nuggets of color from the surface, and to the prospector, each moment not spent on gold recovery was wasted time. As many preachers arrived at this early and frenzied period of mining, Thompson chose to preach to the men while they worked diligently on their diggings. Thompson purchased a boarding home, which he continued to operate to support his preaching. Soon he branched out his ministry, preaching throughout the American River Valley. By 1851, Thompson's success in his ministries afforded him the opportunity of establishing his first church in the town of Stockton, and his congregation, like the general population, continued to grow. While Thompson's success was not replicated by every preacher in the gold fields, he was not alone. In 1850, hundreds of migratory preachers made their way through the gold fields each day and into the cities.

In 1850, San Francisco was home to over 500 saloons and 18 churches. Life in the cities, replete with every known vice available, proved a significant obstacle to living the clean life. However, the 18 churches together reported having over 8,000 congregants in a city of nearly 30,000 inhabitants. The oldest and first Christian church, the Mission San Francisco de Asís, known primarily as Mission Dolores, was founded in 1776. The Mission congregation had peaked in the first decade of the 19th century with over 1,000 members in its congregation. When Mexico gained its independence from Spain in 1821, and following the secularization movement of the 1830s, the Mission Dolores congregation declined, and in 1848 it was barely functioning. However, the Gold Rush breathed new life into Mission Dolores, though not in keeping with the intent of its founders. Rather, in 1850 entrepreneurial-minded individuals took advantage of the strong structural integrity of the building, as well as its choice location, and laid new wood plank roads to the mission and began to operate a gambling hall and saloon in the former chapel and surrounding structures, clearly reflecting the social mores of Gold Rush San Francisco.

The issue of morality was of a significant concern throughout the rapidly growing Gold Rush society, but it was also one of the more common topics for comedy, both on the stage as well as in print. James M. Hutching's 1853 sheet publication *The Miners' Ten Commandments* offered a comical illustration on the benefits of living a moral and respective lifestyle. Beginning with his first

The Rancho era during Mexican California, 1821–1847, witnessed the rise of large agribusiness as Mexican land grants provided ambitious ranchers with vast acreage, typically over 10,000 acres and some over 100,000. While many ranchos continued to operate into the American era of California history, the increased value of the land led many rancho owners to sell off portions or entire ranchos. This image is of a Monterey Rancho in 1849. (William Hahn, *Return from the Bear Hunt*, 1882. Oil on canvas, 55 × 89 in. Collection of the Oakland Museum of California, The Oakland Museum Kahn Collection.)

commandment "Thou shalt have no other claim than one," Hutching addressed the issue of making false claims, abandoning a claim that had not been fully tapped out to ignoring what others do on the Sabbath. Hutching concluded his tenth commandment with a nod to one of the plagues of the Gold Rush, men abandoning their families, the caveat that "if thou hast a wife and little ones, that though lovest dearer than thy life . . ." In 1855, W. C. Butler published the letter sheet *Commandments to California Wives*, which presented a satirical guide for ladies in the Golden State. Advice ranging from "do not put on airs of self-importance" in the first commandment to "thou shalt not substitute sour looks for pickles" in the seventh and in the eighth "thou shalt not neglect to make the person and thy home attractive" were subtle nods to the rise of consumerism and the challenges that women faced in keeping their men from going astray, a commonplace occurrence at the time.

For those who did not intend to remain in California permanently, maintaining a connection with the folks back home was of great importance. While many struck up friendships and cases of amore, they recognized their situation as being one in transience. The genuine fear that plagued many 49ers was that their family and loved ones who did not make the trek to California would forget them or find love in the arms of another. Even though the rate of miners who indulged in the services of the brothels was virtually heroic, the double-standard male belief that while men might stray, women were expected to remain chaste dominated the mindset of the miners. Popular songs of the time evoked this aspect of life far from home, such as James Hutchings's "Do They Miss Me at Home?" As this was an era before the telephone, the mode of communication across great distance was the letter, and thus the importance of the post office and mail delivery was tremendous. It was not an uncommon site to see a crowd of over 100 standing outside of the post office in San Francisco waiting for the doors to open in the hope of a letter or parcel waiting for them. U.S. postmaster general Cave Johnson had sent agents into California in

The romanticized image of the California Gold Rush 49er was commonly represented throughout the art world of the 1850s. In this 1851 painting by E. Hall Martin, mountain men are depicted. (E. Hall Martin, *Mountain Jack and a Wandering Miner*, ca. 1850. Oil on canvas, 39.5 × 72 in. Collection of the Oakland Museum of California, gift of Concours d'Antiques, Art Guild.)

1848 to establish post offices in the wake of the end of the Mexican–American War. However, mail service in Gold Rush California was a contracted affair between government and private merchants. The line that brought the mail into California came from Salt Lake City and utilized the Overland Trail. Absalom Woodward and George Chorpenning were granted the first such federal contract, which yielded them nearly $15,000 per year for the agreement to bring mail from Salt Lake City into San Francisco and conversely deliver the California mail on their return to Utah. They committed to a cycle of 30 days for each leg. Hindered by both a lack of good roads and exposure to the weather, it was rare for the men and their employees to stay on their targeted schedule, though the mail got through, and there were but a few instances of lost mail in the early days of the Gold Rush.

THE SALOONS

The presence of the saloon was arguably, next to the miners themselves, the most ubiquitous component of the ever-growing California economy. While the number of saloons that littered the streets of San Francisco overshadowed the expansion that occurred in every other town or hamlet, there was literally no settlement devoid of a watering hole. While not every miner consumed prodigious amounts of spirits, the mere fact that saloons were the segment of the greater California economy that expanded more than any other industry during the initial years of the Gold Rush is quite telling. The reasons for this radical, disproportionate success in alcohol sales had a few causes that simply did not exist in all other parts of the United States. First, the lack of traditional families and ratio of men to women being roughly 10:1 meant that the men had, on average, fewer responsibilities and a greater amount of free time. Also, life in the gold fields was not easy; rather, the work was physically demanding if one were to be productive in the procurement of gold, and the living arrangements for the miners was not filled with the creature comforts that most had been accustomed to prior to their lives in California. Thus, when a miner had any sort of luck, he was more prone to celebrating in a highly motivated fashion, which typically included a prolonged visit to a saloon and or brothel. Alcohol consumption on a daily basis was also heavily influenced by the harsh life of the miner. Backaches, injuries, the stress of not finding gold on a regular basis as well as ever increasing number of competitors for the precious yellow color played significant roles in the expansion of what would be considered alcoholism by contemporary standards. The miners, who purchased the majority of the liquor from saloons, would consume significant quantities in the gold fields on a daily basis. It was not uncommon for a "seasoned" miner to work through a pint of hard liquor, nor was it unheard of for a miner to get to the bottom of a quart of booze, in a 24-hour period. The most popular alcoholic beverages were whiskey and rum. Both were inexpensive and, by most accounts, distilled in as brief a period of time as possible, which most often produced a harsh beverage. This high rate of alcohol consumption led to many complications in life, such as violence or conflict, but an added physical dimension not prevalent outside of the gold fields became a genuine hazard that claimed hundreds of lives in 1850 alone—the pits dug and either abandoned or left unmarked by miners. These so-called glory holes were anywhere from 10 to 25 feet deep, and if a drunken, or even sober miner, had the misfortune of plummeting down to a bottom of jagged rock and debris, his fate was often sealed.

GAMBLING

In the early months of the Gold Rush, the saloons grew exponentially, and in addition to the vices of alcohol consumption and prostitution, the vice of gambling was available in most establishments and commonplace throughout the camps. Professional gamblers and con artists often went into a partnership with the saloon proprietors. The most common game of chance was the card games. Men, often plied with cheap, abundant alcoholic beverages, were lured to the card tables by the chance of increasing their wealth. It was not uncommon to witness bets that went into the hundreds of dollars per hand, equivalent to tens of thousands of dollars in contemporary America. As one could imagine, the joy of winning large pots was also beset by the anger and rage by losing and the commonplace violence that followed. As the easy gold became more scarce, and the presence of miners more prevalent, gambling began to consume more time of the miners as they began to seek riches that they had not been able to achieve by retrieving gold.

FARMING AND LIVESTOCK

The Mexican–American War had a devastating effect on agriculture in California. Able-bodied men often left their positions at farms as they signed up to fight either on the U.S. or Mexican side during the conflict. Consequently, the undermanned ranchos as well as the smaller farms fell into disrepair. Many crops were either neglected or simply not planted. A good deal of the livestock throughout California was stolen or ignored. In particular, thousands of hogs went feral as they foraged beyond the farms in search of food. The cattle industry, which had expanded considerably during the Mexican period, fueled by the expansion of the hide and tallow industry, shrank due to both neglect as well as pilfering during the conflict. By the end of the war, California's agricultural output had been cut in half; however, by the end of 1849, an incredible resurgence occurred as the flood of Argonauts and the steady increase of gold in the economy and profits in farming fueled a rebirth in agriculture.

In the first few months of the Gold Rush, much of the food, in particular the meat products, were not produced in state as the population expansion far exceeded the capabilities of the local farmers. Initially, gross shortages of food stuffs resulted in an expansion of hunting wild game. By the dawn of 1850, entrepreneurial-minded farmers, strongly encouraged by the inflated prices of food stuffs and livestock, and the willingness of the miners to the exorbitant prices, brought agribusiness back throughout the Golden State. The high profits in agribusiness also produced a frenzy of land claims that so confused the territorial land offices that in the immediate aftermath of statehood, the U.S. Congress formed a commission in 1851 to "ascertain and settle private land claims in the state of California." The board comprised of three men, appointed as commissioners by the president of the United States, who served three-year terms; later in 1856, the tenure was extended to five years. Rather than clear up the massive number of filings, which exceeded 800 in the first five years, the commissioners overwhelmingly passed the claims along to the district courts, many of which ultimately found their way to the U.S. Supreme Court, and they settled only three claims themselves.

AGRICULTURAL EMPIRE

In spite of the confusion or land claims, California agriculture expanded during the Gold Rush. The geography of the rapid growth in agriculture was one of convenience and relative proximity to the gold fields in the Sierra Nevada and the burgeoning city of San Francisco. The central location of the young hamlet, and soon-to-be state capital, Sacramento, which was also accessed by the American and Sacramento rivers, became an obvious marketplace. For over 100 miles to the north and south of Sacramento, the agricultural heartland of California emerged. The farms that seemed to grow nearly exponentially during this period were able to take advantage of the vast water supplied by the Sacramento delta that was able to yield a considerable and easily accessible water supply for planters and herders through the typically dry summers. Flooding in the winter and early spring consistently presented the farmers with ravaging effects. To combat these hostile waters, a series of levees, made principally by the farmers themselves, were built up along the waterways. Transporting the agricultural commodities to market by land was accomplished by horse- and mule-driven freight wagons. Along the water, the steamers soon became the dominant vessels. The consumer demand for foodstuffs in San Francisco escalated each year. This was driven not simply because of the incredible population growth but also because as a city, San Francisco simply could not raise the crops or livestock needed as all the land was used for either residencies or commerce.

The primarily Mediterranean climate of central California along with its rich alluvial soil was and remains a suitable environment to a very wide range of crops. Indeed the well-known wine industry, founded by the Spanish padres during missionization, continued to expand. Reflected the more eclectic tastes of the ethnically diverse Gold Rush California, barley and hops were soon planted by beer and ale brewers. Citrus trees, berries, cereals, and grains all flourish in the long growing season, which runs from March through September. Many enterprising farmers, who had entered California in search of gold, moved back into their original professions and found economic success at levels they never could have imagined in the traditional Midwest farmland of mid–19th century America. Crops of vegetables, potatoes, melons, and poultry products could net a farmer $10,000 in excess of an initial investment in the range of $100 and, of course, his labor. Eggs were one of the most remarkable cash crops as they could be sold for as much as two for $1. The vast amount of open land throughout the surrounding area of the gold fields, south of San Francisco, and surrounding Sacramento was cheap to rent or purchase and served those interested in farming quite well. As the population of California swelled, so did the demand for food, and as the majority of the people lived an urban or mining camp lifestyle, there was very little subsistence farming that took place.

The growth of animal husbandry also mirrored the expanding population throughout California. Cattle, poultry, sheep, and pigs were raised throughout the central valley, and the proteins they yielded were the cornerstone to the diets in the gold fields as well as the towns. The market for hides, as well as the finished leather products, such as shoes, clothing, and bindings, added another dimension to the growing industrial economy. By the close of 1850, over 1,000 livestock farms filled out the Sacramento Valley from the gold fields in the east and to the San Francisco Bay to the west.

RIVERS OF COMMERCE

The San Joaquin and Sacramento rivers were the major transportation arteries between the gold fields and the cities of San Francisco, Sacramento, and Stockton. The Sacramento River, the state's longest river, runs for over 400 miles southward from the Klamath Mountains and empties into Suisun Bay, adjacent to the San Francisco Bay. The shores and surrounding area on the eastern and western flanks of the Sacramento River was home to one of the most densely populated regions of Indians in California prior to Contact. These Native American Nations, such as Yuki, Pomo, Maidu, and Miwok, had benefited from the incredible abundance of natural resources provided by the river for thousands of years. Due to the relatively remote location from Spanish settlement, these Indian societies had little contact with the Europeans, until John Sutter established his fort at the confluence of the Sacramento and American rivers in 1841. After the discovery of gold, the emigrants and immigrants pushed the Indians away from the river by force of arms and also disease; small pox, malaria, and measles brought by the outsiders resulted in epidemics from 1849 to 1850 and decimated Indian villages. As the Gold Rush population increased, along with the discovery of gold itself, the number and types of boats traversing the Sacramento River grew. The first vessels, sailing ships, were a common sight as they carried passenger and cargo. As the ocean vessels turned from wind power to steam, so too did those on the Sacramento River. Driven by consumer demand for products and a high level of competition among the merchandisers, the more reliable steamships began to dominate river transportation by 1850. Passengers were willing to part with $25 to $40 for a one-way ticket to Sacramento. Freight was hauled for a price between $30 and $50 a ton. The San Joaquin River is the second-longest river in California at over 300 miles, connects Stockton with the city of

Sacramento, and at its confluence with the Sacramento River lays the Sacramento–San Joaquin Delta. While less significant in Gold Rush history than its northern neighbor, the San Joaquin River made the booming population and wealth of the city of Sacramento possible, as it provided easy access from the southern Sierra Nevada gold region into the city.

DRY GOODS

One of the most profitable industries to emerge during the Gold Rush was the dry goods stores. Preeminent of the dry goods merchants was Sam Brannan, also one of the most significant Gold Rush boosters. Brannan's first dry good store that catered almost exclusively to the miners was located at Sutter's Fort. Ever the visionary, Sam Brannan recognized the economic potential of selling the miner's all that they might need to live and mine for gold would prove much more profitable than breaking one's back in search of color. Brannan came to this realization when the first wave of Mormon miners, then still employed by Sutter, who found the incredible deposit of placer gold at Mormon Island, were willing to literally bid for the limited number of tools needed to recover the gold and, in so doing, created the first instance of Gold Rush inflation. Brannan, seizing upon the opportunity, and speculating that the amount of gold yet to be discovered, would permit him to sell an unprecedented amount of shovels, pans, picks, and whatever else the miners would need. By mid-1849, Brannan had opened several storefronts throughout the growing gold fields as well as in San Francisco, the port of entry for many miners and the products he sold them. By 1850, Sam Brannan had earned the distinction of being the first millionaire in California history. Brannan is certainly the most famous Gold Rush merchant, though there were many others, such as Stephen Chapin Davis.

At the young age of 17, Stephen Davis made his way into the California gold fields from the eastern United States by way of sea. Davis initially had no intention of opening a store; rather, he dreamed of becoming rich as a miner. However, Davis did not have tremendous luck at finding gold by way of panning or sluicing. The claims he filed brought him land that was without any significant yield, although Davis did make one remarkable observation that served him well. Following a small recovery of gold, Davis entered a dry goods store to purchase provisions, including an upgrade in mining materials. Witnessing the number of successful miners, who also seemed quite willing to purchase goods at what he believed unfathomable prices, Davis decided to change his profession from miner to merchant. His decision proved fortuitous and Davis went from poverty to prosperity. Davis and Sam Brannan were not unique, as the society continued to expand, so did the economy and the growing number of businesses. By the close of 1850, nearly 10,000 businesses operated in San Francisco, and thousands more sprang up throughout the gold fields that offered goods and services on par with those available in New York. Indeed, many Californians, whether in the city or along the rivers and streams, began to see themselves as a cosmopolitan society in just the second year of the Gold Rush.

THE RUSH TO STATEHOOD

The rapid population expansion that occurred in California from 1848 to 1849 virtually secured the territory's right to statehood. Furthering the clamor to leave behind the territorial status was not just the unparalleled economic growth that grew out of the Gold Rush but also significant social and political issues. The number of foreigners within California's borders grew daily, and as the easy gold became less and less plentiful, a once accepting American Gold Rush population became more and more nativist. Men with political and economic ambitions had migrated into California from Midwest, South and East, with the intent of not only elevating their social and economic statuses but also bringing California into the Union as either a free or slave state. The decision by California voters to become a free state accelerated the onset of the Civil War. There was also the issue of the Californios, the former Mexican citizens who, upon the ratification by the U.S. Senate of the Treaty of Guadalupe Hidalgo, became rightful citizens of the United States. However, many Californios faced extreme discrimination and were quite often relegated to second-class citizenship, although some prominent Californios would play a significant role in the Constitutional Convention. Overall, haste marked California's entry as the nation's 31st state. The incredible economic growth and population expansion that occurred in 1849 had rendered California a wealthy, though confused, territory both socially and politically, thus setting the stage for a series of power grab attempts by a myriad of individuals, groups, and organizations. In 1849, Bennett C. Riley served as the last military governor of the California Territory. The seven military governors had virtually no impact on developing a stable political structure, which had not been their charge. Rather, they were in place to maintain order during the period of transition from Mexican to American rule. Not surprisingly, when general elections were held in 1849, voter fraud and confusion ran rampant. In that same year, California also held its first Constitutional Convention in Monterey, which proved a rushed and harried affair. By the close of 1850, California had been granted statehood, though a series of political negotiations bordering on intrigue witnessed California entering the Union as a free state and the passage of the Fugitive Slave Act that same year as a concession to the Southern states. Within California, sentiment for both a slave economy and a wage-based economy by Gold Rush emigrants created a less than harmonious society. Additionally, nativism continued its growth as the resentment of foreigners escalated as gold continued to be more and more difficult and labor intensive to recover.

FRAMING THE CONSTITUTION

On August 1, 1849, Californians elected 48 delegates to design its constitution. Robert Semple served as president and William G. Marcy as secretary, and colorful characters such as Lansford W. Hastings and John Sutter were among the delegates. The delegates, most of whom had no past political experience, never set out to design a territorial constitution; instead they focused strictly on a state constitution as they correctly understood that California's population and economic significance would only continue to rise at a rapid rate and thrust forward statehood. In one of his final official duties as military governor, Gen. Bennett C. Riley oversaw the opening of the convention. Of the 48 delegates, only 14 were attorneys, and 33 of the delegates had been in California for two or fewer years each. On October 10, 1849, after 43 days of negotiations and editorial work, the delegates, all men, signed the California Constitution. On November 13, 1849, the voting people of the California Territory ratified the constitution.

California's constitution reflected its diverse and expanding society, though it generally mirrored the U.S. Constitution. Article I, Section 18 clearly stated that California would not permit slavery. "Neither slavery, nor involuntary servitude, unless for the punishment of crimes, shall ever be tolerated in this State." However, the clause that permitted forced labor as determined by the courts would become a contentious issue as vagrancy law infractions primarily against California Indians led to widespread abuse as employers sought cheap, long-term labor, which they purchased from sheriff departments and the courts.

The right to vote was extended to "every white male citizen" 21 years of age with Article 2, Section 1, which also extended suffrage to Native Americans, as long as the California Legislature authorized extending the vote to "Indians or the descendants of Indians" with a two-thirds majority vote. The constitution also stipulated that no "idiot or insane person, or person convicted of any infamous crime, shall be entitled to the privilege of an elector." Voting was a controlled privilege from the earliest moments. In addition to establishing a court system composed of a Supreme Court, district courts, and county courts, the constitution also laid out the three-branch system of government based on the U.S. federal model, typical practices throughout the country.

The boundary of California was set in Article XII at the ". . . point of intersection of 42d degree of north latitude with the 120th degree of longitude west from Greenwich, and running south on the line of said 120th degree of west longitude until it intersects the 39th degree of north latitude; thence running in a straight line in a south easterly direction to the River Colorado, at a point where it intersects the 35th degree of north latitude; thence down the middle of the channel of said river, to the boundary line between the United States and Mexico, as established by the Treaty of May 30th, 1848; thence running west and along said boundary line to the Pacific Ocean, and extending therein three English miles; thence running in a northwesterly direction, and following the direction of the Pacific Coast to the 42d degree of north latitude, thence on the line of said 42d degree of north latitude to the place of beginning." This rather unique political boundary form took advantage of all, including known gold field regions as well as the incorporation of a dominant run of the Pacific coastline.

The seal of California was designed at the constitutional convention. The dominant figure in the seal is the Roman Goddess Minerva, who, according to mythology, had been born from the brain of Jupiter full grown—an obvious nod to the delegates' full desire that California forgo the traditional territorial period as a society with instant maturity and move directly into statehood. The 31 stars that border the top of the seal represent the first 30 states and California as the 31st state. A miner with a rocker, pick, and pan represent the origins of the great wealth that continued to flow out of the gold fields throughout the convention and what was the cause behind the massive population growth of the territory. The grizzly bear at

Minerva's feet can be seen eating grapevines, "emblematic of the peculiar characteristics of the country." The state motto "Eureka" crests Minerva, and according to the convention records, it applies "either to the principle involved in the admission of the State or the success of the miner at work."

The issue of slavery played a significant role in California state formation. While the 48 delegates had unanimously opposed slavery in California, the growing Southern migration into region fueled pro-slavery sentiment. A motion was made to divide California into two states at the 35th Parallel North, with the southern state being a slave state, and just under one-fourth the size of its proposed northern counterpart. The division proposal was summarily rejected by the delegates, which fueled hostilities between free soilers and slavers in California and throughout the nation. In 1854, just four years after partitioning had been rejected, the California State Assembly once again debated whether or not the state should be divided. Though this time, instead of a North and South California, the proposal was aimed at establishing three states; however, the proposals never made their way out of the committee. Once again, in the pre–Civil War era, the California legislature debated partitioning. However, in a bizarre political twist, then governor, John B. Weller, who had formerly been a disgraced boundary commissioner, attempted to lead California into being an independent republic as the outbreak of succession seemed eminent with the election of Abraham Lincoln. Weller never succeeded in his quest. The apprehension of Southern states to permit California to come into the Union as a free state led directly to the Compromise of 1850. In fact, California's admission as the nation's 31st state was actually the third statute of the Compromise of 1850.

California marked 1850 as a transition year for other reasons in addition to statehood. The growing tensions throughout the state relating to the increased difficulty in locating easy gold, and the expanding, multiethnic, polyglot society resulted in legislation aimed at dissuading non-English-speaking and non-Anglo miners from entering or staying in the gold fields. The Foreign Miners License Law charged all non-U.S. citizens $20 per month. While the motivation behind the passage of the law was clearly nativist, there was also an economic logic as well. Before the passage of this law, untold millions of ounces of gold was recovered by foreigners and removed from California and American soil with the U.S. government receiving no remuneration whatsoever. In contemporary United States, it is unthinkable that any foreign entity, or domestic for that matter, would be permitted to simply remove any natural resources or mineral wealth without being taxed in some form. However, in pre-1850 California, there were no laws governing mining or economic development in place.

The Foreign Miners License Law did have an immediate impact on California society. Many noncitizens abandoned their claims, which had proved increasingly less fruitful anyway, though not all of the foreigners left California. One of the largest foreign-born ethnic groups, the Chinese, moved to San Francisco and either opened small businesses in the service industries or became domestic employees in the homes of well-to-do families. In 1851, the California Legislature repealed the Foreign Miners License fee, though in the following year another, more reasonable, miners tax was established that charged $3 per month. Over the next few years, the expansion of xenophobic beliefs led to an 1856 doubling of the monthly fee, quite reflective of the growing ethnic disharmony emanating out of the gold fields and throughout the state.

The California Legislature also passed the Act for the Government and Protection of Indians in 1850. This title of the legislation was quite misleading. While ostensibly providing for Indian settlement rights by stating that any landowners who had Indians peaceably residing on their property were prohibited from removing the Indians, the act virtually incriminated any Indians found walking about or loitering, for which they could be charged and convicted of vagrancy and incarcerated. Additionally, although slavery had been banned in California, whites could request from the courts a contract for the labor of any Indian convicted of a crime, for which the white petitioner would pay the courts. Further solidifying the divide between Indians and whites in the legal arena, whites could not be convicted upon the testimony given by any Indian. Ten years after the passage of this act, the California Legislature amended the law so that any Indian deemed a vagrant could witness their children being taken and placed into the custody of whites for "training and employment," for which the whites were not required to provide any financial remuneration to the child or the Indian parents.

These social issues did not subside in the early years of statehood and for the generations yet to come, they plagued California. Crime in the cities began to escalate in post-1850 California, which brought about instances of mob rule on a historically unparalleled level. Mining continued and actually expanded, though the days of the independent miner working a claim became fewer and fewer.

Gold extraction techniques became more aggressive, such as high-powered hydraulic mining run by large-scale mining corporations that were bent on getting out all of the gold before any laws might be enacted that would impede their road to riches. After all, California may have had a government and statehood, but at the start of 1851, it was still an open society.

4

POLITICS, DISCRIMINATION, AND LAW

The men and women who rushed into California fueled by the dream of discovering fabulous riches made up the society who soon rushed the territory of California into statehood. The rapid population growth and economic expansion of Gold Rush California also translated into urbanization as cities, in particular San Francisco, experienced tremendous growth during the early years of statehood. A rather ambitious segment of Gold Rush California took hold of politics and governance; however, law and order periodically fell out of the hands of the government officials. Crime became more and more of an issue throughout the state and criminal justice in the young state. Reasons for the rise in criminal activity included the consistent population growth and the increased difficulty in finding gold or the ability to make an honest living outside of the gold fields for many of the immigrants and emigrants, resulting in frustration. Violence, as well as theft, escalated throughout California and became a notorious problem in San Francisco. Periodically, organized mobs formed and took law enforcement into their own hands and in the process instituted reigns of terror in the lives of Californians. These mobs, at times referred to as vigilance committees, were influenced by the growing, and not necessarily incorrect, perception that law and order enforced by elected or appointed officials was often absent in the camps in towns and cities throughout the state. Whether the mobs "cleaned" up ever-present crime is debatable; however, the reign of terror that periodically gripped Californians when these veritable gangs roved the streets was undeniable.

As the overall population rose, a leveling of the gender ratio took place, though men still outnumbered women in the range of 4 to 1. In the first 10 years of statehood, California's population expanded by over 300 percent, was home to nearly 400,000 people, and as the ethnic diversity continued to rise, so too did ethnic tensions and nativism. One of the most striking features of Gold Rush California lay in the obvious discrimination that ethnic groups such as Asians and African Americans faced in their daily lives as local politicians, legislators, and even governors supported exclusionary and prohibitive laws and acts that removed any vestige of social equality for minorities. However, no ethnic group experienced greater injustices during these formative years of statehood than the California Indians. The first people to inhabit the Golden State had known misery since the invasion and colonization by the Spanish nearly one hundred years earlier, and certainly when the Gold Rush began in earnest in 1849, the lives of the diverse California Indian societies were turned upside down, though the harsh realities of the California Indian nations only worsened beginning in 1850, when the mistreatment and removal at the hand of the whites was replaced by reservations and even planned genocide. The early years of California statehood is one of the darkest eras in the history of U.S.-Native American relations.

TENSIONS IN SAN FRANCISCO

Outside of the gold fields, the most notable changes were in the growing cities and towns. California was urbanizing, and San Francisco was the Gold Rush state's crown jewel, though, as with all jewels, before it became polished, it started off in rough form. The changes that took place in San Francisco, which was commonly referred to simply as "The City," during the first decade of statehood were remarkable. San Francisco's population in 1850 was barely over 20,000. In 1860 it was over 56,000 and the nation's largest city west of the Mississippi River and 15th largest overall. San Francisco proved a behemoth in California, a city with streets overflowing with people, commerce and industry, docks that were crowded with ships both abandoned and in use, and languages from around the world being spoken. By 1860, San Francisco had emerged as a city of eastern elegance and Gold Rush ambition. As the city grew, one of its cornerstones was change, which was reflected in every facet of life, though the consequences of the unprecedented growth of San Francisco, and the manner by which it grew, led directly to the problems associated with what many considered to be a wide-open society. Crime itself reached a critical level in early 1851. Overpopulation also led directly to poor urban planning as the people poured into the city and built homes and businesses along with a system of road works of narrow and overcrowded streets of the city, and destructive fires were commonplace. The red-light district, known as the Barbary Coast, in San Francisco was home to dozens of brothels and nearly countless saloons, which only fed the lawless and violent nature of the city.

The flood of emigrants continued into 1851, although unlike the miners who began in 1848 or those who arrived in the following two years, these gold seekers found the gold fields overcrowded, the surface gold hard to find, and an inflation rate that made life incredibly difficult. Tensions in the gold fields escalated, but in the towns and cities they began to reach unanticipated levels that brought about results that no one could have foreseen.

Jurisprudence in California during this early stage of statehood reflected the confusion in governing that plagued a society that was growing at a rate that was well beyond the ability of the newly established, though still under construction, system of laws and governing. In addition to a population growth rate never before seen in the United States, California was the most ethnically diverse state from its genesis, a phenomenon that continued during the early stage of statehood and one that continued to experience economic growth, including economic diversity, at an unprecedented rate. However, this continual economic expansion did not translate into economic equality for one and all, and as California continued its polyglot makeup, nativism and xenophobia added to the combustible formula. One result of these strains on society was popular justice, that is, justice in response to perceived crimes meted out by people not legally in a position of law enforcement or as a duly appointed judge. Other terms for popular justice include *mob rule* and *vigilance committees*, and in California, these began to commonly emerge and, at times, consume society. The high crime rate, and general overpopulation of San Francisco, also led directly to a creative solution for insufficient jail facilities. San Francisco's expansive harbor was filled with ships, many of which became abandoned. Many of these abandoned vessels were converted into jails, either in the harbor directly or brought onto dry land and fashioned into a permanent structure. Other vessels, such as the *Euphemia*, which was sold to the City of San Francisco for a reported figure of over $3,000 by its owner and San Francisco councilman William Heath Davis.[1] During this first decade of statehood, ships were also brought ashore and converted into houses, warehouses, and other places of business. Thus, a converted ship on land was not an altogether uncommon sight throughout San Francisco.

While most historians pay particular attention to the vigilance committees that emerged in California in 1851 and later, there were others that had formed during the course of the Mexican–American War and continued to reemerge into early statehood. Of particular note was the so-called Hounds of San Francisco.

In the summer of 1849, a group of anti-immigrant men, who were specifically opposed to non-English-speaking people, organized with the intent of terrorizing those whom they deemed undesirable and quickly came to be known as the "Hounds." Made up primarily of veterans of the Mexican–American War, these vigilantes commonly attacked encampments of foreigners in their small settlement enclaves in San Francisco and its general surrounding areas. Following an afternoon of heavy drinking on July 15, 1849, this marauding group of men became exceptionally volatile as they turned their attention to a Chilean encampment, commonly referred to as Little Chile. The drunken rioters, who were generally ignored by San Franciscans, moved on the Chileans, tore down their tents, beat them with clubs, stoned several who attempted to flee, and wildly opened fire with the guns creating a state of havoc that was heard nearly a mile away. This raid was carried out in broad daylight and in full view of the residents of San Francisco, none of whom attempted to quell the senseless violence. However, as news of the altercation spread through the elite of San Francisco, a course of action against the Hounds was discussed and agreed upon.

On July 16, Sam Brannan, with the aid of Bezer Simmons, organized a meeting of the economic and political leadership of San Francisco to discuss how to deal with the Hounds and the aftermath of their violent actions. Brannan was able to raise the funds necessary to cover the rebuilding of the Little Chile. Sam Brannan, ever the erudite public speaker, was also able to convince over 200 able-bodied and well-armed men to form a company of deputies who were willing to root out the lawless rabble. Word of the formation of the posse reached the Hounds, who began to scatter south across the peninsula and east across the bay in the hope of reaching the Sacramento River, with the vastness of the California interior at their reach. Twenty Hounds who choose not to flee were quickly apprehended and subsequently imprisoned on one of the floating jails in San Francisco harbor as they awaited their speedy trial.

William Gwin and James Ward were elected as judges to serve in the trial, and within 24 hours, a grand jury of 24 men recognized enough evidence to indict the 20 apprehended Hounds of alleged crimes ranging from conspiracy, robbery, and attempted murder. The outcome of their trial was more generous in its decision. A few Hounds were found guilty of any crimes and required to make fiduciary remuneration to the Chileans, with only two being sentenced to prison. However, following the court's decision, none of the Hounds were actually sent to prison for the restitution or, for that matter, ever imprisoned. Ultimately, those convicted were banished from California, though this decision proved unenforceable due to both popular sentiment being on the side of the Hounds and certainly not in favor of the Chileans. In the coming months, another wave of nativism and xenophobia would take hold of San Francisco. This time, the mob would be different in form and practice and enjoyed widespread support from the citizenry of San Francisco as the infamous Vigilance Committee of 1851 took to the streets and docks to rid the city of its "undesirables."

In early February 1851, violence on the streets of San Francisco began to escalate. Muggings, robbery, and arson occurred daily and nightly. In reaction to the murders of a few prominent businessmen, Sam Brannan organized a mob and went after two Australian men who had reportedly been in the area where the murders and robberies took place. Before the Australians had nooses around their necks, a young and prominent San Francisco businessman, William Tell Coleman, convinced enough people to halt the hangings because, as he explained, the two foreigners had not received a proper trial. While Coleman could not muster more than a trial by mob, he was able to sway enough people to permit legitimate law enforcement agents to take the Australians into custody. The good fortunes that the Australians experienced were virtually an isolated experience as a series of arsons set around San Francisco galvanized the resolve and expanded the ranks of the mob that grew into the first Vigilance Committee.

After a series of fires that were destructive but manageable, on May 3, 1851, a fire was set that proved considerably more significant and led to widespread speculation that all the fires had been the work of the notorious "Sydney Ducks." Nearly 100 people lost their lives in the fire, and the city of San Francisco was in a state

of confusion. Hostility toward foreign-born immigrants intensi-
fied. Random acts of violence committed by Americans against
the foreigners, many of whom were miners in town to spend their
gold, persisted. Remarkably and tragically, a second large-scale
fire cropped up on June 3. The mayor of San Francisco, Charles
James Brennan, had only been in office since May 5, 1851, and was
forced into an unpleasant executive action against leading citizens
of the city as many prominent businessmen of San Francisco not
only called for the formation of an extralegal committee of citizens
to combat what they perceived to be wanton criminal activity but
also organized the First San Francisco Vigilance Committee, officially referring to themselves as "the Committee of Vigilance of San
Francisco."[2]

Initially, Mayor Brennan was able to convince the self-formed
volunteer police to allow the city, under his direct supervision, to
properly investigate the several men that the committee had apprehended and incarcerated, rather than simply hang them based

In this 1853 John Prendergast oil painting, the vigilance committee of San
Francisco is shown bringing to justice a criminal in San Francisco harbor.
(Attributed to John Prendergast, *Justice Meted Out to English Jim by the Vigi-
lantes, San Francisco Harbor*, ca. 1853. Oil on canvas, 18 × 24 in. Oakland
Museum of California, gift of Concours d'Antiques, Art Guild.)

on mere accusations. A grand jury was formed and criminal indictments were handed down, though the inexperienced legal system of San Francisco proved unable to see the process completed and the men placed on trial. Incredibly, the indicted were released and they quickly fled the city, and any hope of a trial vanished with them. Outraged, the citizens of San Francisco turned their back on the mayor and the city administration. On June 10, 1851, the vigilance committee took "law and order" into their own hands and for the next 30 days, the mob roamed the streets in search of offenders. By the time the committee officially abdicated their power and "adjourned," they hung at least four men and forced out from the city limits innumerable others.[3] Five years later, the committee came out of retirement and took control of San Francisco once again.

THE GOLD RUSH POLITICAL ARENA

Politics in Gold Rush California mirrored the society, with all of its successes and failures, that made up the territory-turned-state. California's first 10 governors had all come to California in pursuit of their fortunes during the Gold Rush. Each of the men had made the long journey like all the Argonauts, by foot or by sea. Upon their arrival into California, the men found an expanding society nearly devoid of the structures that defined the East, Midwest, and South. The pace of life itself was different from anything anyone had ever seen before. There was chaos, a sense of urgency, and a quest for riches and domination, and the constantly changing struggles to get rich or simply survive made it difficult for a ruling political class of elites to truly take form. However, nativism and racism ran through all of the political currents as the fast-growing groups, European Americans, expanded their numbers, took over the political arena, and consistently shut out foreigners, African Americans, and, especially, California Indians.

In the first 10 years of statehood, California went through seven governors and all but one, John Neely Johnson, were Democrats with sympathies for the Southern slave states. California's first two governors, Peter Burnett and John McDougal, laid out racist political platforms that were anti-Indian and anti-black; both men had strongly influenced the state's first constitution. Following California's admission into the Union, the Democratic Party, with its core and heavy influence coming from the emigrants who poured into the territory from the Southern slave states, took control of state politics. Its dominance began to falter in 1855 with the emergence of the American Party, whose ranks were filled with members of the Know-Nothing Party, a semisecret political organization with its base platforms resting heavily on racism and nativism. The Democrats who migrated into the Know-Nothing Party tended to view foreign miners, immigrants regardless of trade, and Indians with disdain; they, along with the remnants of the virtually dead Whig Party, filled out the ranks of this third party. While at the birth of the Know-Nothing Party, named as such because if members were questioned about their politics and political colleagues, they were to state that they knew nothing, there seemed to be no real aspect of political life that they could engender change beyond assisting their other rival party, the Republicans. However, the American Party candidate John Neely Johnson was the first non-Democratic elected governor in 1856, and the upstart party did gain elected positions by splitting the Democratic vote. Perhaps most significant, they proved a powerful lobbying bloc that played crucial roles in the passage of racist laws and in the short-lived unification of the factionist Democratic Party that had been split between Southern and Northern lines of alliance. Additionally, election of the nativist and backward thinking John Johnson proved to be a central motivation in the emergence of the upstart Republican Party in California.

The Republican Party was founded in 1854 in Ripon, Wisconsin, and its founders took their name from Thomas Jefferson's Democratic Republican Party. The new political party emerged in reaction against the Kansas-Nebraska Act of 1854, which permitted the expansion of slavery in the United States. Beginning with California's statehood in 1850, the Democratic Party had virtually sealed up politics in the Gold Rush state, though the split in the party and the emergence of the American Party in its wake shook the Democratic hold on the elected offices, though this transition did not occur until 1855. For the first five years of statehood, the Democrats shaped politics and the laws of California.

Peter Burnett was born in Nashville, Tennessee, in 1807 but was raised in Missouri. Burnett was a self-educated man, and he made a comfortable living owning and operating a dry goods store in Missouri; however, like so many others of his day, Burnett had set his ambitions on moving west into the Oregon Territory. Burnett planned for his trek beginning in the late 1830s and, as his attention moved toward his migration plans, his business acumen diminished, which led to a series of loans to cover his losses. By the early 1840s, Burnett found his debts had grown beyond his ability to cover, and in 1843, he finally had his plans in order and made the

· great journey across land, eventually landing in Oregon. In just a few months, Burnett found what he believed to be his true calling: politics.

Peter Burnett set his ambitions on being elected to the Oregon provisional legislature; in 1844 he began his first term, and brutal, racist legislation soon followed. Burnett submitted a proposal to encourage African Americans to move out of the Oregon Territory and the Oregon Legislature passed his bill. The anti-black law barred African Americans from moving into the territory, and those in Oregon who refused to leave faced legalized, public whippings. Burnett's legislation remained on Oregon's books well into statehood, and the state's constitution was not purged of the African American exclusion law, and subsequent racist exclusionary legislation, until after World War I. For his part, Burnett did not remain in Oregon very long after his entry into the legislature. Soon after Burnett received news of the gold discovery in California, Burnett packed his family and headed south into Gold Rush California.

In his first few months, Peter Burnett found and worked a few successful claims that afforded him the opportunity to move his family into a comfortable home in the ever-growing city of San Francisco. Never one to remain outside of the arena, Burnett began to network with the leading political figures in San Francisco, and in 1849, he was emerging as one of the most popular political figures in California. Burnett's political platforms were populist in sentiment, though his maneuvering occurred well before the populist movement that would forever change American politics. Burnett stressed the themes that resonated with the many miners— self-rule, economic freedom, anti-immigrant, anti-Indian, and anti-black. With the election slated for December 1849, Burnett set his sights on his strongest rival, John Sutter, and he distinguished himself from the Swiss immigrant by touting his tenure in office in the Oregon legislature, and by personally engaging as many voters as possible, something that Sutter failed to do. On December 20, 1849, Peter Burnett was elected as the first civilian governor in a landslide.

From the onset, Burnett's social views were an open book. He also successfully called for the exclusion of blacks and Indians from citizenship and recommended that Californians "prevent" those unable or unwilling to assimilate from being permitted entry into the territory that soon became a state. Unwittingly, Peter Burnett ostracized one of his strongest blocs, Southern Democrats, who wanted an expansion of slavery in California, with his push for black exclusion. However, Burnett's views on Native Americans were widely shared by gold miners, who found Indian villages and societies to be an encumbrance on the expansion of their wealth derived from mining and the idea of working alongside blacks repugnant. Also, by 1850, the majority American miners began to view foreigners with disdain, a sentiment fueled by the growing difficulty in finding surface gold and the ever-growing population of miners in the gold fields. This was a position held by Burnett as well, which ingratiated him with many of his fellow Californians. However, a few months into statehood, Burnett began to polarize members of the cabinet and the legislature with his heavy-handed posturing, and members of the assembly reacted by refusing to pass any of his initiatives. Burnett became frustrated and resigned from office after having served less than two years. However, Burnett left his mark on California during his brief tenure as he secured passage of the Foreign Miners Tax, a general increase of state taxes, and successful passage of a bond act that paid bounties for massacre of Indians with the ultimate intent of genocide. Peter Burnett left behind one of the darkest legacies of any governor in California history. In his post-political life, Burnett was far from shunned. He returned to practicing law, served briefly on the California Supreme Court as a justice, and eventually accepted the position of president of the Pacific Bank of California.

Peter Burnett's lieutenant governor, John McDougall, became governor following Burnett's resignation. Born in Ohio in 1818 and raised in Indiana, John McDougall had enlisted in the Indiana Voluntary Militia and fought with distinction in the Mexican–American War and rose to the rank of captain. Following the conclusion of the conflict between the neighboring nations, McDougall moved his family to California, just in time for the Gold Rush. First trying his hand as miner, McDougall found moderate success, though once he changed his profession to merchant, his fortune changed for the better. With his economic outlook on the rise, McDougall entered politics, which was a natural fit due to his affable personality and ability to find the common ground for disparate opinions. With his star on the rise, McDougall was approached by several political insiders to put his hat in the ring for lieutenant governor. McDougall accepted the challenge, and he joined six other candidates in the race and emerged victorious in the December 1849 election.

After Burnett's resignation, John McDougall became governor, and for a brief period of time, the greenhorn politician was led around by the more seasoned political operators as evidenced by

Burnett's tendency to acquiesce to the more loquacious group when pressured into making a decision. In his first few weeks in office, McDougall sided with anti-Indian miners when he commissioned a militia of over 200 men to fight against Indian Tribes in the Mariposa War rather than attempt any negotiations aimed at keeping the peace. In general, McDougall continued the racist legislative path set forth by Burnett, though he supported Chinese immigration into California, not because he cared to extend citizenship to the Chinese but rather because there was a shortage of cheap labor, in particular domestic services, and, like most of the economic elite, McDougall viewed the Chinese as a perfect fit in the service industry. This decision, unpopular with the general views of anti-immigrant Democrats, began to tarnish McDougall's image, which was further hindered when he took a public stance in opposition of the highly popular San Francisco Vigilance Committee of 1851. With his popularity at an all-time low, the Democratic Party refused to renominate the incumbent governor, and after his governorship, McDougall sank into oblivion.

John Bigler succeeded McDougall as the third governor of California and was the first governor to complete a full term in office. A native of Pennsylvania, John Bigler was born to a family of middle-class means. In his youth, Bigler apprenticed in the printing industry, though he was disappointed by the intense labor and minimal economic rewards it offered. An intelligent and ambitious young man, he craved for more than what he perceived the mid-19th-century print industry could offer. John Bigler turned to the study of law, which he felt would be a safe and lucrative career. After over a decade in a successful and lucrative practice, though fairly mundane and uneventful, the call of the California Gold Rush was too strong to ignore. In early 1849, John Bigler moved to California with high hopes to build a successful law practice only to find that the virtually lawless California territory afforded very few opportunities for his trade. What California needed was men of substance who could form the leadership that an ever-changing and ever-growing society desperately needed. In the December 1849 election, John Bigler became a Democratic candidate for the state assembly. As one of 10 candidates, all unknown, Bigler happened to have the good fortune of receiving more votes than the other candidates. Once in office, the experienced lawyer understood the art of politics, and he quickly rose within the party ranks and was voted Speaker of the assembly after being in office for only two months. Following John McDougall's catastrophic plunge in popularity, Bigler became the Democratic Party nominee in the 1851 election and after winning one of the closest races in California history, John Bigler was elected governor.

Once in office, Governor John Bigler demonstrated early on that he was on the side of mining. Bigler was utterly opposed to any restrictions that would curtail mining, and following in the footsteps of his predecessor, he was an avid supporter of racist legislation. The ethnic group that was the focus of Bigler's administration was the Chinese. While Governor Bigler endorsed the reduction of the foreign miners' tax, he insisted that the amended tax policy only require Chinese to pay the monthly charge. Bigler called for Californians to not employ or do business with Chinese, insisting that they were unwilling and incapable of assimilating and would only do damage to the emerging California society. Governor Bigler went so far as to sign into law a $50 charge for Chinese to enter California, a piece of legislation that the California Supreme Court later struck down. Bigler consciously sided with the growing anti-Chinese, anti-immigrant, and anti-Indian movements, and when the Democratic Party over the issue of slavery, Bigler played a key role in the organization of the Free Soil, distinguishing themselves from the predominantly Southern California Democratic Party, who began to refer to themselves as Chivalry Democrats.

The election of 1853 was incredibly contentious. The Chivalry Democrats and the Free Soil Democrats engaged in mudslinging tactics against each other and fairly well ignored the Whig Party candidate, William Waldo. Remarkably, even with the Democratic Party split, John Bigler became the first California governor to be reelected for a second term. Ethnic tensions throughout the state continued to escalate during Bigler's second term and so did anti-immigrant and anti-Indian rhetoric by the politicians. While Bigler did his best to prove his nativist leanings, he was simply outdone by his Know-Nothing American Party adversary, John Neely Johnson, who became the very embodiment of racism. Thus, Bigler became the first incumbent governor to lose a reelection bid.

John Neely Johnson, like his three predecessors, came to California seeking to make his fortune during the Gold Rush. As with his three predecessors, he became embittered against the growing number of foreigners in the gold fields as well as in California in general. Johnson, who had been born in Indiana in 1825, abruptly abandoned a career as a lawyer after hearing about the gold strikes made by the Mormons employed by John Sutter. After one year of chasing the dream of striking it rich and failing to do so at every point that he dug and panned for gold, Johnson returned to law and entered public office as a Sacramento City attorney. After one year in this post, Johnson began to envision bigger and better things for himself in the field of politics, and in 1852, he was elected to the California State Assembly representing the greater Sacramento area.

In the California Assembly, Johnson quickly made a name for himself as a rabid anti-immigrant and anti-Indian Democrat. His combustible personality also led to several public confrontations, including one incident where he attacked and pummeled a newspaperman in public. As with many Democrats in Gold Rush California, Johnson felt as though the party was not in step with the issues gripping California. In 1854, Johnson formally changed his party affiliation and joined the Know-Nothing American Party, which also absorbed not only half of the registered Democrats but also a significant number from the disintegrating Whig Party. With his star on the rise, the leadership of the American Party nominated John Johnson as their gubernatorial candidate in 1855. Johnson gleefully accepted the nomination and subsequently won the election by a significant margin. The growing hostilities throughout the state toward immigrants, in particular the Chinese, as well as the California Indians, were evidenced in the outcome of the election of 1855. Know-Nothing American Party candidates were elected at all levels as they nearly took control of the assembly. Johnson's lieutenant governor was Robert Moon Anderson, and several other key posts, including attorney general, were filled with Know-Nothing candidates. Once in office, Governor Johnson faced a crisis that mirrored the challenges faced by Governor McDougall: a San Francisco Vigilance Committee.

After five years of silence, the San Francisco Vigilance Committee reemerged. While many of the members had taken part in the 1851 episode, many new men comprised the ranks of the second murderous mob. While the growing lawlessness and increased immigration throughout Gold Rush California, particularly in San Francisco, fueled the formation of the second vigilance committee, the flashpoint occurred when a newspaper editor at the *San Francisco Bulletin* was killed by James Casey, a San Francisco politician who had a reputation for corruption and intrigue. Casey was arrested by the police, and while he was in custody, one of the primary organizers of the 1851 committee, William Coleman, organized a new group of armed men to take control of the jail and to try Casey themselves for his alleged crime. The vigilance committee barricaded the streets around the jail and within a few days had overtaken the facility itself by armed force. The fiery mob removed Casey, as well as Charles Cora who had shot a U.S. Marshal, and proceeded to set up the gallows to hang both men. For his part, Governor Johnson reacted swiftly against the vigilance committee.

Governor Johnson arrived in San Francisco along with the state militia's commandant, Major General William Tecumseh Sherman, who would later make history with his brutal war tactics in the Civil War. Johnson, with Sherman present, met with the mob's leader, William Tell Coleman, and stressed the need for him to take the initiative and dissolve the extralegal vigilante force as he was held in highest regard by the members of the mob. Coleman flatly refused, and the two men began a shouting match that Coleman eventually won. Outnumbered, General Sherman was also powerless and was unable to effect any change. The vigilance committee refused all of Governor Johnson's requests to turn over their prisoners to the established state law enforcement agencies and demonstrated their power by hanging both Casey and Cora as Johnson and Sherman watched. Following the hanging, Governor Johnson returned to Sacramento with the understanding that the vigilance committee would disperse; however, that was not how matters played out in San Francisco. Instead, the mob declared itself to be the rightful law enforcement in the city, and its numbers grew, as did their activities as it literally took control of California's largest city.

San Francisco's mayor, James Van Ness, sent word to Governor Johnson that the city's chief executive had lost control of the city as the mob outnumbered his police force. Van Ness pleaded with the governor to send in the state militia and order them to put down the insurrection. Johnson responded by ordering General Sherman to gather the state militia and take action against the vigilance committee as he best saw fit. Sherman pointed out that the state militia not only lacked in numbers but also arms to effectively quash the much larger and well-armed rebellion. Sherman advised Governor Johnson to contact the U.S. Army based in Benicia to provide support. Johnson requested that General John Wool supply the militia with arms and additional troops, but Wool flatly refused as the governor did not have any authority over the U.S. Army and that only the president had the legal authority to make such an order. Making matters even worse, General Sherman became more concerned with his own personal reputation and refused to accept such a humiliating situation, and rather than lead his men into an immanent military failure, he resigned his commission. Johnson reached out to former California land commissioner and lawyer Volney Howard to take control of the militia and put down the vigilante mob.

Volney Howard was a man of action with extensive leadership experience. Before he moved to California, Howard had served as the first attorney general of the state of Texas, where he also served as a two-term U.S. representative. The militia reacted positively to the newly appointed general and their ranks grew, and just as General Howard was ready to supply his soldiers with a significant cache of weapons that had been aboard the militia's clipper anchored in the San Francisco Bay, his fortunes abruptly turned. Probably due to spies within the militia's ranks, the vigilance committee learned of Howard's plans. Scores of vigilantes boarded and seized the vessel and in the process commandeered its arsenal, effectively spoiling any chances that General Howard had of securing victory. For the remainder of the summer of 1856, the San Francisco Vigilance Committee ran the city and as their ranks began to dissipate, an unfortunate situation unfolded. California Supreme Court judge David Terry, a man well known for his temper, was embroiled in a very audible public argument regarding an arrest with Sterling Hopkins, one of the committee policemen. As the argument became more heated, Judge Terry produced a bowie knife and stabbed Hopkins. The mob quickly arrested Terry and confined him at Fort Gunnybags, which served as the headquarters of the committee. Judge Terry was released after 25 days when it was determined that Hopkins had made a full recovery. Terry later gained national notoriety in 1859 when he killed California U.S. senator David Broderick in a duel over slavery. Terry was pro-slavery, while Broderick was a free-soil advocate. Terry was himself later murdered in 1889 by a bodyguard in service to U.S. Supreme Court justice Stephen Field, following Terry's assault of Field for ruling against him in a court case the year before. Eventually the vigilance committee agreed to disperse after Governor Johnson agreed to their proposed Consolidation Act, which set the boundaries of San Francisco County and City as exactly the same. Additionally, the municipal and county authorities were merged, which permitted the San Franciscans to control home rule completely and in the process created the county of San Mateo out of what was formerly southern San Francisco County.

The vigilance committee and the events surrounding their actions had devastated Governor Johnson politically. Johnson was seen as impotent as a leader who could only suppress the uprising by capitulating to the demands of the mob. The Know-Nothings abandoned

Johnson in the 1857 election cycle, resulting in the American Party choosing George Bowie as their candidate, though the pro-slavery, pro-South Democrat John Weller emerged victorious.

John Weller, an Ohioan, was born in 1812 and raised and educated in that state, where he became an attorney, though Weller only practiced law for three years, before he entered a life of politics. After representing Ohio in the U.S. House of Representatives for three terms, he volunteered for service in the Mexican–American War and was commissioned a lieutenant colonel in the Ohio Volunteers Regiment. After the conclusion of the war, Weller ran unsuccessfully on the Democratic ticket for the governorship of Ohio in 1848. Embittered by the close, and highly contested, political defeat, John Weller quickly accepted a post on the U.S. and Mexican Border Commission in 1849. Weller and his commission members were given charge of establishing an agreed-upon California and Mexico border, though John Weller found himself linked to a series of scandals and intrigue in the border commission and was publicly dismissed by President Zachary Taylor. As news from Washington, D.C., traveled slowly, or sometimes not at all, in Gold Rush California, Weller was able to emerge unscathed from the scandals and went back to practicing law, though he remained in California, recognizing the exceptional potential for a man with talent and ambition, in particular in the political arena. Weller tirelessly networked and promoted himself in the Democratic Party. His diligence paid off when he replaced John C. Fremont as a U.S. senator in 1852. Incredibly, Weller lost his bid for reelection in the Senate in 1857 but was elected governor that same year. While each of his predecessors had witnessed their moments of scandal while serving as governor of Gold Rush California, John B. Weller pushed for California to secede from the Union if a civil war between the North and South came to pass. And, rather than join the South, Weller insisted that California become an independent republic. Weller did have some support, though the majority of Californians were opposed to the secession, and when the Civil War began, California sided with the Union. As governor, Weller became known for his failed independent California movement and also for one success.

A private contractor had been given a contract to administrate San Quinton Prison, just north of San Francisco. When rumors of corruption and embezzlement began to surround the private contractor, Governor Weller ordered an investigation. When the allegations were proven accurate, the governor ordered the contractors to surrender. They refused and then actually barricaded themselves in the prison. Governor John Weller reacted by personally leading a militia that forcibly took back the prison. For a brief period of time, he enjoyed widespread approval, but the independent California issue, which he refused to distance himself from, continued to dog him and eventually led to a virtual abandonment by his own party. Weller understood that his drop in popularity would deny him a second term in Sacramento and, rather than face defeat at the polls, he accepted a post as ambassador to Mexico in 1860 but was recalled when Republican Abraham Lincoln took office in 1861.

While Republican Abraham Lincoln won the presidency and had actually secured California's then four Electoral College votes, nearly 70 percent of California voters cast their ballot for other candidates. Democrat Stephen Douglas garnered 31 percent, Southern Democrat John Breckinridge polled 28 percent, and Constitution Union John Bell received nearly 8 percent; Abraham Lincoln received slightly over 32 percent and in the process bested the four-man race. The outcome of the presidential election evidenced California's fractured political makeup. In the gubernatorial race of 1859, the ambitious and popular Lecompton Democrat Milton Latham easily won the race with 60 percent of the vote.

Milton Latham was born in 1827 in Columbus, Ohio. Latham developed his pro-Southern leanings during the course of his first career, school teacher, in Alabama. After just one year as an educator, Latham became bored and began to study law; he was subsequently admitted to the Alabama Bar in 1848. News of the Gold Rush reached Latham in 1849, and over the course of that year, the young lawyer who had been clerking for the circuit court was overtaken by gold fever, or more accurately how he could make his fortune in the rapidly growing territory cum state, and Latham planned out a trip to Gold Rush California. Latham reached San Francisco in 1850, and after surveying the reality that the miners might have pulled the gold from the land, the merchants and politicians were pulling the gold from the miners. Milton Latham quickly put his lawyer skills to work and secured a position in the San Francisco County Clerk's office, which allowed him to meet several other rising stars in Gold Rush San Francisco as well as Sacramento; the latter city soon provided Latham with his first opportunity in politics.

After just one year in California, Milton Latham became the district attorney (DA) of Sacramento—a remarkable feat considering both his brief career as a lawyer and one-year residency in California, but for those who knew Latham, there was no surprise. If ever there was a man who knew how to network, exchange favors, and, most importantly, keep promises, that man was Milton Latham. With his popularity on the rise, Latham segued from the DA office to the U.S. Congress when he was elected to the House of Representatives in 1852. While by any standards Milton Latham was a political success, the tedium and relative inability to accomplish anything of significance in the nation's largest and most divided governing body disappointed Latham, and he decided to finish out his term and head back to California to better his position.

Upon his return to San Francisco, Latham went back to practicing law and with inflation on the rise and an ever-increasing flow of gold into the city, Milton Latham's fortune was on the rise. His success in law, coupled with his political popularity, led to President Franklin Pierce appointing Latham to the post of U.S. customs collector in San Francisco. The customs office was viewed as one of the most corrupt federal agencies in the United States and the San Francisco office was arguably the worst. The reasons behind the corruption that ran young branch were simple. The incredible flow of gold led to incredible bribes that the customs employees found impossible to turn down. Additionally, the lack of any cohesive government or law enforcement in Gold Rush California, and by extension San Francisco, provided the perfect climate to grow government corruption. Recognizing the potential for a tarnished image, Latham turned down the position, though he later acquiesced. After holding the post for nearly five years, during which time Latham had been able to clean up some of the corruption, which he always managed to have recorded by the newspapers, he stepped down from the post in 1857 and began to organize his return to politics. Latham had two elected offices in mind, the California governorship and the U.S. Senate, and while he made known his ambitions to serve as the Gold Rush state's chief executive, his desire to become a senator, which he believed was his best path en route to the U.S. presidency, was kept quiet.

The 1859 gubernatorial election was a heated affair. Once again the split in the Democratic Party between the pro-slavery Lecompton faction, for whom Latham was the candidate, and anti-Lecompton Democrats, who selected John Currey, a rapid anti-slavery candidate, created sensational mudslinging. Many throughout Gold Rush California believed that this election would belong to the Young Republican Party and its candidate, Leland Stanford, though that was not the case as Latham's popularity led to his landslide victory and subsequent shortest tenure in office in California's gubernatorial history.

After just five days in office, Milton Latham was elected by the California State Assembly to fill the U.S. Senate seat vacated by David Broderick, who had been killed in a duel by California Supreme Court justice David Terry. In his short five-day governorship, Latham outlined the various problems the Gold Rush state faced, in particular its inability to effective collect taxes related to gold mining and relative disconnect from the rest of the United States, which hindered California's economic expansion. These were the very problems that the next two governors would find on their desk waiting for them upon entering office. As a Senator, Latham's timing was not the best, the political winds in California shifted tremendously from 1860 to 1862 as the Republican Party grew in its ranks, owing much to the Southern secession and subsequent surge in allegiance to the Union. Latham was not reelected to the Senate by the assembly; instead, the anti-Lecompton Democrat John Conness was elected. Upon Latham's resignation of the governor's office, Lieutenant Governor John Downey assumed the chief executive post.

John Downey was born in Ireland and was California's first foreign-born governor and only foreign-born governor until the election of Arnold Schwarzenegger in 2003. As governor, Downey proved to be pro-industry, pro-mining, and, as many of his critics accused him of, pro-big money, though he came to veto one of the most lobbied bills in the state, the so-called Bulkhead Bill, which was an obvious plot by the San Francisco Dock and Wharf Company as it would have given them an absolute monopoly of the Golden State's primary waterfront. The S.F. Dock and Wharf Company had been able to bribe or cajole enough members of the state assembly and Senate to pass the bill without any serious hindrance or debate, but once it reached Downey's desk, the governor flatly vetoed it and publicly made it known that he would not permit legislation that would increase the rate of shipping for all commerce entering or leaving the San Francisco port. While this proved popular with the throngs of workers and miners, it proved especially popular with the ever-growing large-scale mining corporations, who would have been bled the most had the Bulkhead Bill been enacted. With the Civil War's outbreak in 1861, Downey made it clear that he sided with the Union, though his public proclamation of allegiance, which his adversaries claimed was actually a stance of political convenience, was not enough and the once-popular governor could not even gain the anti-Lecompton Democratic nomination for the 1862 election. And the split in the Democratic Party and the surge of pro-Union Republicans in California finally led to another party capturing the governorship, resulting in the election of Leland Stanford.

THE REPUBLICAN SHIFT

The Republican Party, like the vast majority of the population of the Gold Rush California, was not born in the Golden State. In 1854, an alliance of Free Soil Democrats and anti-slavery Whigs found common ground in their opposition of the Kansas-Nebraska Act of that same year. The main objection that the Republicans held was the codicil of popular sovereignty that permitted territorial settlers to vote on whether or not slavery would be permitted within their respective borders. On April 19, 1856, the Republican Party held its first organized convention in Sacramento, and the Democratic-controlled newspapers poured out negative articles and editorials on the event, castigating the Republicans for their anti-slavery stance. The vitriol of the Democrats only galvanized the resolve of the Young Republican Party to recruit in quantity and in quality, and by the late 1850s, a strong shift in political party affiliation occurred throughout California, much due to the effort of Cornelius Cole.

As one of the most outspoken critics of slavery, and one of the leading advocates in 1850 for California entrance into the Union as a free state, Cornelius Cole, a native New Yorker, had long considered himself a free-soil Democrat, though as the continued evolution within the Democratic Party pushed out or forced into irrelevancy its members who opposed slavery, Cole began to organize other free-soil Democrats with the intent of forming their own political party. While Cole welcomed with open arms anyone opposed to slavery, he also understood the necessity of bringing in as many leading California citizens as possible. Early on Cole was responsible for bringing into the fold the men who would soon comprise the so-called Big Four: Collis P. Huntington, Charles Crocker, Mark Hopkins, and Leland Stanford. These four men were not simply of significant means; they were political and economic visionaries who recognized the incredible social and economic possibilities in the new state. They were also very well known and highly respected. Their words of endorsement and encouragement were of such significance that by the close of the decade, California was a strong Union state, and Leland Stanford was the first Republican elected governor.

Leland Stanford was the first California governor to be financially comfortable from his family lineage and of his own making, and while Stanford came from a well-to-do background, the fortune he amassed in his own lifetime dwarfed what he was born into. A native New Yorker, Leland was born in 1824 and as a young man he studied law at Cazenovia Seminary, and in 1848 he was admitted to the bar and moved to Wisconsin to practice law. It was in Wisconsin that Leland Stanford first became politically active and he joined the Whig Party, which, though appealing to Stanford, was already in a state of serious decline. Following an unfortunate fire at his home in 1852, which destroyed his extensive law library as well as the majority of his and his wife's personal belongings, Leland Stanford, like so many thousands before him, decided to try his luck in the California Gold Rush. Not wanting to put his wife through the ordeal of traveling to California, let alone coping with what appeared to be a society devoid of morals, at least according to the newspaper stories that Mr. and Mrs. Stanford read, the couple decided that Jane would move to Albany for the time being, where she could also care for her ailing father.

In Gold Rush California, Leland Stanford set up a general store in the gold fields, specifically in Placer County, the heart of gold mining activity at the time. From 1852 to 1855, Leland Stanford not only bettered his own position well beyond what he had achieved in his law practice but also put his legal training to work by serving as a justice of the peace, where he gained a reputation for fairness and intelligence. Stanford briefly left California for Albany, where he retrieved his wife; the couple moved back to California in 1856, and Leland Stanford, along with other members of the Whig Party, became one of the organizers of the Republican Party in California that same year. A man who was held in the highest esteem by his colleagues, Stanford was nominated to serve as a Republican delegate at the party's U.S. presidential nomination conventions in 1856 and 1860. Trying his own hand in politics, Stanford was unsuccessful in his 1857 quest for California state treasurer as well as his run at the governorship in 1859 before he was elected governor in 1861. Stanford's two years in Sacramento proved not simply successful but quite fortuitous.

Governor Leland Stanford brought stability to California state politics during his tenure in office. Stanford departed from the economic exuberance at the expense of the state budget that his predecessors had demonstrated. After his first year in office, Governor Stanford managed to bring California's budget under control. The

sound business practices that the first Republican governor implemented also permitted California to establish the first state teachers
college at San Jose. Stanford is best remembered for his part as a
member of the Big Four and his pronounced stand on the side of
the Union, his advocacy of the free-soil movement, and Republican
ascendency in California.

Leland Stanford had been a lifelong opponent of slavery. Originally a devout Whig, Stanford found the platforms of the Republican Party much to his liking; he had also, like many other astute
politicos of his era, come to believe that the tensions between the
South and the free-soil states would eventually lead to a Southern
succession. Whether or not the fateful decision would lead to a full-
blown civil war, Stanford was unsure, though if war did break out,
his convictions would pull him into the fray and onto the side of the
Union. While Cole and the Big Four were ardent anti-slavery activists, most of the Republicans in California were, at best, lukewarm
in their anti-slavery convictions; instead, these hardy souls who
worked long, difficult hours in the gold fields and those who began
the growing agricultural and manufacturing sectors felt strongest
about the establishment of a transcontinental railroad that would
permit the mass exportation of their commodities to the densely
populated east, and it would also encourage migration from the
east to California, but more importantly, it would, hopefully, prime
the pump for easterners to migrate to the whistle-stop towns along
the yet-to-be built rail lines between California and the plains states.
And, while all three political parties supported the construction of
a transcontinental railroad, they differed on where the line should
be built.

The Democrats and their sympathizers strongly preferred a line
that would connect California with the Southern states. The Republicans were utterly opposed to a line that drove east into the
South; instead, they clamored for an eastern terminus in the city
that would connect California with the emerging city of Chicago.
In their political wrangling, the Democrats insisted that they were
the only party in California that could deliver the transcontinental rail road because the Republicans were, at best, merely a sec-
tional anomaly that could not form a national and permanent base
of support. Republicans simply guaranteed that they could build
it, and when in 1862 Congress passed the Pacific Railroad Act, it
was under the Republican-controlled federal government and the
Republican governor Leland Stanford. By this point in time, California had shifted politically and had emerged with a Republican

Railroads sprang up throughout Gold Rush California, before the Transcontinental Railroad was conceived. In this early 1860s image, Chinese workers are working on building the trestle above Colfax. (Unknown photographer, 1860s. Photograph, 11 × 14 in. Collection of the Oakland Museum of California, Museum Purchase.)

majority that reached out to French, Irish, and German immigrants as well as the former Mexican citizenry, the Californios, one of the largest voting blocs, for which the Republicans owed a debt to the flamboyant war hero, pathfinder, and celebrity, John C. Fremont, who, along with William Gwin were the first two U.S. senators to represent California.

FOUNDING SENATORS

Born out of wedlock to Anne Pryor (nee Whiting) and Charles Fremon (John latter added the "t" reverting to the original spelling of his father's surname) in Savannah, Georgia, John C. Fremont appeared to be destined for a life of mediocrity at best. His mother had married Major John Pryor, a Richmond man of significant means and 40 years her senior. Pryor realized he had a jewel in the rough with the young, beautiful, though clearly uneducated Anne. Consequently, he hired Charles Fremon to serve as a teacher for Anne, hoping the Frenchman would teach her French in order for her to fit into the upper classes of Virginia soon after he arrived in the United States from France, though quickly the young and vivacious Anne and the charming Charles began an intense affair that clouded their better judgment, and when the two became careless, John Pryor discovered their affair. Rather than divorce Anne quietly, Major Pryor made it known publicly the extent to which his wife had betrayed him in the divorce process. Anne reclaimed her maiden name, sold some of her inherited slaves, and she and Fremon eventually moved to Savannah, Georgia, where they gave birth to John Charles in 1813.

John C. Fremont demonstrated exceptional intelligence and a strong competitive drive early on. His father educated him to the best of his abilities, and at the age of 16, John C. Fremont entered the College of Charleston. Upon graduation in 1831, Fremont was hired as a mathematics instructor for the U.S. Navy. Fremont's exceptional intelligence led to his commission as a lieutenant in the Corps of Topographical Engineers. Fremont not only drew maps; rather, his post was more akin that of a contemporary intelligence officer. From 1838 to 1839, Fremont explored the Missouri and Mississippi rivers, recording the natural terrain and also the American Indian inhabitants. In the latter, Fremont came to understand the Indian alliances and their military and economic potentials. His reports drew praise from his superiors and helped catapult Fremont into his next post, which would garner him fame and fortune.

In 1842, John C. Fremont made the acquaintance of the already legendary frontiersman Kit Carson, and the two men led an expedition to the far west along the Oregon Trail. From 1842 to 1846, Fremont and Carson combed the Oregon Trail and the Sierra Nevada. Fremont became the first American to see and map out Lake Tahoe, and his reports of the Utah Wasatch Mountains and the valley that lay to their south led to the Mormon migration into the region. Fremont's illustrated report was of such high detail and overall quality that the U.S. Congress published it in 1845, and it served as one of the most valued guides by emigrants in the early part of the Gold Rush.

In addition to his service in the Mexican–American War and the wealth derived from his Mariposa Ranch, John C. Fremont served as one of the first two U.S. senators representing California and he became the first Republican candidate for U.S. president in 1856. Fremont, who had earlier married the daughter of the powerful

U.S. senator from Missouri, Thomas Hart Benton, was unable to secure the endorsement of Benton, which led to Fremont's failure to secure the Republican nomination. Though Fremont had a few chances at securing a fabulous fortune for he, and his wife, through the purchase of a section of the Pacific Railroad in Missouri, a few poor judgment calls in business led to the loss of the rail line. After his failure in Missouri, Fremont never returned to California, the state he helped found and played a significant political role in its infancy. Instead, he and his wife, Jesse, moved to New York, where the two lived for the remainder of their lives as political activists and writers. Fremont's counterpart in the Senate, William M. Gwin, was nearly as colorful and even more significant in Gold Rush California politics.

Born in Tennessee in 1805 and educated at Transylvania University in Kentucky, William Gwin's first profession was medical doctor, which he practiced in Mississippi, before turning to his real calling, politician. Gwin served just one term as a U.S. representative in Mississippi and in 1849 at the start of the Gold Rush and just in time to serve as one of the delegates who wrote the state constitution. In that same year, William Gwin, a Democrat, was elected U.S. senator by the California State Assembly. The year 1849 proved to be a year of tremendous significance in Gwin's life. In addition to his role at the constitutional convention and his position as a senator, Gwin also purchased a large tract of land in Paloma, California, that yielded millions of dollars of gold. Gwin took full advantage of his position in the Senate and pushed for federal patronage programs for California.

Arguing that due to the mass of gold being discovered in California, Gwin successfully insisted that a branch of the U.S. Mint be established in California. Gwin recognized that California's coastal position, and warm weather, afforded it the unique opportunity to serve as the gateway to and from Asia. To prove California to be the prime choice for naval fortifications that would serve to protect its shipping industry, Gwin, who also served as Chairman of the U.S. Senate Committee on Naval Affairs, commissioned a full survey of the California's entire coastline. Soon after the survey team completed their task, a navy yard was established and a fleet of steamers that operated out of the San Francisco Bay were regularly routed through Asia, which proved to be of great economic significance as the international trade brought jobs and wealth to the young state.

Though a Democrat, Gwin sided squarely with Abraham Lincoln and the Union and he attempted several secret meetings between

Secretary of State William Seward and Southern leaders on the eve
of the Civil War, attempting to avert secession. During this process
Gwin became disillusioned with what he perceived to be an extreme stubbornness by the leaders of both the North and South and
he contemplated California's potential break from the United States
and return to its original state of being an independent republic.
Word of Gwin's California secession plan spread, and while on a
trip to New York, he was arrested and held in jail for treason until
President Lincoln ordered his release. Gwin was so stunned by the
brutality of the Union Army as they marched through the Confederacy that he attempted to establish a colony of ex-Confederates in
Mexico, a venture that proved a failure. Eventually, Gwin returned
to California after the Civil War, and for the remainder of his life,
he lived peacefully, outside of the political arena as a gentleman
farmer.

CALIFORNIA INDIANS

   No other ethnic group experienced more suffering and injustice
throughout the Gold Rush and early California than the state's
first inhabitants, the Indians. Firmly buttressed with financial support from the state and federal governments through the California Indian War Bonds, the large-scale mining, and even from the
gold the independent miners dug from the earth themselves, the
whites pushed the Indians off of their traditional lands and made
them virtual outlaws by passing legislation that criminalized their
marginalized existence in California. The conflict between the Indians and whites was born out of the reality that tens of thousands
of emigrants were encroaching on Indian land. The 49ers had no
respect for the Indians, whom they pejoratively labeled as "Diggers," a racial epithet akin to "Nigger." The whites wanted all the
land in California to be under their control to exploit the natural
resources, build towns and cities, and, in the process, make their
fortunes. As the mining communities and overall population expanded, the growing California population viewed virtually all
of the land where the Indians resided as being unused and open
for settlement. But first, the Indians had to leave their traditional
lands. Removal by any means necessary became the mode of operating against Indians. Before California even became a state, militias were organized to attack Indian villages, and laws were passed
to destroy those who were not murdered. The onslaught of terror
waged against the Indians came from every level of California

society, and even the state's first civilian governor, Peter Burnett, called for a war of "extermination" against the California Indians until they were all "extinct." The territorial government, then state government of California, passed a series of legislation, including the dubious "Act for the Government and Protection of Indians" and the "Expeditions against the Indians," which were aimed at the destruction of California Indians. Over the next several decades, the daily lives of California Indians were fraught with a reign of terror that few peoples in the history of the world have ever known. Remarkably, the majority of the California Indian societies survived the genocidal wars that were waged against them.

The Act for the Government and Protection of Indians was passed on April 22, 1850, the year following the composition and ratification of the first constitution. The act, first known as Senate Bill No. 54, titled "An Act Relative to the Protection, Punishment and Government of the Indians," written by state senator John Bidwell, though submitted by state senator Ephraim Chamberlain, grew into one of the most damaging pieces of legislation aimed at California Indians. The text of the act begins ostensibly with regard for the protection of the Indians as their villages were being overrun and their lands stripped from them by the expanding Gold Rush communities. Miners squatted on Indian lands, diverted precious water, chased away the game that was central to the diet of the Tribes, and when Indians attempted to maintain control of their territory, the end result was typically the formation of a well-armed posse or militia made up of miners and businessmen taking the law in their own hands. This was a reoccurring event throughout the gold fields. To provide at least the appearance of a civilized society and encourage further white settlement, the Indians had to be "pacified" and some semblance of adjudication regarding incidents with the Indians needed to be established. Section one of the act indicates that only "Justices of the Peace shall have jurisdiction in all cases of complaints by, for, or against Indians, in their respective townships in this State."[4]

On the surface, one could interpret that the California State Legislature and the governor had the inclination to protect California Indians from white mob rule. Even the second section on the surface appears to be for the protection of the Indians. It states: "Persons and proprietors of land on which Indians are residing, shall permit such Indians peaceably to reside on such lands, unmolested in the pursuit of their usual avocations for the maintenance of themselves and their families: Provided; the white person or proprietor in possession of lands may apply to a Justice of the Peace in the Township where the Indians reside, to set off to such Indians a certain amount of land, and, on such application, the Justice shall set off a sufficient amount of land for the necessary wants of such Indians, including the site of their village or residence, if they so prefer it; and in no case shall such selection be made to the prejudice of such Indians, nor shall they be forced to abandon their homes or villages where they have resided for a number of years; and either party feeling themselves aggrieved, can appeal to the County Court from the decision of the Justice: and then divided, a record shall be made of the lands so set off in the Court so dividing them and the Indians shall be permitted to remain thereon until otherwise provided for."[5] This second section gives the appearance of the state protecting the rights of Indians to live, unmolested in their homes regardless of absence of title deed for the real estate upon which they reside. Though the very next section sheds light on the real cause for existence of this purportedly benevolent codicil as it is clear, the state of California wanted to keep the Indians close to the white settlers to make the kidnapping and enslavement the Indian children a smooth a process as possible.

Section 3 states: "Any person having or hereafter obtaining a minor Indian, male or female, from the parents or relations of such Indian Minor, and wishing to keep it, such person shall go before a Justice of the Peace in his Township, with the parents or friends of the child, and if the Justice of the Peace becomes satisfied that no compulsory means have been used to obtain the child from its parents or friends, shall enter on record, in a book kept for that purpose, the sex and probable age of the child, and shall give to such person a certificate, authorizing him or her to have the care, custody, control, and earnings of such minor, until he or she obtain the age of majority. Every male Indian shall be deemed to have attained his majority at eighteen, and the female at fifteen years."[6] This was later amended in 1860, to allow the Indian children to remain in the custody of whites until the males reached the age of 25 and females the age of 21. Remarkably, any white person had the legal authority over an Indian child. This authority permitted whites to stand before a judge and claim that they were a "friend" of the Indian child, and consequently, they were then legal custodians. At no point were the parents or any other relatives of the Indian children required to approve the solicitation. While the court required the whites to clothe, feed, and properly care for the Indian children, if abuse did take place, only the testimony of another white person was admissible in court. Specifically, section 6 states: "Complaints may be made before a Justice of the Peace, by white persons or Indians: but in no case shall a white man be convicted on any offence upon the testimony of an Indian."[7] Indian children were not alone in this forced labor plight. Furthermore, the act permitted the sale of bonded Indian labor.

Section 14 states: "When an Indian is convicted of an offence before a Justice of the Peace, punishable by fine, any white man may, by consent of the justice, give bond for said Indian, conditioned for the payment of said fine and costs, and in such case the Indian shall be compelled to work for the person so bailing, until he has discharged or cancelled the fine assessed against him: Provided; the person bailing shall treat the Indian humanely, and feed and clothe him properly; the allowance given for such labor shall be fixed by the Court, when the bond is taken."[8] One of the most common convictions that California Indians faced was for being deemed a "vagrant." Throughout the state, county and municipal officials routinely evicted California Indians from the lands upon which they resided to secure the productive lands for the growing white settlements. In these forced removals, it was commonplace for the law enforcement officers to arrest Indians who had resisted the evictions and charge them with not only vagrancy but also with other random crimes. Furthermore, the white settlers behind the eviction paid fees, typically in the range of a few hundred dollars to the law enforcement agents. Quite simply, bonded Indian labor brought income to respective government agencies that oversaw the operation and provided whites with cheap labor. The money derived from this enterprise was deemed the "Indian Fund."[9] It should be noted that Indians were afforded the opportunity to avoid having his labor sold to the highest bidder on one condition—the Indian personally post the bond established by the Justice of the Peace and agree to "conduct himself with good behavior" and find "honest employment" for the next 12 months.[10]

In practical terms, the act was aimed at the removal of California Indians from lands coveted by whites. Also, the fact that Indian children could be legally spirited away from their families and literally thrust into involuntary servitude demonstrates not only a legalization of kidnapping and slave labor system but also that there was a concerted effort to destroy the familial structure of California Indians, eradicate the tribal structures, erase the languages and traditions, and in the process commit what many scholars describe as "culturicide." Ultimately, many California Indians survived the act; however, the damage inflicted upon those who lived through this brutal period is nearly incalculable. It should also be noted that California did not formally repeal this racist, genocidal legislation until 1937.

The brutality of the legislation is seen throughout its language, though one particular codicil stands out. Section 16 originally called for Indians to be given a maximum of 100 lashes as punishment for a crime, though the state Senate reduced the number to 25 before passing along the document to the governor's desk for signing, though it pales in comparison the direct and forthcoming legislation that aimed at achieving what Governor Peter Burnett called for in his Annual Message to the Legislature on January 7, 1851, that being the "war of extermination" against the California Indians.[11] In this spirit, the state of California issued a series of War Bonds for "expeditions against the Indians."[12]

The first instance on record of a governor calling for an establishment of a militia to take on arms against Indians took place in 1850, which also illuminates Burnett's reprehensible call for "extermination" the following year. In April 1850, an altercation between California Indians and white miners took place at the convergence of the Colorado and Gila rivers, in southeastern California. While it is unclear what prompted the conflict, the miners in the area coveted the land that the Indians were living on and took the measure to the governor's office, requesting that military action be taken against the Indians. Governor Burnett responded swiftly. Burnett sent his emissaries to enlist the sheriffs of both San Diego and Los Angeles Counties to establish posses or militias of 100 men to hunt down the Indians accused of premeditated violence to send the message that the emigrants would be protected in California. In October of that same year, another altercation between miners and Indians occurred in El Dorado County, and once again Governor Burnett ordered the establishment of a militia, though he doubled the size of the militia with his call for 200 armed men. Governor Burnett, again acting under the authority vested to his office under Article 7 of the first California Constitution, called forth for the establishment of a militia to "suppress" an "insurrection" and "repel" an "invasion."[13] In addition to these bloody massacres, one of the best documented and well known of these earliest of these large-scale conflicts was the Mariposa War, 1850–1851.

John D. Savage, a former Sutter employee and Bear Flagger, had set up a trading post on Mariposa Creek as well as other locations along the southern run of the Sierra Nevada at the start of the Gold

Rush. Several of Savage's regular customers were in fact Indian miners from the Ahwahneechee and Chowchilla tribes, who had found significant success prior to the flood of emigrants into the region began. As the number of white emigrants grew with each passing week in 1850, the competition for establishing new claims increased. Furthermore, whites also forced Indians to work the mines and turn over the gold recovered; often these were the very same mines that the Indians had previously held as their own. When the Indians did not submit, the whites began to randomly attack the Indians, stealing their property and on occasion committing murder. Savage had become not only a friend and trading partner to the surrounding Indians; he had also taken several Indian women as wives. By some counts, Savage had over 20 wives. Though when the whites organized raids aimed at extermination of Indians in early 1850, which led to the Ahwahneechee and Chowchilla retaliating against all whites, including Savage's trading posts, James Savage decided to side with the 49ers. As hostilities continued to escalate, miners pressed California's second governor, John McDougall, for assistance. The governor quickly acquiesced and authorized not only enough militia to form a few squads but rather a battalion of 200 men. McDougall's justification for the formation of the battalion of militia was that the Indians were challenging the sovereignty of the California state government and society. McDougall's personal views of Indians were quite similar to his predecessor, Peter Burnett: The Indians should be removed and blacks should be kept out of California.

Initially, Mariposa County sheriff James Burney was placed in charge of the battalion, though Burney, claiming his position as sheriff precluded him from commanding the battalion, did not accept the commission. However, Burney had previously attempted a small militia raid of some Indian villages, and in the process, he realized defeat would be his fate and subsequently retreated. McDougall then reached out to Savage, who accepted the commission of major. McDougall organized the men into three companies, who then each waged war against three Indian villages. Beginning in March 1851 and ending on July 1, 1851, the three companies of the Mariposa Battalion combed the region for Ahwahneechee and Chowchilla villages and warrior patrols. The battalion more often than not were unable to find any Indians, though on at least three occasions, Ahwahneechee and Chowchilla were ambushed in their respective villages, and in each case, the outnumbered and outgunned Indians were forced to capitulate and the core component of the peace treaties was the removal of the Indians from the gold fields and placement on reserved land, known as reservations.

Beginning in 1851 and concluding the following year, the U.S. federal government sent Indian commissioners into California to negotiate treaties with Indians throughout the state. The intent of the federal government was to force the Indian Tribes to accept a negotiated existence that even further marginalized their very existence. In what became known as the "18 Treaties," the Indian commissioners entered into agreement with dozens of distinct Indian Tribes, which recognized that nearly 8 percent of the land within California's borders would be set aside for the Indians. However, lobbyists in California pressured the state assembly to recommend that the U.S. Senate not ratify the treaties because of the great value of the land guaranteed to the Indians. The treaties were considered, though ultimately rejected by the Senate. Incredibly, the very existence of the failed treaties was not entered into the public domain until 1905.[14] From 1850 until 1905, the vast majority of California Indians were effectively made homeless until public knowledge of the treaties was made known and public outrage led to the establishment of Indian Rancherias, similar to reservations, throughout the state.

AFRICAN AMERICAN REALITIES

Beginning in 1848, the African American population in California began to rise. While the draw was the gold fields and the fact that many of the blacks were brought in by their white masters from the South to mine for gold that would belong to someone else, following statehood, a migration of blacks into San Francisco and Sacramento began. The initial social realities for African Americans was relatively free from any significant discrimination, though once the easy-to-recover surface gold waned and the number of miners continued to increase along with inflationary prices on all goods and services, whites became more hostile towards blacks. The European and white American miners by and large resented working side by side with the blacks in the mine fields, in particular when their black counterparts had been slaves brought out by their white masters from the South to work claims while their masters reaped the rewards. To the whites, it was demeaning to labor in the same fashion as the men that they widely regarded as below their own station, and when legal changes derived from the Compromise of 1850 either forced blacks out completely or simply into hiding, the white miners' desire to rid the fields of blacks was nearly realized in full. However, many African American mining camps had sprung up throughout the gold fields, as evidenced by the names of several camps, such as Negro Hill, Negro Bar, and Negro Flat.[15]

While California was officially a free state, there were many blacks who had been brought in from the South by their masters during the Gold Rush era prior to the Civil War. The most common labor performed by the slaves was mining for gold, though many slave holders contracted out their slaves as laborers, kitchen help, servants, and agricultural workers. The slave holders could expect to make $100 or more per month for the labor of his slaves.[16]

In 1852, California passed its own Fugitive Slave Law with a state senate vote of 14–9. The state law supported the return of slaves to their owners if they had crossed into California before statehood. The law was confined to a one-year period, though it was open to renewal. After two successful renewals, the changing political climate in California no longer held a majority interest in maintaining the state's Fugitive Slave Law, which passed into oblivion in 1855, though before its demise and as the federal act continued, African Americans faced not only discrimination but also the threat of being kidnapped and sold in auction.

By 1854, the Fugitive Slave Act had driven out scores of free blacks from the mining camps, either from bounty hunters capturing blacks and bringing them into the South for auction or because of blacks entering the cities and organizing strong, tight-knit communities. By 1859, nearly 50 percent of California's African American population resided in the cities, which were considered relatively safer than the countryside or mining camps for blacks. African Americans successfully founded several churches, predominantly African Methodist Episcopal and Baptist, the *Mirror of the Times* newspaper, which ran from 1856 to 1862, schools, and the political organization "Convention of the Colored Citizens of the State of California," which convened for decades, beginning in 1855.[17]

CHINESE

While Chinese miners bore witness to significant racism against them from the earliest moments of the Gold Rush, over the first few decades of California statehood the discrimination grew. Indeed, the foreign miners tax had been lowered from the initial $20 per month to just $5, out of sympathy, though at the same time anti-Chinese clubs and organizations formed throughout the gold fields as well as in the cities. One of the major points of contention that the Euro-American Californians had against the Chinese was the fact that they did not appear to make any effort to assimilate or conform to the norms and perceived culture of Americans. Another common grievance by the white population was that many of the Chinese were not concerned with citizenship but were only in California to plunder its wealth and return home. In both of these cases, ironically, the bigotry experienced by the Chinese at the hands of the whites only encouraged such allegedly unwanted behavior on behalf of the Chinese. From 1863 to 1869, the call by the Central Pacific for Chinese labor to build the Transcontinental Railroad line from the west to the east did pull a minimal number of Chinese from the cities and gold fields, although the majority of the workers were new arrivals from Asia and not the so-called Gold Mountain Men. Though less

Hydraulic mining proved to be one of the most significant and detrimental forms of gold mining. While responsible for recovering remarkable levels of gold, the environmental disasters were even more significant. Throughout California's gold fields, the scars that hydraulic mining left behind can still be seen. (Unknown photographer, June 3, 1919. Gelatin silver print, 8.25 × 10 in. Collection of the Oakland Museum of California.)

prone to abandoning their position on the rail lines and heading into the cities and gold fields than their Irish counterparts on the west heading Union Pacific line, some Chinese did leave the difficult position of carving a rail line out of nature and head for a new life in California, and in the process, the state witnessed a Chinese population growth, which the federal government, in the minds of the anti-Chinese, only exacerbated with the Burlingame Treaty of 1868.

The treaty, named for American minister to China, Anson Burlingame, had three major objectives. The first was to encourage Chinese immigration into the United States to meet the growing

In this image, the incredible environmental damage wrought upon the environment by hydraulic mining is obvious. This image is of an abandoned hydraulic mining site just outside of Nevada City, California. (A. J. Russell, n.d. Lantern slide, Collection of the Oakland Museum of California, Museum Purchase.)

demand for cheap labor, which put the Chinese into a direct collision course with the European immigrants as well as whites in
search of jobs. Second, it permitted free Chinese entry into the
United States, and once in country, the Chinese could travel freely,
attend school and/or college, and also reside. The third codicil, at
the bequest of China, was a commitment by the United States not to
interfere with domestic Chinese issues.[18] In response to the federal
accord, California politicians began to pass some of the first state
anti-Chinese legislation, though the weak legislation did little to
nothing to stem the ever-growing migration of Chinese into California, which, consequently, only fueled the anti-Chinese sentiment
and reaction by whites.

By 1875, over 16,000 Chinese lived in San Francisco alone and their
numbers continued to expand statewide and of particular note in
the growing city of Los Angeles, incredible considering the hostile
reality the immigrants faced. Just four years earlier, a massive mob
in Los Angeles had roamed the streets in pursuit of Chinese. The
mob eventually lynched 19 Chinese, and an embarrassed Los Angeles mayor and city council were forced to act, eventually indict-
ing over 100 men, though only six were convicted and incarcerated

San Francisco's Chinatown quickly emerged as the largest Chinatown in
the United States, a distinction that it holds into the contemporary. In this
stereograph image, a wealthy Chinese couple sits for their portrait in 1875.
(John James Reilly, *Chinese Merchant and Wife*, San Francisco, California,
ca. 1875. Albumen stereograph, 3.4375 × 6.875 in. Collection of the Oakland Museum of California, gift of an anonymous donor.)

for a matter of hours and days. Throughout the state, Chinese were denied citizenship, access to the courts, education, and the right to vote. Referring to themselves as anti-Coolie, a derisive term for Chinese laborers, unions grew in numbers and strength. In the gold fields, the reality was much harsher for the Chinese following the Burlingame accords. Chinese laborers and miners were constantly threatened, and the burning of their property was commonplace. The lynching and subsequent burning of Chinese corpses was nearly as common as murder by shooting. Nonetheless, the Chinese population of California nearly broke 50,000 by 1870. However, in the coming years, the Chinese Americans would face a series of legislative acts aimed not only at restricting their rights

Many photographers combed through the gold fields and cities in Gold Rush California as Daguerreotypes became a fashionable manner by which Californians demonstrated their level of wealth through conspicuous consumption. In this picture are Sarah Anne MacDougal with daughter Elizabeth. January 1851. (Unknown photographer, *Sarah Anne MacDougal with Elizabeth, January 1850, upon Arrival in California*, 1850. Quarter plate daguerreotype, 5 × 4.0625 in. Collection of the Oakland Museum of California, gift of Joan Murray.)

The vigilance committees, though being unlawful assembles, were actually well regarded in polite Gold Rush society as they were seen as the only means by which law and order was upheld in an otherwise unruly society. This picture is of sharpshooters from the 1856 vigilance committee in San Francisco. (Unknown photographer, Untitled (Sharpshooters of the 1856 Committee of Vigilance), May 15, 1856. Whole plate ambrotype, Collection of the Oakland Museum of California, Museum. Purchase.)

but also focused on stripping them away any chance they would have at attaining the American dream.

NOTES

1. William Heath Davis, *Seventy-five Years in California*. (American Memory, Library of Congress, 1929). calbk 025, http://hdl.loc.gov/loc.gdc/calbk, p. 306.

2. William T. Coleman, "San Francisco Vigilance Committees. By the Chairman of the Committees of 1851, 1856, and 1877." *The Century* 43, no. 1 (November 1891), pp. 133–150.

3. Ibid.

4. Section 1, An Act for the Government and Protection of Indians April 22, 1850 (Chapter 133, Statutes of California, April 22, 1850).

5. Ibid. Section 2.

6. Ibid. Section 3.

7. Ibid. Section 6.

8. Ibid. Section 14.

9. Ibid. Section 8.

10. Ibid. Section 20.

11. Peter H. Burnett, "Governor's Annual Message to the Legislature," January 7, 1851.

12. The General Laws of the State of California, 8402, Civil Loans and War Bonds, 1852.

13. Constitution of the State of California, 1849. Article VII.

14. Kimberly Johnson-Dodds, *Early California Laws and Policies Related to California Indians* (Sacramento: California Research Bureau, California State Library, 2002), pp. 29–29.

15. Rudolph M. Lapp, *Blacks in the Gold Rush California* (New Haven, CT: Yale University Press, 1977), pp. 49–50.

16. Ibid., p. 133.

17. Ibid., pp. 101, 210.

18. Text of the Treaty Between China & United States, Generally known as the "Burlingame Treaty of 1868," signed by Secretary of State, William Seward, Ambassador to China, Anson Burlingame, Chinese Diplomats, Chih-Kang, Sun Chia-Ku. Washington, July 28, 1868.

5

EXPANDING ENTREPRENEURIALISM

By 1852, the majority of the gold was collected not by the toil of the individual miners or even the small partnership companies that had proven quite successful at attaining great wealth. Later, mining corporations were formed, hiring formerly independent 49ers and anyone else willing to work for a wage. New technologies, investment capital, and a very laissez-faire state government opened doors for the real growth in industrial mining, where large-scale operations took place and highly effective crushers pounded and pummeled the rock, permitting an easy separation of the precious gold from the unwanted debris. Rivers and streams continued to be dammed and diverted, though not just by miners. Rather, professional engineering and construction companies completed large-scale projects that did not simply permit the collection of yellow from now dry stream or river beds but instead provided water as a tool that was incredibly effective at moving tremendous amounts of earth and separating gold from debris. Hydraulic mining was responsible for bringing an incredible amount of gold into the California and national economy, though it was also the bane of the environment. Regardless, newspaper accounts across the nation, sometimes factual, sometimes fictional, continued to print fanciful reports of gold deposits being found, individuals striking it rich, and people finding their dreams of riches, which kept the flood of emigrants and immigrants into California alive.

By the end of the 19th century, the easy surface gold had dried up. Miners, and corporations, began to mine beneath the surface, to as great a depth as possible. The miner in this image reflects the most common form of yeoman miner in the post-Rush era. (Unknown photographer, ca. 1904. Glass plate negative, 6.5 × 8.5 in. Collection of the Oakland Museum of California, gift of Tom Springer.)

While no one can say for certain who actually brought hydraulic mining into the Gold Rush, there is evidence that Edward Matteson was the first prospector to put the effective, though environmentally destructive, to work. Around 1852, in the Sierra Nevada, Matteson assembled a rather crude system of canvas hoses that utilized water flow and gravity to blast away at the cascading sides of valleys, bringing down soil, debris, and gold, which was then sifted and sluiced by attentive miners in search of color. The excess debris, or tailings, was then dumped back into the rivers and streams, and in the process, forcing those downstream to wade through not only the expected levels of unwanted materials given by nature; rather, these unfortunate souls were forced to deal with a mass of debris that at times would literally cut off the flow of the water, the key element necessary for success in this form of mining. As the easy gold continued to be more and more a rare find, hydraulicking added to the tensions in the gold fields and quickly became a politically divisive topic not only in Sacramento but throughout California.

Hydraulic mining quickly spread throughout the state. As a result, more gold was recovered, ditches grew wider and longer, and rivers, streams, and creeks became mudflows; some of the smaller tributaries simply became extinct. In other cases, small valleys literally became large, open pit mines. One of the best examples of this physical geographic change during the early years of the Gold Rush was the Malakoff mine, opened in 1851, which quickly became known as the Malakoff hydraulic pit, after the mining methodology switched. Just north of Nevada City, the Malakoff diggings, as it was originally known, rests at an elevation of over 3,000 feet on the San Juan Ridge, providing a temperate climate that permitted year-round mining and an ample supply of water to make it not only possible but large scale. By 1853, the sluicing flume was over 40 miles long. Within a few months, the news of the growing gold take became a beacon to masses and also inspired more attempts in similar geographic locations to take to the hydraulic mining system. Within a decade, the Malakoff hydraulic pit was at the center of several legal wranglings that played a significant role in the eventual outlawing of hydraulic mining, though in the early 1850s, hydraulicking flourished.[1]

Located 12 miles north of the town of Orville, in Butte County, is the Cherokee mine (so named for the first emigrant miners, Cherokee, who arrived in 1849), which became one of the most famous and active of the hydraulic mines. The Cherokee hydraulic gold pit became famous not only for its incredible yield of gold but also for the diamonds discovered in the flumes in the first few years of mining in the early 1850s. The actual count of diamonds discovered is not known, though most estimates place the haul at 400–600, with the largest at over 5 carats. When the diamonds were first discovered, the men working the flumes erroneously tested their authenticity by smashing them with hammers on metal sheets as they believed that since diamonds are the hardest natural substance on earth, if genuine, they would remain unscathed. Fortunately for the miners, a few were taken into San Francisco for further examination by gemologists, who confirmed that these hard little gems were in fact diamonds. Ultimately, the Cherokee pit produced a great deal more gold than diamonds with a yield of nearly 10 million ounces of gold before it was deemed dry at the dawn of the 20th century. The scars left from the Michigan City mines were first discovered by 49ers in 1850, and by 1853, hydraulic mining had become the most common form of retrieving color, which by 1855 was collectively netting miners over $100,000 per month. The word spread quickly throughout the gold fields, which in turn encouraged miners to pour in to the picturesque Michigan Bluff District in Placer County and to expand hydraulicking in previously unmined zones as well as in mining camps that had been previously believed to have run dry. Not surprisingly, merchants from San Francisco began to open satellite stores in Michigan City, with future California governor Leland Stanford being one of the most successful entrepreneurs to supply whatever the miners needed, though at a significantly inflated "field" price.

One of the most dramatic changes associated with hydraulic mining came within the first few years of its incarnation. Miners realized that to mine with water cannons all year and not simply seasonally, depending on the rains, water needed to be harnessed in reservoirs or diverted from annual streams and rivers and then brought to the sites. These diversions were massive in comparison to the earlier stream diversions that permitted sand bar diggings, and the physical impact on the land amplified the effect of the water cannons blasting away at the earth. As William Henry Brewer, a former chemistry professor-turned-California state geologist, noted in his journal his observance of the Sacramento River in 1862: "Previous to 1848 the river was noted for the purity of its waters, flowing from the mountains as clear as crystal; but, since the discovery of gold, the 'washings' render it as muddy and turbid as is the Ohio at spring flood—in fact it is perfectly 'riley,' discoloring even the waters of the great bay into which it empties." This transformation was commonplace, and while the waterways were ecologically impacted, the towns and villages that rested on and were dependent on the flows were at times devastated, not simply because of the loss of freshwater and game but because of the mudflows that brought the unfathomable events that at times literally buried the settlements and destroyed the farms. The classic example of this tragedy was Marysville and Yuba City.

The Yuba and Feather rivers reach a confluence at the point where Marysville was established, while Yuba City rests upon the banks of the Feather. Upstream from these farming towns, miners worked for some of the largest hydraulic companies in the region, the Spring Valley mine and the Malakoff pit. The flow of sediment was a constant nuisance, as the tailings killed off the fish and drove away game that would have otherwise come to the banks of the two rivers for their water. The farmers too found that the canals they dug from these two previously pristine rivers would become so filled with silt and tailings that constant re-dredging was required to bring the precious water to irrigate their crops and keep their livestock watered. Remarkably, in 1868, another tragedy that was unforeseen occurred. The constant heavy flow of silt in the two rivers had created floodplains where once there had been rivers. In addition to the natural catastrophe, Marysville now found itself in a very precarious situation. The beds of the rivers had actually become higher than the town itself. To cope with the rising waters, the townsfolk built and maintained levees that kept pace with the rising waters, though the consequences would come. Ironically, hydraulic mining had originally been viewed as a means by which man could not simply cull more gold but could also wield power over nature itself, though, as events unfolded over time, it became clear that nature was truly in control.

By 1870, the bed of the Yuba River was nearly 15 feet higher than it had been in 1848, and Marysville had become a walled city as the levees had reached a height of a two-story building. Many people in town as well as the farmers who had watched their water supply turn from fresh to mud brought the miners to court and won their case, though the early 1870s were known for seasons of very heavy rain, and as the levees breached, roads and farms became fields of mud and debris. The years 1875 and 1876 were the worst to that point as the heavy winter rains destroyed Marysville, and the subsequent rebuilding of the levees, this time even higher than before, resulted in the town being known, unflatteringly, as the walled city. The farmers and townsfolk once again took legal issue with the miners, though this time they brought their case before the California Assembly and petitioned for the politicians to outlaw hydraulic mining. In response to their plea, the miners argued that the town and the farms were dependent upon the economic strength of the mines. The assembly sided with the miners, and understandably, as the hydraulic mining companies earned millions of dollars, many times over the economies of the towns, they stood little chance of victory. The mining companies contended that the towns and the farms only existed because of the miners. The bill submitted by the farmers failed; the assembly voted against it. The loss for the farmers and towns also brought about a change that they could not have wanted. The mining companies formed a new coalition, the Hydraulic Miners Association. For the next 30 years, hydraulic mining continued to grow, though it was far from unchallenged, and a flurry of lawsuits brought against hydraulic mining outfits from 1879 to 1884 changed the course of mining history.

In 1883, a significant case against hydraulic mining was organized, and in the following year, *Woodruff v. North Bloomfield* was heard by the Ninth Circuit Court. Central Valley farmers had been a growing force in the anti-hydraulic mining camp for decades. As one of the farming regions that had experienced wave after wave of tailings dumped into their waterways, each time effectively destroying their businesses, this group of agricultural entrepreneurs had a significant stake in forcing change. Additionally, there was one ally of the farmers on the bench, Judge Lorenzo Sawyer.

Nearly 30 years before the Gold Rush, Lorenzo Sawyer was born into a farming family in upstate New York. While he never demonstrated much interest in plowing the earth or raising livestock, the young Sawyer impressed his family and all who knew him with his keen intellect and quick study abilities. Initially, Sawyer's chosen profession was teaching, although all the while his ambitions drove him to study the law, and in 1846, he was admitted to the Ohio Bar. Soon after becoming a lawyer, Sawyer moved to Chicago, where he worked for then Illinois state attorney general and future California congressman, James McDougall. Even though Sawyer began to rise in his profession, like McDougall, the call of the Gold Rush was simply too strong to deny. In 1850, Sawyer joined a wagon train and headed West for the Golden State.

After a brief, unsuccessful and highly forgettable attempt at gold mining, Lorenzo Sawyer went back to his profession before the bar and set up a law office in the rapidly growing city of Sacramento. Like many others, he found the flood-prone city not to his liking and for two years he moved into the gold fields before settling in San Francisco in 1853. In that same year, Sawyer's luck took a good turn as he was elected San Francisco City attorney. His star was on the rise; over the next decade, he would expand his business and open offices throughout the more economically advantageous regions of California and Nevada, with a focus on mining interests. In 1863, Sawyer began a six-year term on the state supreme court, which included a two-year stint as chief justice. After the Civil War, President Ulysses S. Grant successfully nominated Sawyer to the Ninth District Court, where he presided until his death in 1891. On the bench, Sawyer's most significant case became *Woodruff v. North Bloomfield Mining and Gravel Company.*

As with many of the former mining regions of the early part of the Gold Rush, the Malakoff mine attracted the wave of speculators

In this romanticized painting of 1849 San Francisco, by George Henry Burgess in 1891, the idealized image of the youthful city is commemorated and was a popular style of commission painting in San Francisco, which had emerged as one of the 20 largest cities in the United States by then. (George Henry Burgess, *San Francisco in July, 1849*, 1891. Oil on canvas, 62 × 132.75 in. Collection of the Oakland Museum of California, gift of the Women's Board.)

who were intent on squeezing out every possible ounce of what many had considered to be exhausted claims. The North Bloomfield Mining Company happened to be the lucky one who secured the enormous Malakoff mine in 1866; they quickly turned on their water cannons and began to blast the yellow color out of the earth, one ton at a time. North Bloomfield quickly became a monstrosity and the dominant hydraulic mining interest in Nevada County, California; the Malakoff mine was their favored and most productive interest. Extensive geologic research led the concern to dig a drainage tunnel nearly 8,000 feet long through bedrock, through which they were able to process over 50,000 tons of gravel; the tailings poured into the Yuba River and wrought havoc as far away as Sacramento. Edwards Woodruff, a Marysville farmer, had his fill of ruined land, destroyed by the incredible and uncontrolled tailings of North Bloomfield, which by 1883 was the largest and most productive hydraulic mining operation in California. Woodruff knew that all previous legal attempts against the gargantuan mining interest had failed; regardless he filed suit, and the trial of *Woodruff v. North Bloomfield Mining and Gravel Company* began in June 1883. After six months, Judge Lorenzo Sawyer rendered his decision in favor of Edwards Woodruff. While the decision did not

outlaw hydraulic mining, it forced an end to the uncontrolled production of tailings, which, by extension, rendered hydraulic mining
dead. Unknowingly, Judge Lorenzo Sawyer rendered a verdict that
ended large-scale hydraulic mining's productive, yet destructive,
run in gold mining. It was also the first significant and major environmental court decision in California.

THE FIRST INDIAN RESERVATIONS
AND THE OWENS VALLEY WAR

As the flood of immigrants and emigrants in Gold Rush California
continued to increase and the settlements patterns began to fan out
across the state, the tensions between the Americans and the California Indian societies only escalated. Many came to believe that
the Indian societies would soon become extinct, and with growing
militia attacks on Indian villages, the outlook for the Indians was
bleak. From 1851 to 1852, the work of the Indian commissioners
O. M. Wozencraft, George Barbour, and Redick McKee to establish
a system of treaties between California Indian societies effectively
came to a halt as the U.S. Senate, bowing to the heavy pressure from
the California State Legislature, refused to ratify the documents,
which would have reserved nearly 7.5 million acres of the state's
lands for its first inhabitants. In an attempt to court political favor
as well as find a scapegoat for the failed diplomacy, President Millard Fillmore dismissed Wozencraft, the lead Indian Commissioner
in 1852. The following year, President Fillmore appointed Edward
Fitzgerald Beale to the post of Superintendent of Indian Affairs for
California and Nevada. The failure to ratify the 18 California Indian
treaties in Washington, D.C., cast a dark cloud over any ambitions
that Beale might have had, though he was a man who had found
success in virtually all of the difficult tasks that he had undertaken
in life. Many felt that if anyone could solve the so-called Indian
problem, it was Edward Fitzgerald Beale.

Born in the District of Columbia in 1822, Edward Beale followed
in his father's footsteps by serving in the navy. In 1845, Edward
Beale had the good fortune of serving under Captain Robert F.
Stockton during the U.S. annexation of Texas, which was formally
carried out under Stockton's supervision. Beale's talent for logistics
and his obvious intelligence did not go unnoticed. Robert Stockton quickly promoted Beale and placed him in the highly sensi-
tive position of his secretary, though Stockton's real plans for Beale

were much grander. The United States and Britain were reaching a near crescendo in their dispute over the exact location of the Oregon border. Stockton instructed Beale to go undercover and gather as much intelligence as he could on the true sentiment of the British and what, if any, plans had they made. Beale found the Britain was in fact planning a military movement to improve their land holdings in the Oregon territory. The launch of military operation was most probably one that would be predicated on a U.S.-Mexican war, which was inevitable following the U.S. annexation of Texas. Beale reported his findings to President James Polk, becoming the first person in history to bring California gold back East, and in the process, he further elevated his already rising star.

Following his service in California during the Mexican-American War, Edward Beale was selected as the individual to find and then provide evidence on the extent of the gold deposits in California for the federal government. Beale did just that with aplomb. This last post provided Beale with exceptional firsthand knowledge of the economic potential in California. He subsequently resigned from the navy and accepted the lucrative position of property development manager for W. H. Aspinwall and the promoted Commodore Robert Stockton, who had carved out significant land tracks for themselves in the new Golden State. After two years, Beale found himself back in government service when he accepted the post of Superintendent of Indian Affairs for California and Nevada.

President Millard Fillmore needed someone who could effectively and quickly establish a system by which the California Indians could be removed from the lands desired by whites in the wake of the immense population growth. Additionally, a system other than simply waging wars of extermination against the Indians, which was costly and impossible to manage from the perspective of the federal government, had to be arrived at. Beale found the reality for Indians in California quite shocking, and for the first couple of years, he was virtually impotent in facilitating any positive change, though in 1854 Edward Beale conceived of a reserved land system for Indians in California that would have a lasting impact.

After witnessing the harsh realities for California Indians, Edward Beale conceived of a land reserve for tribes that would protect the Indians from whites, eliminate the need for raiding by the Indians living on the fringes of society, which was not only drawing the wrath of white settlers but also effectively pitting Indians against each other as they attempted to survive in a California that sought their annihilation. Beale's solution became the Indian reservation system, beginning in 1853 with the Sebastian Indian Reservation in southeastern San Joaquin Valley.

The economic design of the Sebastian Indian Reservation was agricultural. The daily lives of the Indians on the reservation, while certainly not regimented in any fashion similar to the previous form of forced confinement at the Spanish Missions, was anything but ideal. The Sebastian Indian Reservation, like all subsequent 19th-century reservations in California, was akin to a prison camp. The freedom of movement off of the reservation was regulated by the U.S. federal agents. The movement of goods or visitors onto the reservation was also under the supervision of the agents. While economies emanating outward from the reservation did emerge in a slight fashion, these systems of trade were essentially a black market economy. Often, any sort of commodity exchange involved the sale of liquor, or was an act of coercion aimed at taking advantage of the limitation imposed upon the Indians. While the Indians could raise crops, and they certainly had significant success in agriculture and animal husbandry, it was also common for whites to literally steal from the Indians, who in turn were denied the right to file charges against the whites or to testify against whites either in court or through a sworn affidavit. Often, when Indians did move beyond the borders of the reservation, they were arrested, very often in an unlawful fashion, and charged with vagrancy, the most common offense then; their labor was sold via the courts. The hostile living situation certainly encouraged Indians to remain on the reservation, and this also led to their high level of productivity in agriculture, which also brought on unwanted consequences.

Given the temperate climate and relative proximity to the waters drawn from Tejon Creek, the Sebastian Indian Reservation had early economic success. However, their achievements in raising crops and animal husbandry caught the attention of neighboring white farmers, who became outraged with what appeared to be government interference in their chosen industry. In the second year of the Sebastian Reservation's existence, local whites began to regale Washington, D.C., with allegations of improprieties being committed by Beale as they attempted to both unseat the agent and bring about the closure of the reservation. Beale's support in Washington dried up, as did any significant support for the Sebastian Reservation. Thomas J. Henly, a former congressional representative from Indiana, replaced Beale as the designated California Superintendent of Indians, who placed James Russell Vineyard as

Indian Agent for the Sebastian Reservation, and a turn of fortunes for the Indians began.

In 1855, several Indians became disenchanted with the new government agent and left the reservation. The following year, a severe 24-month drought threatened nearly all the crops, though an aggressive irrigation project saved most of the farms, and the population of the Sebastian Reservation once again began to grow as more and more Indians witnessed the loss of their lands throughout the interior of California and whites continued to systematically remove them. The heightened tensions between the U.S. citizens and Native American societies in the region also led to a series of conflicts that quickly became known as the Owens Valley Indian Wars.

In the mid-19th century, the Owens Valley was of the most fertile crescents of the eastern central valley. This was before the establishment of the Los Angeles Aqueduct, which would divert the waters of the Owens River and turn this rich crescent into a desert. Pre-aqueduct, the potentials of this region had, for millennia, drawn and fostered significant settlements. In the Gold Rush era, business-minded farmers and developers followed in the traditions of Paiute, Kawaiisu, and Shoshone, as they carved out homes and villages along the rich shorelines and throughout the valley. From the earliest moments of white settlement, conflict with the Tribes began, and as more Indians from neighboring areas moved into the Owens Valley in an attempt to extricate themselves from the growing mining camp populations that surrounded the valley, it became more and more difficult for all of the people who relied on the water and land of the Owens Valley as the abundance of resources continued to dwindle. These tensions reached a crescendo in late fall of 1861, when an exceptionally severe winter brought record snowfalls, followed by a series of devastating floods through the following spring. Much of the natural game that the Indians depended on was either chased out of the area or simply killed by the devastating weather. Additionally, the livestock and crops of both the Indians and Americans were greatly impacted. While the whites could purchase the food necessary to maintain life elsewhere, the Indians, in particular the Paiute, did not have any such options as their freedom of movement and industry was virtually nonexistent. By the close of the month of December 1861, Indians began raiding the herds of the white settlers for the food they so desperately needed to survive. Within a few weeks, the conflict escalated as both sides organized.

In late January 1862, a few attempts were made to end the conflict, though when raids conducted by starving Indians as well as whites continued to occur, violence once again picked up. By early March, volunteers on the side of the white ranchers began to migrate into the valley, and by late that month, they numbered at least 60. Led by a retired U.S. Army officer, William Mayfield, the militia began to wage war against the Indians. In an attempt to bring the situation under the control of the Department of War, the U.S. Calvary entered the field at the start of April, and over the next few months, skirmishes occurred on a regular basis. While peace appeared to be on the horizon by January 1863, in early March, attacks on miners were reported and attributed to Indians. Subsequently, the military presence increased, and more bloodshed followed.

On April 10, 1863, the 2nd California Volunteer Calvary, commanded by Captain Moses McLaughlin, responded to a request for military protection from the town of Keyesville as the locals reported several attacks by Indians. McLaughlin and his militia arrived and set up camp and, after listening to several of the local ranchers and farmers, began to formulate an attack aimed at forcing the Indians out of the area either through negotiation or through military force. When it became apparent that not only would the Indians not depart but were also most probably increasing their strength in the area, McLaughlin devised a plan to eradicate one of the Indian villages in the hope of spreading fear throughout the Indian communities and thus encourage their departure. Just after 1 A.M. on April 19, the so-called Keyesville Massacre took place, and under direct orders from McLaughlin, at least 35 Indian men, women, and children were killed. While intermittent skirmishes continued over the next several months, the Owens Valley Indian Wars were effectively over by early summer, and nearly 1,000 Indians from various Tribes who had lived in the area were led by military escort and confined at nearby Fort Tejon. In the end, the Indian presence in Owens Valley was eliminated.

CONTINUED URBANIZATION

Housing in Gold Rush San Francisco reflected the churning population of the state. While single homes were being built, the most common form of housing in the early years was the boarding home. There were two primary reasons for this unique feature of daily life in the biggest Gold Rush city. Initially, most people who came lived in San Francisco from 1850 to 1855 were simply passing through, or at the very least, they initially had that idea in mind. Either they arrived at the docks and were en route to the gold fields, or they were coming from the gold fields into San Francisco for business. Though the population of the city consistently grew, its itinerant population was even larger with each successive year.

This dramatic, and constant, population increase led to real estate price inflation and a general housing shortage in San Francisco. The transient nature of the growing miner population also fueled the growth of temporary housing as well as general domestic services. Coupled together, these two trends led to an expansion of boardinghouses in San Francisco and the gold fields. Many of the boardinghouses were founded by the wives of 49ers who ventured into California with their husbands in search of riches. While some women toiled alongside their husbands in the diggings, others attempted to hold together the familiar life that they had left behind by carrying on the traditional domestic responsibilities. Women were, of course, a rarity in Gold Rush California and, justifiably so, drew the attention of the single males. In the gold fields, the observance of a woman tending after her husband was rare and frequently drew the request for cooked meals and assistance with clothing repairs from the bachelors, which often was the origin of boardinghouse development in the mining camps.

Whether in the mining camps or in the cities, boardinghouses provided and exceptional means by which women, families, or male entrepreneurs could earn a living. Depending on the number of boarders, it could also prove a rather labor-intensive business that operated each day before the sunrise to substantially after sunset. In 1852, Mary Ballou wrote to her son Selden on the daily life that she and her husband experienced as boardinghouse operators in the mining camp of Negro Bar. Mrs. Ballou discussed the variety of dishes that she prepared for her customers, including a wide range of desserts such as fruit pies, turnovers, and donuts. Her main courses ranged from ham, chicken, cod, steak, and fresh salmon. Other dishes included cabbage plates, quail, and even cooked squirrel. The price for each meal was in the range of $4, a significant fee in the mid-19th century, but the miners were willing to pay, and as long as their luck held out in the diggings, they handed over their gold dust in exchange for a good meal. Also, Ballou's varied menu was representative of what one could expect from the boardinghouse kitchens as competition for clients drove up the level of service. Not all women were inclined to perform domestic work, and childcare became one of the featured services

In this 1887 work by Henry Raschen, the California Gold Rush miner is depicted with all of the typical and romanticized gear, including the pack horse. Additionally, by this early Progressive era, the romanticized vision of the Gold Rush had become one of the most popular genres of folklore depicted in art as well as literature. (Henry Raschen, *California Miner with Pack Horse*, 1887. Oil on canvas, 40 × 30 in. The Oakland Museum Kahn Collection and the Museum Donors Acquisition Fund.)

performed by the Ballous, with a hefty charge of $50 per week. While the income was great, Mary Ballou emphasized for Selden that the labor was grueling.[2]

In San Francisco, the boardinghouse development was on a grander scale than the mining camps as was the diversity of the clients. The buildings themselves quickly evolved from converted adobes into large four- to six-story buildings made of wood, brick, and mortar. While the mining camp boardinghouses only served a relatively small population of miners who were typically known to each other, the urban experience was quite the opposite as a constant influx and exodus of boarders led to an ever-changing clientele. Different ethnic groups comingled on a much greater level than in the gold fields, though not always amicable, but in the first decade of statehood, it was not uncommon to witness Asians and European Americans eating side by side in the dining halls. Other notable distinctions between the San Francisco boardinghouses and those in the gold fields were the predominance of prostitution, the highly varied ethnicities of the boarders and the operators of the boardinghouses, the high rate of crime and violence, and the number of boardinghouses that one might find along any one street. The boardinghouses in San Francisco, in particular, had a raucous environment. One of the main thoroughfares of the city, Market Street, had a gamut of boardinghouses that provided every conceivable service and vice. Most were amalgamations of bars, brothels, barbershops, billiard halls, hotels, and general stores. Some had active stables complete with blacksmiths, while a few even held religious services. By 1860, San Francisco boardinghouses matured to include a greater range of accommodation levels, and in the process, ethnic and class segregation became commonplace.[3]

While it was clear by 1850 that San Francisco was the premiere city in Gold Rush California, the state's second city was Sacramento. While located much closer to the gold fields than San Francisco, Sacramento was relatively distant, roughly 90 miles, from

This romanticized depiction of a bear hunt by artist William Hahn, in 1882, demonstrates the lingering interests in the fictionalized accounts of the California Gold Rush. (Alfred Sully, *Monterey, California Rancho Scene*, ca. 1849. Watercolor on paper, 8 × 10.75 in. Oakland Museum of California Kahn Collection.)

the Pacific Ocean. Its location, at the confluence of American and Sacramento rivers, also placed it midway between the Golden Gate and the Gold Rush mines and nearly assured its development into town and later city. Before the onset of the California Gold Rush, the Nisenan Maidu had called the gentle Sacramento Valley their home since the beginning of time. The Spanish explorers, beginning with Juan Bautista de Anza in the late 18th century, regarded the region as less than desirable; consequently, no Spanish colonization or missionization of any significance took place in the region. However, once gold was discovered by James Marshall at Sutter's Mill, less than a day's journey from what would soon become Sacramento, life along the intersection of the two rivers would be forever changed.

John Sutter himself established a small port or embarcadero in 1849, which he placed in the hands of his son, John Sutter Jr., who in turn hired future Union Civil War hero William Tecumseh Sherman, who is rumored to have laid out the first plan for the city that would become Sacramento. By the end of 1849, Sacramento, though compared to San Francisco, was relatively free of brothels and saloons and had several churches, a public theatre, and even a newspaper, *The Placer Times*. The following year, 1850, the growing settlement and business center officially incorporated as Sacramento City and received official recognition by the California State Legislature. While the generous flow of water along the Sacramento and American rivers brought significant economic resources and conveniences to Sacramento City, their flood waters, often buttressed by snowmelt from the Sierra Nevada, also brought crisis after crisis. Also, as the city is just 25 feet above sea level and it effectively lies at the base of a valley, flood waters recede slowly and in the process can transform the terrain into a dismal swamp.

In January 1850, Sacramento City was hit by a monumental flood considered to be of biblical proportions. The American and Sacramento rivers each crested well above their levies, and the torrid waters took down any and all buildings that were in the floodplain. In the months that followed the devastating natural disaster, residents of Sacramento City cleaned up and rebuilt. Laborers came from the gold fields and San Francisco, as well as off the ships and from the Overland Trail. The gold continued to pour into the economy, and along with the continued flood of immigrants and emigrants, the rebuilding process itself steamed along. Politically, Sacramento City was ripe for the pickings. The growing business community needed leadership that would be able to take Sacramento City down the road of stability, while understanding the needs of a growing urban center. One man whose sensibility and engineering acumen brought him great respect was Hardin Bigelow.

In the immediate aftermath of the January 1850 flood, Hardin Bigelow set to work on the great problem that beset Sacramento City: control of the flood waters. As the economy and growth of the city was shackled to easy access to the rivers, moving the marketplace of Sacramento City a few miles to the east and to a higher elevation was not practical. For that matter, few residents felt secure with the weak systems of levies that had been constructed in a most haphazard fashion during the prior decade.

THE BIG FOUR AND THE TRANSCONTINENTAL RAILROAD

With tremendous riches and an economy that seemed to double with each passing month, quite nearly as often as the inflationary rate, Gold Rush California was more than simply a beacon for emigrants and immigrants, and its far-flung geographic location in relation to the rest of the states was a concern for those on the rise in California and those back East hoping to share in the perceived abundant material wealth of the Golden State. After 10 years of statehood, California was still primarily accessed by the Overland Trail and by way of the oceans. For a state economy that was rapidly becoming one of the American powerhouses, this was a hindrance that was simply not acceptable. The idea of a transcontinental railroad had been bantered about for more than a generation. The first railroad to connect the East with the West, in terms of the Atlantic and Pacific Oceans, had been the Panama Rail Road, which opened its nearly 50 miles of track in 1855. But, Panama was not the United States. However, there was one daunting task that seemed, at least to most sane individuals, laying track through the Rocky and Sierra Nevada mountains. The one man who, at least in his own mind, had resolved how this could be accomplished was Theodore "Crazy" Judah.

Born in 1826 in Bridgeport, Connecticut, Theodore Judah seemed destined to be a part of railroad construction from his teenage years, when he left behind his formal classroom training and joined the local firm that was building a rail line connecting Troy and Schenectady in upstate New York. Judah was a quick learner, nearly devoid of humor and was utterly committed to learning every facet of railroad construction. He mastered engineering, design, and surveying by his early twenties and eventually served as one of the lead managers of a new section of the Erie Canal, which garnered significant attention for the young Judah.[4] In 1854, the talented Theodore Judah accepted a business offer to build a rail line connecting Sacramento with the gold fields of the Sierra Nevada foothills. After completing the 18-mile track, Judah began to seriously conceive of a rail line connecting Gold Rush California with the rest of the nation; though not a man of significant means, Judah needed to look for investors to back what was quickly viewed as a "crazy" notion.

In 1857, Theodore Judah embarked upon his first real foray into the Washington, D.C., political arena, hoping to secure enough support from members of Congress and any other potential moneyed interests. After two years of hard work, with no positive outcome, Judah was able to meet with President James Buchanan, who was not interested in a transcontinental railroad, though Judah did have a successful and fortuitous meeting with Senator Abraham Lincoln, who had not only worked with railroads himself but had also consistently backed the railroad businesses during his tenure in the Illinois legislature. Of course, it would be President Lincoln who would eventually back the legislation establishing the transcontinental railroad. Judah would have to wait for three more years before being able to put together business investors who would actually agree to raise the capital and also build the railroad. In the winter of 1860, Theodore Judah's fate changed, and so too the course of history; when following one of the multitude of Judah's public speeches on the feasibility of a transcontinental railroad, he was approached by Collis P. Huntington, who asked him to stop by his Sacramento office for further discussion on Judah's proposals.[5] Judah had just made the acquaintance of one of the men who would come to be known as California's Big Four.

Of the hundreds of thousands of fortune seekers that poured into Gold Rush California, the four men who formed a business association, collectively referring to themselves as the "Associates," impacted the economic and political forces in the state for over a generation to a greater degree than any others. Popularly known as the Big Four, Leland Stanford, Collis P. Huntington, Charles Crocker, and Mark Hopkins, had all found their way into Gold Rush California, seeking to build their fortunes, and through Theodore Judah's incarnation, they would become some of the richest and most powerful men in the nation. Remarkably, each of these four men were not from any significant means; rather, like the majority of the Emigrants, they were most blessed by their remarkable ambitions, though in their case, good luck also played a role in their success that no other 49er had ever experienced.

Collis P. Huntington, a Connecticut Yankee born in 1821, had experienced very moderate success as a merchant in New York State, when, in 1849, he heard fanciful tales of the gold being discovered in California. Free for the pickings and in abundance no less, the dream of collecting his weight in gold appealed to both Huntington's business-oriented mind and his sense for adventure, though what had cemented his resolve was the news that dry goods in the gold fields were remarkably more expensive than anywhere else, and thus Huntington the salesman saw the real chance at making a fortune. Huntington came to California by way of traversing through the jungles of Panama, where Huntington and the other Argonauts found themselves stranded for two months, waiting on the arrival of the steamboat that was to take them to California. Recognizing the opportunity that others viewed as an unwanted predicament, Huntington left the stranded beachcombers behind and made his way back to a village where he loaded up with provisions that he knew could be sold at a considerable profit to his fellow sojourners. As Huntington later noted for posterity, he left New York with $1,200, and by the time he left Panama for California, he had $5,000.[6] Collis P. Huntington proved to be one of the very few individual Argonauts to generate a considerable profit en route to the gold fields. By the time Collis Huntington became acquainted with Judah, he had become one of the more successful businessmen in Sacramento, partnering in dry goods with Mark Hopkins.

Mark Hopkins Jr. was born in New York State in 1813, though following his father's premature death, he was raised by his mother in Michigan. First trying his hand at the study of law, Mark Hopkins found his real calling in the business world as his talents for both accounting as well as management became apparent. While Huntington's personality was outgoing and brusque, Hopkins was introverted and methodical. Huntington was a risk taker and Hopkins was conservative. When the two men met in Sacramento and subsequently formed a business partnership, Huntington & Hopkins, their blended personalities brought balance to the business dealings serving as counterbalances that prevented the two men from either being too stubborn or too compulsive.[7] Together the two men would make a careful study of Theodore Judah, and his proposals, in the private meeting with the dreamer.

Just one day after Theodore Judah's first encounter with Collis Huntington, Judah met with Huntington and Hopkins at offices above storefront of Huntington & Hopkins on K Street in Sacramento. For a few hours, Judah spoke and described in impossible detail his plans for a transcontinental railroad. Huntington and Hopkins were virtually silent through the entire meeting and asked only a few short questions, and by the time the men were getting ready to adjourn, Judah thought he had failed to sway his potential investors. He was wrong. Collis Huntington suggested that the men have another meeting, which would include other potential investors. Judah had never been asked to attend a second meeting before, let alone a second meeting that would comprise more investors. It was in this second meeting that two other men in attendance, Charles Crocker and Leland Stanford, would decide to join with Huntington and Hopkins in this business venture. Judah, though on paper he was originally listed as a partner, would soon find himself on the outside looking in, once the process of building the railroad began.

Charles Crocker was a bull of a man. Standing over six feet in height and typically weighing in at well over 250 pounds, Crocker was an imposing figure. Born in 1822 in Troy, New York, Charles Crocker spent his formative years in Indiana. From an early age, Charles Crocker demonstrated an impatient personality. He quit school at the age of 12 and by the age of 17 was on his own and found work at a sawmill. In 1849, Charles Crocker responded to the call of the gold fields and joined a small company of local men, becoming the leader in the process, and headed to California. Crocker and his company arrived in California in the early spring of 1850, and he soon found failure in the mining camps. Wherever Crocker dug, there was not even a hint of gold. However, Charles Crocker recognized another economic opportunity. Crocker, with one of his brothers, opened a store in the one of the richest regions of the gold fields in El Dorado County. Within two years, Crocker had three stores. In 1856, Crocker, by then a leading businessman in Sacramento, met Mark Hopkins and Collis Huntington through the fledgling Republican Party, where the three men also met Leland Stanford, who was by then a rising political figure with star potential.[8] Leland Stanford, like Huntington, Hopkins, and Crocker, answered the siren call of the Gold Rush and found his way up the economic ladder by profiting off of the miners and the growing California economy and not through swinging a pick and panning for gold himself. Within a few weeks, the Big Four agreed to form a corporation that would seek to first gather more investors and then take on the politicians in Washington, D.C., to guarantee a monopoly, and government assistance, to build the Central Pacific line from Sacramento heading east. Judah, for the moment, believed that his dream would be fulfilled. And though the Civil War would slow the start of the railroad, it did not mean its demise.

On July 1, 1862, President Abraham Lincoln signed into law the Pacific Railroad Act of 1862. Over the next dozen years, the act would be amended 10 times, each time accommodating the railroad companies and the tycoons who ran them. The Union Pacific was awarded the contract to build the line coming out of the East and the Central Pacific from the West. While other investors were a part of the shareholders of Central Pacific, Huntington, Stanford, Hopkins, and Crocker were in control. These men met in secret, away from not only the other major investors but also Theodore Judah. The Big Four understood business, not just how to develop an interest but also how to successfully control all the operations even when working with other significant investors. Stanford was elected president of the Central Pacific, Collis Huntington its vice president, and Hopkins its treasurer; only their signatures were the ones required for hiring contractors. The men hired one of their own, Charles Crocker. This obvious manipulation outraged Judah, who vociferously protested. The response by the Big Four was succinct but not subtle; Crocker resigned from the board of directors of the Central Pacific and formed Charles Crocker & Company, which was subsequently awarded the contract to build the railroad. Theodore Judah had become obsolete. Leland Stanford had been elected governor of California the previous year, though he also retained his position as president of the Central Pacific. By virtue of his two positions, Stanford was able to convince the California legislature to chip in $15 million in state bonds to help build the railroad as well as subsequent county ballots.[9] No men, laws, or regulations were going to stop the Big Four from building, and controlling, the Central Pacific.

The Pacific Railroad Act itself, signed into law by a business- and railroad-friendly Lincoln and U.S. Congress, provided exorbitant aid and considerations in addition to the funds generated by the sale of stock to investors and the local government bonds. Stanford, the attorney, read and studied the act in great detail, in particular the sections relating to the land grants and monetary grants made by the federal government. Section 2 of the act provided for the right of way for the construction of the railroad, effectively gifting the land over to the railroad companies where the tracks were laid, along with 200 feet of real estate in both directions emanating from the track itself. Also, all of the materials needed for the construction process gathered from the lands and surrounding vicinity were free for the pickings.[10] The very next section allowed for alternating five-square-mile sections, resembling a checkerboard pattern to be given to the railroad companies, which further expanded their landholding potential.[11] These gifts of real estate, unprecedented in American history, encouraged a break-neck pace of rail line construction that consistently placed the workers in physical jeopardy, as the Big Four only saw the value of adding more mileage as fast as possible because repairs could always follow behind, but nothing could make up for the lost feet of track to the Pacific Union.

The men who swung the picks and hammers up and down the emerging rail line for the Central Pacific overwhelmingly came from China, though they were not the first laborers. Crocker first tried to hire men of European and American stock, though the work was difficult and the men were prone to work just through the first couple of pay days to have the funds necessary to purchase mining wares and then depart quickly to seek their fortune digging for gold. Others not just worked the rail line for a quick paycheck but also utilized the transportation that the emerging railroad provided into and past the Sierra Nevada Mountains, which led to yet another series of gold and silver mines. Frustration drove Charles Crocker to reexamine his hiring practices. The one ethnic group that proved most loyal was the Chinese. These men, most of whom came over in search of gold just like nearly everyone else in California, were more willing to work the long shifts and under the most harsh conditions than anyone else. Daily life on the construction of the rail line consisted of working a minimum of an eight-hour shift, with one short break somewhere in the middle for a quick intake of sustenance. Working in the great outdoors may have provided for remarkable scenery for the laborers, though the extreme weather conditions certainly made an even greater impact.

For the leg from Sacramento to the Sierra Nevada, the hot burning summer sun brought temperatures up to 100 degrees Fahrenheit, and with the arrival of the fall came the rains, followed by the winter snows in the mountains. The weather, though a significant inconvenience, did not stop the construction of the line. Nor would the mountains, through which no real road, let alone railroad line, had ever been established. It was here in the Sierra Nevada that the job turned deadly. Rockslides were common. Accidental deaths related to mishaps with the explosives used to either begin the cuts through the mountain or establish flats for the rails along the sheer sides were commonplace. Cave-ins that occurred while the men were digging out tunnels claimed hundreds of lives. All in all, no one knows the exact number of deaths that occurred as the Central Pacific made its way East, though estimates range from 1,000 to 1,500. The Chinese workers were aware of the hazards, as it was impossible for one to be oblivious, and the bleak economic realities they faced back home in China made the grueling, back-breaking work of building a railroad desirable and quite simply the best option for making a living that the majority of them had. And, compared to their non-Chinese counterparts, they were the most productive employees of the Central Pacific, which pleased Crocker tremendously.

Charles Crocker was also drawn to the lower wages that the Chinese initially commanded, between $25 and $28 per month, as well as their form of self-management, which placed the clan leader in the role of group foreman, which allowed for the railroad engineers to only have to communicate with a few, rather than many, Chinese. It was a system that proved fruitful for the first few years, which led to a significant escalation of recruited Chinese laborers. By early 1867, over 4,000 of the Central Pacific workers were Chinese, and following their remarkable work progress during the harsh winter of 1866–1867, they decided to strike, demanding that their wages be raised to at least $40 per month. Their demands were not unreasonable. In addition to the vast land grants and natural resource grants that were virtually gifted to the Central Pacific, the railroad corporation received an additional fiduciary incentive of $16,000 per every mile of track laid on flat land, $32,000 in the foothills, and $48,000 in the mountains. It was in the mountains that the strike took place, which only firmed Charles Crocker's resolve to not increase the wages and to cajole the men back into work by any means necessary. In this regard, Charles Crocker decided to starve the men into submission; after all, they were in the Sierra Nevada Mountains, where there was virtually no access to food stuffs, and Mr. Crocker controlled two donkey carts that brought in all supplies. In just one week, the hungry Chinese gave in, were fed, and went back to work.[12] Over the next two years the rate of construction picked up as the Central Pacific and Union Pacific competed for miles. Finally, on May 10, 1869, the two engines met at Promontory Summit in Utah.

In a ceremony that was transmitted live from California to New York City via the telegraph line that was built alongside the rail lines, four special spikes were hammered into place, commemorating the event. Hundreds, perhaps thousands, of spectators and VIPs were present, and photographers did their best to capture the moment for posterity, though their craft still required then that the men stand still, a virtually impossible request given the celebratory atmosphere that was further enhanced by the consumption of alcohol. Just before the Central Pacific No. 60 met the Union Pacific No. 119, the first of the four final spikes was driven into place. It was of a low blend of gold, followed by a second, a silver spike from Nevada, a blended gold, iron, and silver spike from Arizona, and finally the golden spike. As president of the Central Pacific, Leland Stanford was given the honor of driving home the last spike. In his initial, gingerly tap, Stanford missed, but in anticipating the event, the telegraph operator tapped out the message that Stanford had hit his mark, and in doing so, California was finally connected to the rest of the United States, and within a few minutes, it actually was. Remarkably, in just one generation, Gold Rush California had been transformed from its position on the map of being a remote western territory with virtually no connection to the rest of the United States to the fastest-growing segment of the American economy, which would only pick up steam now that all of the incredible riches it harbored could be easily exploited and distributed across the continent. In effect, the opening of the Transcontinental Rail Road was the beginning of the second California Gold Rush.

NOTES

1. Susan Lindström, *A Historic Sites Archaeological Survey of the Main Hydraulic PitBbasin, Malakoff Diggins State Historic Park, North Bloomfield, Nevada County, California* (Sacramento, CA: The Division, 1990).

2. Christiane Fischer, ed., *Let Them Speak for Themselves: Women in the American West*, 1849–1900 (New York: E. P. Dutton, 1977), pp. 42–46.

3. Barbara Berglund, *Making San Francisco American: Cultural Frontiers in the Urban West*, 1846–1906 (Lawrence, KS: University Press of Kansas, 2007), pp. 16–40.

4. Oscar Lewis, *The Big Four: The Story of Huntington, Stanford, Hopkins and Crocker, and the Building of the Central Pacific* (New York: Alfred A. Knopf, 1941), pp. 3–5.

5. Richard Raynor, *The Associates* (New York: W. W. Norton & Company, 2008), pp. 29–34.

6. Raynor, pp. 19–20.

7. Lewis, pp. 124–129.

8. Lewis, pp. 56–59.

9. Raynor, pp. 47–49.

10. An act to aid in the construction of a railroad and telegraph line from the Missouri River to the Pacific Ocean, and to secure to the government the use of the same for postal, military, and other purposes. Section 2.

11. Ibid., Section 3.

12. Raynor, p. 81.

6

CIVIL WAR, SOCIAL UNREST, AND OTHER GOLD RUSHES

THE CIVIL WAR

Gold Rush California has a special and unique relationship with the Civil War. The Compromise of 1850, which was passed in order for the members of Congress from the South to vote in favor of California statehood, contained the proviso that also permitted the Fugitive Slave Act of that same year. This act led to an expansion of bounty hunters who combed American lands well beyond the South in search of any blacks whom they could capture and drag back into the South to set on the auction block regardless of their status of freedmen, which was quite often the case. Internally, Californians were divided on their allegiances. The popular sovereignty vote to become a free labor state was within a small percentage victory for the free-labor movement in the decade before, and as many emigrants from the slave states of the South had brought with them their slaves, who became free, at least in their legal status.

Vast amounts of gold from California found its way into the growing industrial economy of the Northeast and burgeoning Great Lakes economies. While some of this capital wealth trickled into the Southern slave states, including Texas, the biggest beneficiary, outside of California, were the banking centers of New York, Boston, and Philadelphia, with New York having a clear advantage. While California was seen as both different and distinct from American society east of the Mississippi River, it had a real economic connection with the free-labor industrialized sections. Many farmers who had settled in California on the heels of the Gold Rush did come from South, but they also came in more significant numbers from the Midwest. This duality of heritage within the emigrants would come to play a significant role in terms of loyalty to the two sides in the Civil War.

In the wake of the battle at Fort Sumter in South Carolina in 1861, which most historians recognize as the first military action in the Civil War, patriotism for both sides picked up steam. However, given California's distance from the rest of the states, and the fact that no railroads connected the West to the East, any travels to join the either side in the growing conflict were just as time consuming as they had been in the first years of the Gold Rush itself. While pro-Union Republicans were swept into office, Southern sympathies pulled many a young man into the Rebel camps. Over the next four years, California's internal civil war was waged and secessionist movements were a constant threat to the integrity of the Golden State.

In Southern California, the majority of the Americans came from the South or were Californios who had been denied many of the rights that came with full citizenship. To these groups, the Union represented a foreign imperialist state that had never given them the freedoms that they believed to be their rights. Slavery had been outlawed in California, which to those from the South who had brought their slaves with them was tantamount to the theft of property. The Californios found that during the transfer of power from Mexico to the United States, many, if not most, of their land claims were ignored, even when there was substantial documentary evidence to support their veracity. While many Southern emigrants were, in fact, guilty of bilking Californios out of their real estate holdings, the general sentiment was that the real culprits were the lawyers and bankers from the North who had been the most active agents in these nefarious acts. These two groups felt cheated, and the former rivals found a common enemy in the Union.

Signs of a divided California were everywhere. In the 1860 presidential election, Abraham Lincoln did receive all of California's Electoral College votes, though he received less than 40 percent of the popular vote. Federal troops in California were under the command of Brig. Gen. Albert Johnston, a Kentucky native who had strong sympathetic ties. Many of the leading secessionists in California quickly sought out General Johnston and implored him to take control of the troops and have them fight for the Confederate cause. Johnston, one of the finest commanders in the U.S. Army, had opposed secession, though once the split began, he tendered his resignation and migrated from the San Francisco Bay Area to Los Angeles, where he joined up with the Confederate Los Angeles Mounted Rifles. Johnson evaded Union forces in California and led his growing Confederate army into Arizona territory, which was a part of the Confederacy. Confederate president Jefferson Davis placed him in command of the Western Confederate forces. The Confederacy pulled Johnson and his troops, which numbered in the range of 5,000, out of the West as their strategy became centrally focused on the East. Johnson drove his men through Kentucky and throughout the border states, and though his forces were always fewer than his adversary generals, including Gen. William Tecumseh Sherman, his practice of guerilla warfare beguiled the Union armies. General Johnston's luck in commanding the Los Angeles Mounted Rifles ran out at the Battle of Shiloh against Gen. Ulysses S. Grant, where he was killed, and in this bloody two-day battle, the Confederates suffered a significant defeat.

Fighting within the state of California was sporadic. There were attempts made by Confederates to seize the San Francisco Mint, which had been established in 1854 and contained the largest deposit of gold in the state. However, these attempts were haphazard at best and none proved successful. Stagecoach robberies were a different matter. There were a handful of incidents of successful heists carried out around Placerville by men claiming to be Confederates. Union and Confederate sympathizers alike saw their personal property stolen and real estate damaged for the "cause" throughout California. Wells Fargo and Company stepped up the number of rifles protecting their stagecoaches, and the well-armed Union-backing company took over mail delivery along the Butterfield Line to keep communications and business open during the conflict. The most notorious outlaws, who also claimed to be Southern sympathizers, the so-called Mason Henry Gang, proved to be the most destructive in the Gold State during the Civil War.

In late 1863, the former American soldier who participated in the Mexican–American War and subsequent 49er who rose up through the political and economics ranks in Central California, eventually becoming the first real boss and later judge in the town of Stockton, George Gordon Belt, organized what he thought would become a legitimate Confederate force of raiders within California. Judge Belt, as he preferred to be called, had made his fortune, as so many other 49ers had, not in mining, but by doing business with the miners, mining camps, and large-scale mining concerns. Belt also secured a lucrative trading license at the Merced Indian Reservation, which guaranteed a steady flow of federal funds. Belt expanded his enterprises to include a ferry system across the Merced River. By the mid-1850s, Belt had emerged as the economic hub of the region and secured the post of judge, which only enhanced his financial stranglehold on that portion of the Central Valley. Though on the receiving end of a significant flow of federal funds due to his store at the Merced Reservation, Belt came to resent what he came to view a bureaucracy that he had no real sway over, in effect one that never came to view him as more than a small-time businessman. In time, Judge Belt matured into a man full of rage who, early on in the Civil War, came to view the Union as the enemy. He also saw, wrongly, what he saw as an opportunity to weaken the Union cause in California. Judge Belt formed and ostensibly trained a murderous band of outlaws that he incorrectly believed could be a Confederate force in the Golden State. But in reality, what emerged, the Mason Henry Gang, was nothing more than a notorious, organized criminal element that plagued whomever they encountered, regardless of politics.

Two Southerners came to lead the Mason Henry Gang on their two-year rampage throughout Central and Southern California, John Mason and Tom McCauley, the latter preferring his pseudonym "John Henry." Judge Belt was impressed by the leadership qualities that he perceived Mason and McCauley possessed. This was a significant mistake. Both men had long criminal backgrounds. Mason was actually a stagecoach robber, who made a living by robbing, and sometimes killing, people like Belt. McCauley, after getting out of prison for murder, took to calling himself John Henry, to evade recognition. Hardened by the time he spent behind bars, Henry emerged as a man with a singular cause, getting rich, and the road he took to get there was one of violent criminal activities. The two men convinced Belt to turn over the reins of the recently formed "Confederate Rangers," and with no other men willing or able to challenge Mason and Henry, they were given the command.

In early 1864, the two men began their search for men that they believed would aid their cause. They centered their search on finding "Copperheads," Northern Democrats who were opposed to the Civil War. Mason and Henry believed that Copperheads would be the most malleable as they lacked the moral conviction of the true

Confederates, who were engaged in the war effort as they wanted men to work for them and not for a cause. However, as the tide of the war was strongly tipping on the side of the Union, and as the promise of a Transcontinental Railroad beckoned, Mason and Henry could not find the hundred men they sought to fill out the ranks that spring. As the fall began, Mason and Henry were able to secure the assistance of several outlaws, and under the false flag of the Confederacy, they began their series of raids that took them across several counties. For the duration of the Civil War, they robbed, murdered, and destroyed property throughout the central and southern parts of the Golden State, leaving a wake of destruction and instilling fear throughout. After the war concluded, the Mason Henry Gang migrated into the Lytle Creek vicinity, just outside of San Bernardino. Loyal Unionists discovered their encampment and notified San Bernardino sheriff George Fulgham, who assembled and led a posse in an attack on the band of outlaws. The end result was brutal as the posse took the charge with the intent of annihilation. Hundreds of shots rained down from the posse upon the murderous horde. Jim Henry was shot over 50 times, and his corpse was brought back into town where it was put on display. John Mason, who was either not encamped with his outfit or who had escaped, was not among the dead. The following year, Ben Mayfield, a man that Mason had failed to recruit and subsequently attempted to murder, shot and killed the outlaw John Mason, bringing the nightmare to a close.

The most active Union militia to come out of California was the California Column; however, their military engagement was more centered on the Navajo and the Apache as opposed to the Confederates, as the Column marched through Arizona and New Mexico before ending their sojourn in Texas. Along this trek of over 900 miles, the Column had simply not encountered and Confederate resistance of significance. The Column, under the command of Col. James Henry Carleton, who was promoted to general en route through the Arizona Territory, where he was primarily engaged against the Navajo, employed the tactic of Total War that would later become the calling card of General Sherman in his march through the South. After his war against the Navajo, Carleton engaged the Apache and, in the process, became known for his prowess as an Indian fighter as he moved through New Mexico. Without ever joining up with the Union forces, the Column effectively set up garrisons along their route as they carved out a pathway through the Indian territories.

By the conclusion of the Civil War, California's attention, economically and politically, was focused on the future and soundly behind the Transcontinental Railroad. Agriculture and industries in general expanded, as did immigration that fed the construction of the Central Pacific as well as the state's expanding economy. However, social harmony proved elusive.

SOCIAL UNREST

Beginning in 1849, the Chinese began migrating into California, as so many others from around the world, in search of gold. The Chinese also began to open and operate businesses across California, though primarily in the cities and emerging towns, finding, as so many other immigrants and emigrants, that the abundance of gold and the growing California economy in general provided many avenues by which one could make a living. One arena of employment that was a beacon to the "Gold Mountain Men" that was outside of the gold fields and growing urban centers, the construction of the Transcontinental Railroad, brought in thousands of men from China. This second surge of Chinese immigration really built up steam by 1864 and, just as the significant numbers in the earlier period less than a generation earlier, a strong wave of nativism against the Asian immigrants quickly followed. By the 1870s, anti-Chinese laws, with specific language that targeted the Chinese, and virtually all Asians by extension, grew out of this racism, the origins of which can be understood within the context of the Chinese Americans being viewed as a group of immigrants that did not conform to American society but was one that held onto their customs and language even after generations had passed in the United States. This perception of cultural aloofness was in part accurate, though not necessarily self-imposed. A significant factor, too, rested in the desire of a great many of the Chinese Argonauts to come into Gold Rush California only for a range of time and not permanence, therefore having a mind-set of temporality as opposed to permanent, let alone establish a family line. The reality for many was one of transience, though tens of thousands became permanent residents of an American society that was steeped in racism that manifested itself in the form of racial exclusion. To understand how U.S. federal legislation such as the Chinese Exclusion Acts came about, it is necessary to look at the evolution of the myths and real history of the Chinese in Gold Rush California and beyond.

While the immigrant and first-generation European Americans in California played a central role in the emerging anti-Chinese movement, the one immigrant ethnic group that proved to be one of the most powerful, politically, was the Irish American constituency. Historians have examined this phenomenon with significant attention. The Chinese had proven exceptionally resilient during the Gold Rush; whatever the obstacles that were thrust upon them, nothing seemed to be capable of thwarting their overall economic success. However, though as a group they succeeded in capturing a piece of the American Dream, in reality, as individuals, from the onset of their arrival, their daily lives were anything but serene.

All other immigrants that came into the California Gold Rush assimilated faster than the Chinese, of whom it can be said did not assimilate, but rather kept to themselves within the confines of their Chinese ethnic enclaves. It was true that the Chinese miners did, in fact, work side by side with all other ethnic groups across the gold fields of California, and many migrated into employment with the large miner concerns that began to evolve in the early and mid-1850s. Additionally, the Chinese population with the largest California city, San Francisco, was one of the five largest ethnic groups. The same could be said of Sacramento, the state's second most important city. And, although the other immigrant settlements also reflected the desire of so many people to live among those speaking a common language, only the Chinese settlements came to be named by those from the outside as well as the inside, with a moniker that evoked a sense of isolation and difference. These were the so-called Chinatowns. The construction of the Chinatowns afforded the Chinese a level of security and prosperity, though they also created a near permanent state well into the mid part of the 20th century of subordination and exclusion.

Inside the Chinatowns, with San Francisco's being by far the largest in population, geographic size, and economic importance, a romanticism or exoticism cloaked a harsh reality of the difficult life that these immigrants faced as a group of people who were forced, by both laws and ethnocentrism and nativism, to be a virtual subculture, visible, yet invisible.

At the center of the Chinatowns' economy was the broadly defined service industry. The second most important economic component was tourism. Both became intertwined in the success of the Chinese in the Golden State. The Chinese were not the only ethnic group to profit in these areas of endeavor; however, their manner by which their professions evolved was unique.

Seen as an ethnic group that was below the European Americans on the social and economic ladder, as were the African Americans and Native Americans, the Chinese were able to parlay one of the initial outcomes of racism into their favor. By taking on tasks of labor that the European Americans viewed as menial or as in the case of the opium dens, morally beneath their standards, the Chinese came quite close to monopolizing segments of the California economy. The most common mental images of the Chinese industries during this period were the laundries, public eating establishments, and, of course, the opium dens and brothels. All of these did exist and were in significant demand in both the cities as well as the gold fields. Additionally, prostitution proved to be one of the most significant draws. However, it would be the connections to these vices that not only romanticized the history surrounding the Chinese realities but also played a central role in casting them in the overly hyped negative and disingenuous stereotype of being a menace to society, which was the basis for all of the Chinese exclusionist laws and policies.

While it is unknown how Chinese prostitution really began in Gold Rush California, the most commonly referenced madam was San Francisco's Ah Toy. Both legend and oral tradition have recorded that, Ah Toy, a Chinese woman who presents herself as being from some means, though in reality she was sold into her situation, was en route to Gold Rush California with her husband in 1849. The two departed Hong Kong with dozens of other Chinese, predominantly males, and while on their Ocean voyage, Ah Toy's husband died of unknown causes. Ah Toy, a statuesque beauty, with a sharp mind for business and steely personality, recognized her situation as a young widow traveling alone to a foreign land. Though she had brought some of her late husband's wealth along for the voyage, she and her husband were anticipating remarkable, though different, opportunities, as did so many other 49ers. Free from the confines of her arranged marriage, Ah Toy quickly took into account her situation and recognizing that the one man who could offer her more than any other during her migration across the Pacific, the ship's captain, had more than made his interests in her known, Ah Toy seduced him, and in return, the captain showered her with as much gold as he could in return for her affection. By the time the ship docked in San Francisco, Ah Toy had enough capital to start her own business. She opened a brothel and exotic theater specializing in stripteases, during which she offered clients a glimpse of what they purchased a more sizeable investment.

Ah Toy was viewed as exotic, not just by Westerners but Chinese men as well. She was a tall woman, full figured, though not obese, a woman who furthered the perception that she was gentile, including the "bound feet" of the upper-class Chinese ladies. Though her physique did much to attract the male gender, it was her powerful personality, poise, and skill as a seductress that wins her their affection and willingness to pay her exorbitant fees, which were reportedly well above the going rate for such services. Ever the entrepreneur, Ah Toy did not confine her income to her own personnel services rendered; rather, she expanded her enterprises by developing an elaborate brothel system, stocked with young Chinese women and girls, some reportedly as young as pre-teens. Ah Toy negotiated with Chinese men back in her homeland in the development of what became the first international criminal sex trade organization in Gold Rush California. While the vast majority of the Chinese brothels were owned by men, Madam Ah Toy successfully kept her business free of their clutches, and consequently, she rose to a remarkable level of wealth, even to the point where, unlike other Chinese, including men, she was even afforded the opportunity to sue white men in court for not having paid her in full for services rendered.

The opium trade made its way into the Gold Rush through the port of San Francisco and through that city's Chinatown as well. The opium dens that first emerged in the gold fields were overwhelmingly confined within the Chinese men as the first patrons, though, by 1849, the purchase and use of opium had made its way throughout California. The sale, distribution, and use of the narcotic were not illegal, though it was generally viewed as a vice and its use drew disdain. Unlike Ah Toy's brothel, there never emerged any one significant opium den; however, what did evolve was a well-managed Chinese warlord system that ruled the opium enterprises in San Francisco and beyond well into the early part of the 20th century. These warlord organizations, the so-called Tongs, built an economic empire that influenced policemen, politicians, and judges. Though the Chinese were denied many of the social rights of the other Americans, the ruling Tongs found their access to the American dream of wealth and power by negotiating effectively with the European Americans to leave the Chinatowns and their devices to their strict management. One of the most striking components of this "gentlemen's agreement" was that the Chinese would be permitted to own real estate and inherit property, though it had to be within the agreed-upon confines of Chinatown.

Beyond the romanticized stories that circled around Ah Toy, the sex industry of the Chinatowns of Gold Rush California was far from glamorous. While their European American counterparts suffered from the abuses that were rife in this dangerous endeavor, the laws that were in place to protect people in the underworld of prostitution from physical assault, theft, and murder were overwhelmingly ignored by police, none of whom were Chinese. In the place of the absence of the legitimate law enforcement, the Chinese criminal organizations flourished and expanded beyond the role of maintaining order in the Chinese American communities. By the 1870s, the Chinese Tongs controlled a vast network of vice-oriented businesses beyond prostitution and narcotics. Gambling houses and the slave trade grew along with a steady increase of population across California. However, their perceived abilities to maintain order vanished as war between the Tongs ravaged Chinatown and the Chinese communities outside of San Francisco that were beholden to their grip. Clamor for American political reactions aimed at controlling the violence grew and included a good number of political platforms that called for the expulsion of the Chinese from American soil.

While the politicians and political agitators focused heavily on the vice and criminal elements to justify their push for laws that ranged from limiting Chinese immigration to full exclusion from the prospect of citizenship, the majority of the Chinese American wealth and success came from legitimate and well-respected enterprises. Indeed, one of the more commonly known endeavors was domestic services; Chinese had branched out into agriculture and fishing, the former of which captured the attention of their social and political adversaries as it involved the control of significant amounts of land. The proponents of Chinese exclusion founded a political party and made this racist policy their platform. They called themselves the Workingmen's Party. In just a few short years, their numbers and their political power would reach throughout California, across the continent, and into the Congress of the United States and even the Presidency.

This migration into the politics of ethnic exclusion was a sharp departure from the economically motivated reform diplomacy that the United States had been previously engineering. American manufacturers wanted more cheap Chinese labor and also open trade with the largest nation on the earth. The former, more so than the latter, was the prime motivation that led to a more open door to the East; the Transcontinental Railroad would also play a significant role. The process for normalization between the two nations began when the United States and China had entered into formal talks aimed at making Chinese immigration a more fluid and open process in 1861. President Abraham Lincoln appointed Anson Burlingame as minister to China.

The post was one filled with great challenges and great potential. The United States and China had a less than productive relationship; in the previous year, the United States played a secondary way in the Opium Wars, which pushed for the Chinese to open more ports for international trade. The negotiations were heavy handed and overly favored the Westerners, with the ports more akin to a sphere of influence operated by foreigners on Chinese land. In an attempt to develop a more equitable relationship with China, one that would increase American profits, though provide economic incentives to the Chinese, Anson Burlingame would work tirelessly for over seven years to create a more symbiotic and productive relationship. If any man were capable of engineering and brokering such a deal, Anson Burlingame was one of a very select few who had the intelligence, empathy, and strength of character needed for such a feat to be successful.

Born in upstate New York in 1820 and raised in Ohio and Michigan, Anson Burlingame demonstrated from an early age a remarkable intelligence. Graced with a fantastic memory, superior debating skills, an eye for details, and the ability to negotiate far better than any of his peers, the young Burlingame studied at the University of Michigan and completed his studies at Harvard Law School. Staying in the Boston area following law school, Burlingame became highly active in the short-lived Free Soil Party, an amalgamation of Whigs and Democrats who were deeply opposed to slavery that was one of the precursors to the Republican Party. Burlingame not only opposed slavery but also called for the equal rights of blacks, and this placed him in the more radical camp of his political allies. Burlingame was elected first to the Massachusetts state senate and later he served in the U.S. House of Representatives, where he drew national attention and also the future president, Abraham Lincoln.

As the debate around slavery in Congress became more heated in the 1850s, following the Compromise of 1850 that permitted California and all of its riches to come into the Union as a free state, members of Congress began to act more aggressively against their opponents. In 1856, Burlingame's first term in Congress, his fellow congressman Preston Brooks of South Carolina, one of the most rapid pro-slavery political advocates in the nation, had severely beaten the intellectual and moral giant of the Senate, Charles Sumner of Massachusetts. The attack came on the heels of Sumner delivering one of his remarkable and passionate attacks on the institution of slavery. Brooks went to Sumner's Senate office and beat the Senator with his metal-based cane to near the point of death. The attack was in retaliation for Sumner's acidic criticisms, in particular to Brooks own uncle, Senator Andrew Butler of South Carolina, who was also one of the authors of the Kansas-Nebraska Act of 1854. Congress never acted to impose any censure of Brooks for his assault, and in the South, Brooks was lauded as a hero of pro-slavery and states' rights advocates. Burlingame seized the moment and called upon Brooks to settle the matter in open public, in a duel, which he did in public during an impassioned speech delivered in Congress. Burlingame offered to accommodate Brooks with any sort of weapon of his choosing. Brooks, who was fully aware of Burlingame's rightful reputation as an expert marksman, backed down. Brooks was exposed for his cowardice; Burlingame's reputation for courage and character grew. When it was time to choose a man of character and courage who would not succumb to criticism, President Abraham Lincoln went with Burlingame to head the delegation to China. From 1861 to 1867, Anson Burlingame negotiated the forward-thinking treaty with China, which came to bear his name. The end result was an economic advantage for both nations as well as one that fostered better political and diplomatic relations, though the surge of Chinese migration into Gold Rush California and along the Central Pacific's growing construction of the Transcontinental Railroad led to growing conflicts between the Chinese and growing immigrant population in the U.S. west. While it is impossible to recognize any one individual as the originator of the anti-Chinese movement in California, one man did more for growth of the party and labor organization that embraced this racist cause than any other, Denis Kearney.

An immigrant from Ireland, Denis Kearney was a man who possessed great skills as an orator and agitator. After his arrival in 1868, Kearney was singularly focused on amassing great wealth. He moved his young family to San Francisco in 1871, where he developed his land based freight business and, by 1877, was a man of significant means. Kearney connected with his fellow Irish immigrants and recognized that their real competition was not the native-born European Americans of the middle and lower classes, who it is worth mentioning looked down upon Kearney and his fellow Irish immigrants regarding them as rabble. Rather, Kearney focused his vitriol on the wealthy, in particular California's Big Four and their Central Pacific Railroad and the Chinese. Kearney massed great protest marches throughout San Francisco and gathered as much economic support as he could bring together to influence politicians of the Golden State and beyond, to pass legislation that would encourage Chinese migration out of the country as well as make immigration from China come to a halt. While Kearney and his followers called for more "reforms" beyond Chinese exclusion, he was most adamant about what he considered the one issue that he refused to compromise on, that the Chinese "must go." Ironically, when Kearney began his quest for political attention from his fellow Irish immigrants, he called upon them to follow the example of the Chinese in being focused on their business acumen.

The anti-Chinese sentiment gained steam in California during the brief, post–Civil War stagnated economy. Though never even close to being a full-scale economic depression, or even a recession of great significance, the memory of the great economic expansion that seemed to add truth to the moniker of "Golden State" was fresh in the minds of its residents and also growing immigrant population. As laborers found their wages lowered across all industries, and as the Chinese seemed to accept the dip in salaries, they became the most common scapegoat. California governor John Bigler, himself a racist and anti-Chinese advocate, found great support and a good number of voters in the ranks of the Workingmen's Party as well as another growing nativist organization, the Supreme Order of Caucasians. Violence against Chinese grew and Bigler and other like-minded politicians began to cite the need for Chinese removal for the safety of the Chinese themselves. Building on the tradition established by the Page Act of 1875, which was strictly focused on baring the immigration and importation of Asian prostitutes and bonded laborers, Congress passed the first such attempt at racial exclusion 1875, though President Rutherford B. Hayes promptly vetoed the legislation. However, in 1882, Congress once again sent up to the executive a new and more sweeping version, which the more amenably minded President Chester Arthur signed into law.

The Chinese Exclusion Act of 1882 had an immediate impact on the daily lives of the Asians in California. It immediately brought to a halt any immigration from Asia. Though its language focused on barring immigrants who were in the mining industry, the act had a far sweeping impact on the Chinese and all other Asians, who were simply lumped in with the Chinese, in the Golden State. The language of the Chinese Exclusion Act bears witness to the racial or ethnic exclusion. In its introductory paragraph, it states: "Be it enacted by the Senate and House of Representatives of the United States of America in Congress assembled, that from and after the expiration of ninety days next after the passage of this act, and until the expiration of ten years next after the passage of this act, the coming of Chinese laborers to the United States be, and the same is hereby, suspended; and during such suspension it shall not be lawful for any Chinese laborer to come, or having so come after the expiration of said ninety days to remain within the United States." Section 14, in relation to citizenship, states: "That hereafter no State court or court of the United States shall admit Chinese to citizenship; and all laws in conflict with this act are hereby repealed."[1]

If any Chinese returned, even on a temporary basis to China, they were barred from reentry into the United States. Furthermore, the act also cast the Chinese as permanent aliens who were not eligible for citizenship. This codicil prevented the immigrants from holding public office or voting and thus cast them into a state of being a subordinate component in American society. In California, the state as well as counties and cities established even more laws that made life a living hell for the Chinese. While many, literally thousands, of Chinese Americans attempted to bring their cases against the act to court but found that their access to due process had dried up as well. Over the next two successive decades, more restrictions were added as amendments to the Chinese Exclusion Act of 1882, which was not repealed until 1943 with the passage of the Magnuson Act of that year, when the appearance of such racist legislation ran afoul of the American and Chinese alliance against the Japanese in World War II.

LIFE IN OTHER GOLD RUSHES

Beginning in 1804, the first real Gold Rush in American history began in the state of Virginia. The earliest known account of gold being discovered in Virginia came from notations made by Thomas Jefferson in 1782, who recorded for posterity that he had come upon rocks with gold veins, though nothing beyond Jefferson's initial accounts had been unearthed until 1804, when spotty and fragmented reports began to appear, resulting in migration by gold seekers, numbering in the hundreds, into the fields. By 1806, the first significant strike of placer gold was recovered, which resulted in a noticeable increase of miners, predominantly squatters, throughout the Virginia countryside. For the next 20 years, miners found relative success, in effect extracting an ounce per every hundred to two hundred pounds of earth, though the easy, surface-level placer gold was gone by the mid-1830s, resulting in a major exodus from the fields, rivers, and streams. A few hearty miners formed partnerships in the post–Gold Rush era and began to dig mine shafts throughout the countryside that had once offered the easy surface gold for the pickings. Though unlike the incredible mother lodes offered in future decades in the west, these mines produced busts more often than strikes and the technology of the day did not bring any innovations such as hydraulic mining, as would be the case in California. The greatest blow to the Virginia gold mining industry was literally the California Gold Rush as evidenced by the near complete abandonment of all mining activity in Virginia starting in 1849. While a trickle of mining began to pick up again in the mid-1850s, the outbreak of the Civil War in 1861 brought all mining activities to a screeching halt. Gold mining virtually vanished from Virginia until the 1870s, but the yields throughout the entire state, recently re-mapped as the northwestern section of pre–Civil War Virginia ceded to join the Union as West Virginia, proved very weak. Gold mining never proved to be a significant source of revenue in Virginia, and consequently, Virginia never witnessed the rise of any real mining towns, nor was there ever any population explosion. One of the greatest significances of the Virginia Gold Rush was that once the news of California's gold fields reached its borders, it lost the workforce of the entire mining industry within one calendar year. While Virginia may have been the home of the first Gold Rush, albeit small, its neighbor to the south, Georgia, was anything but insignificant.

Reports of gold in Georgia began long before the territory was a part of the United States. The Cherokee had reported to the Spanish that gold could be found in several of the hilly sections that lay far from the ocean shores. The Spanish, though intent on finding gold wherever they could, did not explore the interior of Georgia in any serious fashion after initial attempts to locate any color proved fruitless. However, in 1828 the discovery of surface, placer gold would lead to very different results.

Unlike the birth of the California Gold Rush, there is no agreed-upon point of discovery, as had been the case with James Marshall at Sutter's Mill. What is known is that in 1828 there were a handful of reports of individuals finding gold, independent of each other, and all were surface placer gold discoveries. The two locations for this initial discovery were both creek beds, similar to California, though certainly not as covered as the glistening beds in the west. Word of mouth first spread the news, though within a few months newspapers carried the stories of the mining exploits across the young United States, which had barely progressed any further west than Ohio in the north and whose population overwhelmingly clung to the Atlantic along the nation's northeastern seaboard. Consequently, miners from around the state and emigrants from other regions began their journey to Georgia, in search of riches and adventure.

Within one year, the trickle of gold seekers, numbering in the hundreds, turned into a deluge of prospectors. By 1830 close, there were nearly 25,000 miners throughout Georgia. As would be the case later in California, prospectors were highly motivated and quite willing to dig wherever they believed a gold deposit might be. Some strikes rivaled even the best in the west. For example, in the southeast section of Cherokee County, hundreds of ounces were being recovered daily in 1830. Boom towns and mining camps sprang up, bringing with them the culture that would later spread into California; prostitution, gambling and a boom–bust economic cycle. The rapid influx of emigrants also impacted the Cherokee Nation, as hundreds and subsequently thousands of squatters peppered the Cherokee land, attempting to strip away as much gold as they could as well as utilize any of the Cherokee resources they could appropriate along the way. Not surprisingly, significant conflicts between the gold seekers and the Cherokee began. Additionally, white plantation holders who coveted the prized, nutrient-rich Cherokee land took full advantage of the growing tensions as they first pressed the state of Georgia to act, by supporting the removal of the Cherokee. The Tribe responded to the illegal attempts to roust them from their land by suing for their rights in court. Georgia pressed for an interpretation of the *Compact of 1802*, issued by President Thomas Jefferson, which promised the fledgling state that the federal government would not recognize Indian land claims in Georgia. President Andrew Jackson signed into law the Indian Removal Act of 1830, which permitted the president to negotiate directly with Tribes for their relocation further west to appease the whites who coveted the Indian lands. However, the Cherokee rejected Jackson's edict and proceeded with their own case, which they presented to the U.S. Supreme Court.

The case *Cherokee Nation v. Georgia* of 1830 was an attempt by the Cherokee, led by Chief John Ross, to literally prevent the annihilation of the Tribe itself. The brief filed by the legal representatives for the Cherokee, led by former U.S. attorney general William Wirt, argued that the Cherokee Nation was a sovereign and foreign nation in relationship to the United States and because of this status, the laws of the state of Georgia could not be applied to the Cherokee. However, Chief Justice John Marshall ruled that the framers of the U.S. Constitution did not recognize Indian societies as independent and sovereign, rather, he interpreted the relationship as more akin to a dependent state (Indian society) to the sovereign state (the United States), and in the process, Marshall further wrote in his decision that as the Cherokee were in effect "wards" of the federal government, the U.S. Supreme Court could not issue a ruling on the case. This was a significant blow to the Cherokee as well as all other Indian societies.

In 1832, the U.S. Supreme Court heard yet another case emanating from the Cherokee Nation with *Worcester v. Georgia.* The heart of the case brought before the U.S. Supreme Court by a missionary, Samuel Worcester, who along with six other missionaries was arrested in Georgia due to his protest against the forced relocation of the Indians, was that as he was on sovereign Indian land, law enforcement agents from Georgia had no jurisdiction over his affairs. Remarkably, Chief Justice John Marshall ruled that Worcester's conviction in Georgia for his alleged crime of being on Indian land without a license from the state of Georgia was void as Georgia laws did not extend onto sovereign Indian land. Furthermore, Marshall ruled that the Cherokee Nation was a "distinct community" and therefore Georgia could not impose its legal codes and statutes on Cherokee land. While on the surface the decision appears to protect the Cherokee from a forced relocation, President Andrew Jackson and the executive branch of the U.S. federal government were not a part of the case. Jackson proceeded with his support of the state of Georgia, which included the military, for the removal of the Cherokee and the other Tribes in the region. The result became known as the Trail of Tears. From 1836 through 1839, over 4,000 Cherokee perished en route to Indian Territory, present-day Oklahoma. This great tragedy foreshadowed those yet to come for the California Indians in the California Gold Rush.

In addition to the conflicts between the indigenous societies and Georgia, the state of Georgia attempted to control the flood of gold seekers and others fortune seekers who were creating chaos throughout the region by bringing about a system of land management. Prior to the Gold Rush, Georgia had issued land lotteries to distribute real estate in an equitable fashion to settlers attempting to develop farmlands. In December 1831, the state government brought back the lottery system, though this time tied it to gold recovery. The parcels were 40 acres, and for those who were lucky winners in the lottery, a filing fee of $10 was required to handle the property transfer and registration. Eligibility requirements were quite specific. Eighteen-year-old men, widows, and orphans were eligible to apply, as long as they were residents of Georgia for at least three years, U.S. citizens, and who had not resided previously on Cherokee lands, previously been a miner in the state, or have been convicted of a felony. The gold lottery was successful in that it partially managed the flood of gold seekers, though it did not entirely cut off the rush of squatters who were willing to take the chances of illegally mining for gold.

The Gold Rush in Georgia continued on into the late 1830s, and while most of the placer surface gold had been recovered by that point, there were still hundreds of working mines throughout the state. In 1838, the U.S. Mint opened a branch in one of the boom towns of the Gold Rush, Dahlonega, which remained in operation until 1861 when, after the outbreak of the Civil War, Confederates seized the mint and all of its materials and operations. Following the conclusion of the Civil War, the U.S. federal government decided against reopening the mint. The mint had been opened as a market place for the miners to have their gold assessed and purchased. Gold coins bearing the American Bald Eagle were stamped at the mint throughout its operating years. While the Civil War signaled the end of serious gold mining in Georgia, the real death blow to the state's Gold Rush was the discovery of gold in California. After the news of the California Gold Rush reached the East, Georgian miners migrated to the west coast in droves. Also, the former residents of Georgia, the Cherokee, many of whom had become adept miners prior to the Trail of Tears, also migrated into California to partake in the Gold Rush. While sporadic mining once again picked up throughout Georgia in the late 19th century and through the Great Depression years, no significant gold mining on the scale of what had taken place in the 1830s ever occurred in the Peach State again.

While the California Gold Rush signaled an end to the one in Georgia, it spurred forth several other rushes of significant magnitude as fortune seekers dreamed of replicating the success they, or others, had in the Golden State. One of greatest significance that took place on the heels of the California Gold Rush was Pike's Peak.

During the California Gold Rush, many a speculator entered the great Rocky Mountains in search of color. While there were dozens of reports of rivers, creeks, and streambeds that yielded a few ounces or at times even pounds of placer gold, the first significant strike that brought about a rush for riches happened along the Pikes Peak country of what was then the Kansas and Nebraska territories. The first discovery in the region occurred on the South Platte River in mid-1857 by miners who had prospected in California but had found very little success, but significant discouragement as the gold fields in California were full of miners and growing mining concerns that had taken all of the rich spots. Word had spread into California about the Southern Platte, but as had been the case with reports during the 1850s, very few took the news with any seriousness. However, William Greenberry Russell, blistered by what he considered a defeat in the gold fields of California, gave prospecting the West one last effort. The native Georgian headed to the Southern Platte in early 1858. He formed a company with several other prospectors, including two of his brothers, and at the confluence of the South Platte Cherry Creek, they began panning, digging, and sluicing in earnest. The natural geography, a large river, a confluence at a smaller creek, both of which were fed not only by rainfall but also snowmelt, was reminiscent of the places where the great strikes in California took place. After nearly a month, the hearty souls were met with no success. The camp that went up overnight was coming to a close nearly as fast. William Russell, exhausted by his nearly decade-long quest for riches that only seemed to yield heartache, packed up and was one of the first to leave, while his brothers continued to be a part of the few who remained and toiled the harsh land that produced no gold. Russell's departure from the South Platte and Cherry Creek would actually lead to a drastic change in his fortunes.

In July 1858, William Russell and fellow Argonaut, Sam Bates, had momentarily stopped in the course of their dejected wanderings and began to work a dry creek bed, Little Dry Creek, just south of contemporary Denver. The two men found gold, and within a few days, Russell's brothers joined them, and within a few days, the men found nearly two pounds of placer gold. Energized by their findings, the men began to comb the area for gold, and by the following year, news of their growing success spread into California and throughout the United States. Newspapers, eager to sell copies, exaggerated the success that the men were having, though as real gold deposits around the Russell diggings did consistently yield results, albeit meager ones in comparison to California, gold seekers began to migrate into the harsh county. In June 1859, significant strikes of placer gold began to materialize and the Pike's Peak Gold Rush was in motion.

The eastern flank of the Rocky Mountains proved to be a substantial draw for prospectors, and the continual discovery of gold veins and placer gold brought in, just as had been the case in California, more miners than productive gold claims. The mining camps grew into villages and towns and quickly gave birth to Denver and Boulder. Countless other camps appeared and vanished within a week's time; other boom towns persisted as long as the discovered gold could support the economy of a dry goods-, saloon-, and brothel-oriented society. The miners in the Pike's Peak Gold Rush were great in number, with most estimates placing the draw at over 100,000 and had taken to calling themselves "59ers." While large-scale mining took a few years to resort to massive open pit mines and mechanized crushers in California, the easy-to-find surface placer gold dried up much faster in the Pike's Peak Rush, compelling those in search of gold to take more aggressive means of recovery. Through the first half of the 1860s "hard rock" mining made many rich, though the extraction deposits of gold in the sulfide ore were beyond their ability. That changed in 1868.

Nathaniel Hill, a professor of chemistry at Brown University, developed and implemented a process by which he could effectively smelt out the gold sulfide ore. He moved to Colorado and partnered with James Lyon, and together the men became quite rich, with Hill eventually being elected a U.S. senator representing Colorado, which in 1876 became a state. While Hill certainly benefited from his chemical extraction process, so did the gold industry in Colorado. From the early moments of the Pike's Peak Rush and through the remaining 19th century and into the early part of the 20th century, gold deposits continued to be discovered, and over the two generations of the peak of gold recovery in the Centennial State, dozens of tons of gold fed the growing population and economy of the state of Colorado, which, as a territory, became the second to have statehood bestowed upon it following its rapid population growth as a result of a Gold Rush. The Pike's Peak Gold Rush of Colorado proved to be one of the most significant discoveries of gold in American history and was, unlike the California Gold Rush, one that did not yield any great conflicts with Native Americans;

however, the next significant Gold Rush that followed Pike's Peak would prove to be very consequential in American Indian history.

In 1873, Col. George Armstrong Custer led the 7th Cavalry into the Dakota Territory to provide protection for a railroad survey party against the Lakota. After minor skirmishes, Custer, who had been making a name for himself beginning in the Civil War and most recently as an Indian fighter, pushed his cavalry into the Black Hills in search of resistance. Rather than encountering any significant Indian resistance to report back to the press, Custer and his men reported finding gold. Custer and his thousand men combed the Black Hills looking for further deposits, and as news of the find spread, miners began to pour into the region, which was actually on Lakota land. Tensions and war would soon follow as the major strike of gold at Whitewood Creek and Deadwood Gulch. While the Treaty of Laramie in 1868 guaranteed the Lakota that the United States would not permit settlement or encroachment in the Black Hills, the discovery of gold that launched the Black Hills Gold Rush in 1874 led to a flood of emigrants and gold seekers and soon thereafter the conflict began.

The Northern Black Hills provided many a miner with gold, and in the first year, new discoveries were being made every day. By 1876, all of the land in the Black Hills was under claim by the thousands of invaders who were tearing up as much soil that they could with their shovels. Towns quickly grew out of the mining camps, with some of the more famous being Deadwood and Custer, both in what would later become the state of South Dakota. Just outside of Deadwood, four enterprising men, Alex Engh, Hank Harney along with Moses and Frank Manuel, took a gamble on finding the source of the pacer gold being scooped up in Deadwood. Their gamble paid off. The men found what became one of the richest gold strikes in history, and the four men founded the Homestake Mine. While the men retrieved vast amounts of gold, it was labor intensive as the gold had to be separated from rock by crushers. The year following the establishment of Homestake, George Hearst purchased their interests for a reported $70,000, and over the coming generations, Homestake became the second most productive mine in American history. Perhaps the greater historical significance of the Black Hills Gold Rush was that it led directly to the Battle of Big Horn, by far the most known battle of the Sioux Wars, which resulted in the eradication of the men under the command of George Armstrong Custer, who also perished in the battle.

The same year as the Battle of Little Big Horn and the Centennial of the United States, a small mining camp, nearly due east of San Francisco along the California–Nevada border, that had virtually vanished in a harsh blizzard in 1859 found new life when a gold strike began a rush. Bodie was founded as a mining camp the same year that a blizzard of remarkable strength pushed out any settlement potential, or so it seemed. A few, feeble attempts at mining reemerged in Bodie in the late 1860s; however, gold recovery proved insignificant, and the miners once again abandoned the camp. However, in 1876 agents of the Standard Company discovered a very rich gold deposit, and within two years, Bodie was transformed from a near ghost camp into a mining boom town.

From 1877 to 1879, Bodie's expansive economy had powered the population explosion that resulted in a settlement of 8,000. Given its proximity to one of the mining and ore-processing centers in Nevada, Carson City, Bodie never developed the expansive stamping and separation process that would have only fueled a greater population expansion. Most of the gold that was mined and processed out of Bodie in the neighboring Carson City, eventually made its way into San Francisco. The wealth that remained in Bodie, which was considerable, was reflected in the evolution of one of the most wide open Wild West cities in the history of California. Bodie was, perhaps, the city that most fit the image of the Wild West that so many Hollywood films and dime novels popularized.

While it was never more than a boom town, the population supported a relatively diverse consumer-based industries. At its peak at the start of the 1880s, over 60 saloons peppered the streets along with a thriving red-light district that was populated by one of the largest selection of working girls outside of San Francisco in the American West. By the time Bodie reached its peak of mining production in 1881, the city received its first train with the arrival of a narrow gauge line, the Bodie Railway & Lumber Company, which also brought in much needed materials for the construction of homes and businesses. Following the establishment of the rail line, the Standard Company hoped to further Bodie's development into more of a family-oriented community, which they had believed would also bring in a higher caliber of worker in their mines. Two churches did emerge in Bodie, one Roman Catholic and one Methodist, as did one Taoist Temple that was supported by Bodie's Chinese population in the city's Chinatown, which constituted about 10 percent of the townsfolk. Bodie's most successful newspaper, *The Standard Pioneer Journal of Mono County*, evolved into a multi-edition press after starting out as merely a weekly. While several attempts were made at banking, Wells Fargo maintained the only permanent branch, which also happened to be the most heavily fortified.

Coinciding with the growing trend in labor across the United States, Bodie also witnessed the rise of labor union activism, though unionization was not necessarily a good cultural fit in the mining town and no union of miners of great significance emerged, with the Miners Union Hall primarily serving as a town hall and currently a ghost town museum.

The economy of Bodie went into a slow decline after 1881 as the Standard Company, which was highly mechanized for its time, required fewer and fewer workers. Most of those who departed Bodie during the 1880s were independent miners, saloon keepers, prostitutes, and the Chinese, in the wake of the Chinese Exclusion Act. The town that in the late 1870s was predicted by many to grow beyond Sacramento appeared to be going in the opposite direction: however, the infrastructure, which was significant, slowed its decline. For example, Bodie had a telegraph line that connected it to the outside world, given its relative distance to Sacramento and the Reno-Carson City settlements, which were continuing to grow.

Bodie experienced a brief bounce beginning in 1890, when improvements in the cyanide extraction process afforded entrepreneurs the opportunity to comb through the tailings for gold and silver that had been discarded in previous years. In 1891, the Standard Company began the construction of a hydroelectric facility outside of the town, which permitted Bodie, and the Standard Company, to utilize electricity well before most of the rest of the country. Though the inevitable decline occurred as the gold recovery dried up. Bodie limped into the 20th century, and the Standard Company closed its doors in 1913. Within a couple of years, people began to refer to Bodie as a "ghost town"; in the 1920 U.S. Census, Bodie's population was recorded at 120. In 1962, the once-glorious Wild West town became an official California State Park as a relic of the past, a California Gold Rush boomtown.

The last great Gold Rush was the Alaska-Klondike Gold Rush from 1896 to 1899. Gold had been known to exist by the Indigenous peoples in the region, though any external discovery of gold was hampered by the relative isolation from the populations of the United States and Canada as well as the exceptionally rugged terrain and inhospitable long winter of the Yukon and Alaska borderlands.

In mid-August 1896, George and Kate Carmack and Kate's brother, Skookum Jim, were fishing along the Klondike River when they were told by a passing gold prospector that there was gold in one of the river's tributaries. Intrigued, and as George had previously, but unsuccessfully, tried gold prospecting, they started out for the location, and as their story tells, they found a significant deposit. Carmack and his family proceeded to file their claims, and within a few days, they were actively pulling placer surface gold out of the water and along its shores. By the end of the month, dozens of miners were panning for gold along what became named Bonanza Creek. Word did not travel as fast in the Alaskan-Yukon territories as it did in California, or anywhere else in late 19th-century America. This relative isolation allowed the Carmacks and handful of other gold seekers several months of uninterrupted mining, except of course for the heavy snow and below zero temperatures, which brought a halt to gold recovery until the early part of the spring thaw. By then, the news of the gold discovery had been carried by regional newspapers. At the end of the spring of 1897, the gold began to make its way into the marketplace and thus began the rush into the north.

While the most common estimate places the hoard that rushed into the Klondike in excess of 100,000. The arduous nature of the trek limited the number of those who actually arrived to somewhere between 30,000 and 50,000, still a sizeable number of emigrants to land in the gold fields, the majority of which came from the United States. The Alaska-Klondike Gold Rush also happened to coincide with the recession that had the United States in its grips through the middle part of the decade, and which was also one of the most virulent in American history, and had brought the nation's economy to its knees and from which it took several years to fully recover. The idea of striking it rich appealed to many in the wake of the economic panic, and, consequently, many who would have been otherwise not inclined to make such a demanding and potentially perilous trip, those from the upper classes, threw their hats into the ring.

Newspapers and photographers covered the event from the docks of San Francisco through the entire voyage and into the gold fields. The photographs recorded nearly every moment of the rush itself, and consequently, it is the most documented Gold Rush in history. The two main routes were either completely overland from the Pacific Northwest through Canada and by water into Alaska and then by land across from the Alaskan port of St. Michael. As had been the case in the California Gold Rush, along the routes, the price of commodities skyrocketed. Food, provision, and beasts of burden made many an entrepreneur of trade quite wealthy. Canada had learned from the lessons of the California Gold Rush and from the onset of the rush began to send its Mounties into the region to charge a tariff on the importation of goods, whether they were to be sold in market or used in the process of mining. Unlike the California Gold Rush, given the physical geography of the Yukon, in addition to the challenging journey just to get there, it required a significant investment in materials. Most miners, those who would actually arrive in the gold fields, found that they had to spend several thousands of dollars just to get their respective camps in operational form and to support their very lives as well. Also another lesson in economics learned from the California experience, Canada required all miners to pay for a claim before they became operational and then an annual fee was required to continue work on the diggings. People paid the fees and made the investments, because the gold was there, the territory in which it lay was vast and the relative number of miners was small when taking the geography into account.

Boom towns sprouted up, just as they had in the gold rushes to the south, and with them came the usual array of businesses; saloons, brothels, dry goods stores, and confidence men. On the Alaskan panhandle, the town of Skagway became notorious. Gunfights and murders were commonplace in the small trading hamlet that grew to a town of over 20,000 in the first year of the rush. By 1898, a permanent encampment of businesses kept the residential population at over 8,000 and a steady stream of thousands of gold seekers heading into the Yukon during the spring and summer and those leaving the gold fields in the fall made it a town of transience, opportunity, and peril. Dawson City, situated along the Yukon River, came into existence during the rush itself. Consequently, it became the boom town most associated with, and most reflective of, the Alaska-Yukon Gold Rush. Compared with its American counterparts, both contemporary and historical, Dawson City was tranquil. It was also quite rich as long as the gold kept pouring in. While gambling and prostitution were rampant, they were contained and permitted. Violence was abhorred, and justice was swift in the early part of the rush; consequently, historians note that the culture of this town evolved into one where everyone knew the consequences and the inability for criminals to thrive kept many from making their move into town. For a brief time, Dawson City was, by many contemporary accounts, a right fine place to live and work. However, the Alaska-Yukon Gold Rush ended as quickly as it had begun. By 1899, the Yukon was, by all accounts, bone dry of gold. That stark fact, culminated with word of a similar gold deposit in Nome, Alaska, which never yielded the equivalent of the Yukon, also in 1899, resulted in Dawson City drying up as fast as it had started. For all intents and purposes, the last Gold Rush of the 19th century actually came to a close in the last year of that century.

NOTE

1. An Act to Execute Certain Treaty Stipulations Relating to the Chinese, May 6, 1882.

GLOSSARY

Alluvial Gold—Gold that has been deposited by the process of moving water; gold that has been separated from debris by the process of moving water.

Alluvium—Loose soil and sediment that has been eroded by the passage of water. Can be made up of several types of minerals or debris.

Amalgam—Gold or silver mixed with mercury.

Argonaut—Person who travels a great distance to take part in the California Gold Rush.

Assay—Analysis of materials aimed at determining the amount and quality of gold within a vein.

Bullion—Refined, formed, and weighted measures of gold or silver.

Claim—A specific miner's or corporation's legal title to a specific track of land for the purposes of mining.

Claim-jumper—A person or group of people who illegally mine for gold on a plot of land that they do not have legal title for, but someone or some other corporation does.

Color—The common term used by miners for gold.

Diggings—The location where mining, most typically by hand, takes place.

Dredging—The process of scraping the bottom of a creek, stream, river, or other body aimed at recovering gold that is on the bed.

Excavation—The process of digging and examining the soil and rocks for the presence of gold.

Flume—A form of hydraulic mining, in that the process of separating gold from unwanted debris involves the use of a man-controlled flow of water.

Fool's Gold—Pyrite; a mineral that to the untrained eye resembles gold.

Forty-niner—The moniker given to the miners that either set off for the California Gold Fields in 1849 or arrived in 1849.

Glory Hole—The location wherein a significant deposit of gold has been discovered in a small mine or claim.

Gold—The soft, malleable metal; a chemical element, symbol: AU; atomic number 79.

Gold Fever—Colloquial term referring to someone who is obsessed with mining for gold.

Hydraulic Mining—The use of water jets to separate soil and rock from hillsides or the use of water jets to separated gold from unwanted debris.

Lode—A significant deposit of gold in one fixed locus.

Long Tom—A type of sluicing box that is used to separate gold from unwanted debris with the use of water that is either flowing or stagnant.

Malleable—Material that one can reshape with relative ease.

Mercury—Chemical element, symbol Hg; atomic number 80. Was referred to as quicksilver and utilized in the separation of gold from debris.

Mine—The location wherein gold recovery takes place.

Miner—A person who is attempting to find and recover gold.

Mother Lode—A very significant gold deposit.

Nugget—A small, natural forming gold deposit.

Ore—Gold after the process of debris separation has taken place.

Panning—The process of using a pan, either with water or dry, to separate gold from unwanted debris by swirling soil and small rocks and removing gold when made visible.

Placer—Surface gold that has through the process of erosion been separated from other debris.

Placer Mining—Recovery of surface gold, typically lying on the beds of rivers, streams, and creeks.

Prospecting—Attempting to find gold by digging and other forms of mining.

Quartz—The second most common mineral on the crust of the earth after feldspar; gold is commonly found in the form of veins in quartz.

Rocker—A type of moveable box that either hydraulic mining or dry mining is used to sort gold from unwanted debris by tilting the box in one direction to another, a rocking fashion, causing movement and separation.

Sluice—A hydraulic channeling box that utilizes both water and gravity to separate gold from unwanted debris.

Stamp Mill—A machine, either mechanized or hand operated, that crushes rock or minerals into smaller debris that is sifted through in search of gold.

Strike—An encounter with a deposit of gold.

Tailings—The residual materials left behind following the process of separating gold from unwanted debris primarily through the use of moving water.

Vein—A formation of gold that occurs within another mineral, such as quartz, or in rock.

BIBLIOGRAPHY

ARTICLES

Apostol, Jane. "Adventures at Sea: A.M. Ebbets's Voyage to California in 1849." *Southern California Quarterly* 95, no. 1 (Spring 2013): 24–46.

Bakken, Gordon Morris. "The Courts, the Legal Profession, and the Development of Law in Early California." *California History* 81, no. 3/4, Taming the Elephant: Politics, Government, and Law in Pioneer California (2003): 74–95.

Bethel, A. C. W. "The Golden Skein: California's Gold-Rush Transportation Network." *California History* 77, no. 4, A Golden State: Mining and Economic Development in Gold Rush California (Winter, 1998/1999): 250–275.

Bringhurst, Newell G. "Samuel Brannan and His Forgotten Final Years." *Southern California Quarterly* 79, no. 2 (Summer, 1997): 139–160.

Burns, John F. "Taming the Elephant: An Introduction to California's Statehood and Constitutional Era." *California History* 81, no. 3/4, Taming the Elephant: Politics, Government, and Law in Pioneer California (2003): pp. 1–26.

Caughey, John Walton, and Walter Gardner. "A Yankee Trader in the Gold Rush Letters of Walter Gardner, 1851–1857." *Pacific Historical Review* 17, no. 4 (November, 1948): 411–428.

Chalmers, Claudine. "Françoise, Lucienne, Rosalie: French Women-Adventurers in the Early Days of the California Gold Rush." *California History* 78, no. 3 (Fall, 1999): 138–145, 147–153.

Chan, Sucheng. "A People of Exceptional Character: Ethnic Diversity, Nativism, and Racism in the California Gold Rush." *California History* 79, no. 2, Rooted in Barbarous Soil: People, Culture, and Community in Gold Rush California (Summer, 2000), 44–85.

Chaput, Donald. "The Civil War Military Post on Catalina Island." *Southern California Quarterly* 75, no. 1 (Spring, 1993): 37–50.

Clair, David J. St. "The Gold Rush and the Beginnings of California Industry." *California History* 77, no. 4, A Golden State: Mining and Economic Development in Gold Rush California (Winter, 1998/1999): 185–208.

Clair, David J. St. "New Almaden and California Quicksilver in the Pacific Rim Economy." *California History* 73, no. 4 (Winter, 1994/1995): 278–295.

Clay, Karen, and Randall Jones. "Migrating to Riches? Evidence from the California Gold Rush." *The Journal of Economic History* 68, no. 4 (December, 2008): 997–1027.

Costello, Julia G. "Gold Rush Archaeology: Excavating the Mother Lode." *Archaeology* 34, no. 2 (March/April, 1981): 18–26.

Curtis, Kent. "Producing a Gold Rush: National Ambitions and the Northern Rocky Mountains, 1853–1863." *The Western Historical Quarterly* 40, no. 3 (Autumn, 2009): 275–297.

Delgado, James P. "Gold Rush Jail: The Prison Ship 'Euphemia.'" *California History* 60, no. 2 (Summer, 1981): 134–141.

Delgado, James P., and Russell Frank. "A Gold Rush Enterprise: Sam Ward, Charles Mersch, and the Storeship 'Niantic.'" *Huntington Library Quarterly* 46, no. 4 (Autumn, 1983): 321–330.

Dilsaver, Lary M. "After the Gold Rush." *Geographical Review* 75, no. 1 (January 1985): 1–18.

Dutka, Barry L. "New York Discovers Gold! In California." *California History* 63, no. 4 (Fall, 1984): 313–319.

Eales, Anne Bruner. "Paoli and Placerville: Correspondence of a Hoosier in the Gold Rush." *Indiana Magazine of History* 95, no. 1 (March 1999): 14–30.

Gardner, Albert Ten Eyck. "A Relic of the California Gold Rush." *The Metropolitan Museum of Art Bulletin*, New Series, 8, no. 4 (December, 1949): 117–121.

Goodman, John B. III. "The 1849 California Gold Rush Fleet: The Magnolia." *Southern California Quarterly* 67, no. 1 (Spring, 1985a): 72–87.

Goodman, John B. III. "The 1849 California Gold Rush Fleet: The Ship 'Harriet Rockwell.'" *Southern California Quarterly* 67, no. 3 (Fall, 1985b): 310–320.

Goodman, John B. III. "The 1849 California Gold Rush Fleet: The Ship 'South America.'" *Southern California Quarterly* 68, no. 2 (Summer, 1986): 183, 185–195.

Gordon, Mary McDougall. "Overland to California in 1849: A Neglected Commercial Enterprise." *Pacific Historical Review* 52, no. 1 (February, 1983): 17–36.

Gordon, Mary McDougall. "Life in the California Goldfields in 1850: The Letters of Bernard J. Reid." *Southern California Quarterly* 67, no. 1 (Spring 1985): 51–69.

Hamilton, Gary G. "The Structural Sources of Adventurism: The Case of the California Gold Rush." *American Journal of Sociology* 83, no. 6 (May, 1978): 1466–1490.

Hamilton, Marian. "California Gold-Rush English." *American Speech* 7, no. 6 (August, 1932): 423–433.

Hardeman, Nicholas P. "Sketches of Dr. Glen Owen Hardeman: California Gold Rush Physician." *California Historical Society Quarterly* 47, no. 1 (March, 1968): 41–71.

Hayes-Bautista, David E., Cynthia L. Chamberlin, and Nancy Zuniga. "A Gold Rush Salvadoran in California's Latino World, 1857." *Southern California Quarterly* 91, no. 3 (Fall 2009): 257–294.

Higley, Caroline. "The Rise and Fall of Sutter's Golden Empire." *Montana: The Magazine of Western History* 14, no. 3, Mining and the West (Summer, 1964): 26–36.

Holliday, J. S. "Reverberations of the California Gold Rush." *California History* 77, no. 1, National Gold Rush Symposium (Spring, 1998): 4–15.

Honeysett, Elizabeth A., and Peter D. Schulz. "Burned Seeds from a Gold Rush Store in Sacramento, California." *Historical Archaeology* 24, no. 1 (1990): 96–103.

Hurtado, Albert L. "Controlling California's Indian Labor Force; Federal Administration of California Indian Affairs during the Mexican War." *Southern California Quarterly* 61, no. 3 (Fall, 1979): 217–238.

Hurtado, Albert L. "Sex, Gender, Culture, and a Great Event: The California Gold Rush." *Pacific Historical Review* 68, no. 1 (February, 1999): 1–19.

Johnson, Susan Lee. " 'My Own Private Life': Toward a History of Desire in Gold Rush California." *California History* 79, no. 2, Rooted in Barbarous Soil: People, Culture, and Community in Gold Rush California (Summer, 2000): 316–346.

Jung, Maureen A. "Documenting Nineteenth-Century Quartz Mining in Northern California." *The American Archivist*. 53, no. 3 (Summer, 1990): 406–418.

Kirk, Anthony. "Seeing the Elephant." *California History* 77, no. 4, A Golden State: Mining and Economic Development in Gold Rush California (Winter, 1998/1999): 174–184.

Kowalewski, Michael. "Imagining the California Gold Rush: The Visual and Verbal Legacy." *California History* 71, no. 1, Landmarks of Early California Painting: Art in the Ninet (Spring, 1992): 60–73.

Kowalewski, Michael. "Romancing the Gold Rush: The Literature of the California Frontier." *California History* 79, no. 2, Rooted in Barbarous Soil: People, Culture, and Community in Gold Rush California (Summer, 2000): 204–225.

Kurutz, Gary F. "Popular Culture on the Golden Shore." *California History* 79, no. 2, Rooted in Barbarous Soil: People, Culture, and Community in Gold Rush California (Summer, 2000): 280–315.

Levinson, Robert E. "American Jews in the West." *The Western Historical Quarterly* 5, no. 3 (July, 1974): 285–294.

Libecap, Gary D. "Economic Variables and the Development of the Law: The Case of Western Mineral Rights." *The Journal of Economic History* 38, no. 2 (June, 1978): 338–362.

Limerick, Patricia Nelson. "The Gold Rush and the Shaping of the American West." *California History* 77, no. 1, National Gold Rush Symposium (Spring, 1998): 30–41.

Littlefield, Douglas R. "Water Rights during the California Gold Rush: Conflicts over Economic Points of View." *The Western Historical Quarterly* 14, no. 4 (October, 1983): 415–434.

Lonnenberg, Allan. "The Digger Indian Stereotype in California." *Journal of California and Great Basin Anthropology* 3, no. 2 (Winter, 1981): 215–223.

Marshall, Thomas Maitland. "The Road to California: Letters of Joseph Price." *The Mississippi Valley Historical Review* 11, no. 2 (September, 1924): 237–257.

Mattes, Merrill J., and Esley J. Kirk. "From Ohio to California in 1849: The Gold Rush Journal of Elijah Bryan Farnham." *Indiana Magazine of History* 46, no. 3 (September 1950): 297–318.

Mazzi, Frank. "Harbingers of the City: Men and Their Monuments in Nineteenth Century San Francisco." *Southern California Quarterly* 55, no. 2 (Summer 1973): 141–162.

McDowell, Andrea. "Real Property, Spontaneous Order, and Norms in the Gold Mines." *Law & Social Inquiry* 29, no. 4 (Autumn, 2004): 771–818.

McGloin, John B., and Martin Francis Schwenninger. "A California Gold Rush Padre: New Light on the 'Padre of Paradise Flat." *California Historical Society Quarterly* 40, no. 1 (March, 1961): 49–67.

Merriam, Paul G. "Riding the Wind: Cape Horn Passage to Oregon, 1840s–1850s." *Oregon Historical Quarterly* 77, no. 1 (March, 1976): 36–60.

Nasatir, A. P., and J. Lombard. "A French Pessimist in California: The Correspondence of J. Lombard, Vice-Consul of France, 1850–1852." *California Historical Society Quarterly* 31, no. 2 (June, 1952): 139–148.

Nash, Gerald D. "A Veritable Revolution: The Global Economic Significance of the California Gold Rush." *California History* 77, no. 4, A Golden State: Mining and Economic Development in Gold Rush California (Winter, 1998/1999): 276–292.

Owens, Kenneth N. "The Mormon-Carson Emigrant Trail in Western History." *Montana: The Magazine of Western History* 42, no. 1 (Winter, 1992): 14–27.

Paddison, Joshua. "Capturing California." *California History* 81, no. 3/4, Taming the Elephant: Politics, Government, and Law in Pioneer California (2003): 126–136.

Palais, Hyman. "Some Aspects of the Black Hills Gold Rush Compared with the California Gold Rush." *Pacific Historical Review* 15, no. 1 (March, 1946): 59–67.

Pastron, Allen G., and James P. Delgado. "Archaeological Investigations of a Mid-19th-Century Shipbreaking Yard, San Francisco, California." *Historical Archaeology* 25, no. 3 (1991): 61–77.

Paul, Rodman W. "A Tenderfoot Discovers There Once Was a Mining West." *The Western Historical Quarterly* 10, no. 1 (January, 1979): 4–20.

Peterson, Charles E. "Prefabs in the California Gold Rush, 1849." *Journal of the Society of Architectural Historians* 24, no. 4 (December, 1965): 318–324.

Peterson, Richard H. "Anti-Mexican Nativism in California, 1848–1853: A Study of Cultural Conflict." *Southern California Quarterly* 62, no. 4 (Winter 1980): 309–327.

Peterson, Richard H. "The Frontier Thesis and Social Mobility on the Mining Frontier." *Pacific Historical Review* 44, no. 1 (February, 1975): 52–67.

Pisani, Donald J. " 'I Am Resolved Not to Interfere, but Permit All to Work Freely': The Gold Rush and American Resource Law." *California History* 77, no. 4, A Golden State: Mining and Economic Development in Gold Rush California (Winter, 1998/1999): 123–148.

Pisani, Donald J. "The Squatter and Natural Law in Nineteenth-Century America." *Agricultural History* 81, no. 4 (Fall, 2007): 443–463.

Raup, H. F. "Place Names of the California Gold Rush." *Geographical Review* 35, no. 4 (October, 1945): 653–658.

Raup, H. F, and William B. Pounds, Jr. "Northernmost Spanish Frontier in California: As Shown by the Distribution of Geographic Names." *California Historical Society Quarterly* 32, no. 1 (March, 1953): 43–48.

Rawls, James J. "Gold Diggers: Indian Miners in the California Gold Rush." *California Historical Quarterly* 55, no. 1 (Spring, 1976): 28–45.

Ridge, Martin. "Disorder, Crime, and Punishment in the California Gold Rush." *Montana: The Magazine of Western History* 49, no. 3, Special Gold Rush Issue (Autumn, 1999a): 12–27.

Ridge, Martin. "The Legacy of the Gold Rush." *Montana: The Magazine of Western History* 49, no. 3, Special Gold Rush Issue (Autumn, 1999b): 58–63.

Rodman W. Paul. "After the Gold Rush: San Francisco and Portland." *Pacific Historical Review* 51, no. 1 (February, 1982): 1–21.

Rohe, Randall. "Origins & Diffusion of Traditional Placer Mining in the West." *Material Culture* 18, no. 3 (Fall, 1986): 127–166.

Rohe Randall. "Chinese River Mining in the West." *Montana: The Magazine of Western History* 46, no. 3 (Autumn, 1996): 14–29.

Rohrbough, Malcolm J. "The California Gold Rush as a National Experience." *California History* 77, no. 1, National Gold Rush Symposium (Spring, 1998): 16–29.

Rohrbough, Malcolm J. "No Boy's Play: Migration and Settlement in Early Gold Rush California." *California History* 79, no. 2, Rooted in Barbarous Soil: People, Culture, and Community in Gold Rush California (Summer, 2000): 25–43.

Rohrbough, Malcolm J. " 'When a Person Gets to California It Is Hard to Say or Tell When He Gets Away': Why the Forty-Niners Were Reluctant to Come Home to the Families They Loved." *Montana: The Magazine of Western History* 49, no. 3, Special Gold Rush Issue (Autumn, 1999): 28–41.

Rojas, Maythee. "Re-Membering Josefa: Reading the Mexican Female Body in California Gold Rush Chronicles." *Women's Studies Quarterly* 35, no. 1/2, The Sexual Body (Spring–Summer, 2007): 126–148.

Roske, Ralph J. "The World Impact of the California Gold Rush 1849–1857." *Arizona and the West* 5, no. 3 (Autumn, 1963): 187–232.

Roth, Mitchell. "Cholera, Community, and Public Health in Gold Rush Sacramento and San Francisco." *Pacific Historical Review* 66, no. 4 (November, 1997): 527–551.

Rotter, Andrew J. " 'Matilda for Gods Sake Write': Women and Families on the Argonaut Mind." *California History* 58, no. 2 (Summer, 1979): 128–141.

Sauder, Robert A. "The Agricultural Colonization of a Great Basin Frontier: Economic Organization and Environmental Alteration in Owens Valley, California, 1860–1925." *Agricultural History* 64, no. 4 (Autumn, 1990): 78–101.

Shields, Scott A. "Stay East Young Man: California Gold Rush Letter Sheets." *California History* 78, no. 2 (Summer, 1999): 98–102.

Sisson, Kelly J. "Contract Laborers and 'Patrones' in the California Gold Rush, 1848–1852." *Southern California Quarterly* 90, no. 3 (Fall, 2008): 259–305.

Slawson, L. R., and Russell E. Bidlack. "To California on the Sarah Sands: Two Letters Written in 1850 by L.R. Slawson." *California Historical Society Quarterly* 44, no. 3 (September, 1965): 229–235.

Spier, Robert F. G. "Tool Acculturation among 19th-Century California Chinese." *Ethnohistory* 5, no. 2 (Spring, 1958): 97–117.

Starr, Kevin. "Rooted in Barbarous Soil: An Introduction to Gold Rush Society and Culture." *California History* 79, no. 2, Rooted in Barbarous Soil: People, Culture, and Community in Gold Rush California (Summer, 2000): 1–24.

Steffen, Jerome O. "The Mining Frontiers of California and Australia: A Study in Comparative Political Change and Continuity." *Pacific Historical Review* 52, no. 4 (November, 1983): 428–440.

Taniguchi, Nancy J. "Weaving a Different World: Women and the California Gold Rush." *California History* 79, no. 2, Rooted in Barbarous Soil: People, Culture, and Community in Gold Rush California (Summer, 2000): 141–168.

Thompson, Gerald. "Edward Fitzgerald Beale and the California Gold Rush, 1848–1850." *Southern California Quarterly* 63, no. 3 (Fall 1981): 198–225.

Umbeck, John. "A Theory of Contract Choice and the California Gold Rush." *Journal of Law and Economics* 20, no. 2 (October, 1977): 421–437.

Vaught, David. "Putah Creek: Water, Land, Wheat, and Community in the Sacramento Valley in the 1850s." *Agricultural History* 76, no. 2, Water and Rural History (Spring, 2002): 326–337.

Virtue, G. O. "Public Ownership of Mineral Lands in the United States." *Journal of Political Economy* 3, no. 2 (March, 1895): 185–202.

Webb, Warren. "The California Gold Rush and the Mentally Ill." *Southern California Quarterly* 50, no. 1 (March 1968): 43–50.

Weinstein, Robert A. "San Francisco, 1851: The Golden City as the Argonauts Saw It . . ." *California Historical Society Quarterly* 47, no. 1 (March, 1968).

Weinstein, Robert A. "The Search for California Gold: A Photographic View." *California Historical Society Quarterly* 48, no. 1 (March, 1969).

White, Richard. "The Gold Rush: Consequences and Contingencies." *California History* 77, no. 1, National Gold Rush Symposium (Spring, 1998): 42–55.

Wilson, Karen S. "Seeking America in America: The French in the California Gold Rush." *Southern California Quarterly* 95, no. 2 (Summer 2013): 105–140.

Zanjani, Sally S. "To Die in Goldfield: Mortality in the Last Boomtown on the Mining Frontier." *The Western Historical Quarterly* 21, no. 1 (February, 1990): 47–69.

Zerbe, Richard O., Jr., and C. Leigh Anderson. "Culture and Fairness in the Development of Institutions in the California Gold Fields." *The Journal of Economic History* 61, no. 1 (March, 2001): 114–143.

Zhu, Liping. "No Need to Rush: The Chinese, Placer Mining, and the Western Environment." *Montana: The Magazine of Western History* 49, no. 3, Special Gold Rush Issue (Autumn, 1999): 42–57.

BOOKS

Altman, Linda Jacobs. *The California Gold Rush.* Springfield, NJ: Enslow Publishers, 1997.

Andrist, Ralph K. *California Gold Rush.* Kansas City, MO: Andrews McMeel Pub., 1961.

Axon, Gordon V. *The California Gold Rush*. New York: Mason/Charter, 1976.
Brands, H. W. *The Age of Gold: The California Gold Rush and the New American Dream*. New York: Anchor Books, 2003.
Brodbeck, J. Christoph. *California Gold Rush: Tales of a Swiss Prospector*. Canada: ArtBookbindery.com, 2009.
Brown, Marjory W., and Margaret Fitzwilliam. *Gold Fever: The Story of a Young New England Couple and the California Gold Rush, 1849–1853*. Wellesley, MA: Windsor Press, 1989.
Butruille, Susan G., and Kathleen R. Petersen. *Women's Voices from the Mother Lode: Tales from the California Gold Rush*. Boise, ID: Tamarack Books, 1998.
Byrd, Cecil K. *Searching for Riches: The California Gold Rush*. Bloomington: Lilly Library, Indiana University, 1991.
Caughey, John Walton. *The California Gold Rush*. Berkeley: University of California Press, 1975.
Chartier, JoAnn, and Chris Enss. *With Great Hope: Women of the California Gold Rush*. Helena, MT: TwoDot, 2000.
Chidsey, Donald Barr. *The California Gold Rush: An Informal History*. New York: Crown Publishers, 1968.
Claes, Jean V., and Howard L. Martin. *The California Gold Rush*. San Francisco: Golden Gate College Administrative Services Center, 1972.
Conrotto, Eugene L. *Miwok Means People: The Life and Fate of the Native Inhabitants of the California Gold Rush Country*. Fresno, CA: Valley Publishers, 1973.
Davies, J. Kenneth, and Lorin K. Hansen. *Mormon Gold: Mormons in the California Gold Rush, Contributing to the Development of California and the Monetary Solvency of Early Utah*. North Salt Lake, UT: Granite Mountain Publishing Company, 2010.
Davis, Stephen Chapin. *California Gold Rush Merchant: The Journal of Stephen Chapin David*. San Marino, CA: Huntington Library, 1956.
Delano, Alonzo. *On the Trail to the California Gold Rush*. Lincoln: University of Nebraska Press, 2005.
Delgado, James P. *To California by Sea: A Maritime History of the California Gold Rush*. Columbia: University of South Carolina Press, 1990.
Derbec, Etienne, and Abraham Phineas Nasatir. *A French Journalist in the California Gold Rush: The Letters of Etienne Derbec*. Georgetown, CA: Talisman Press, 1964.
Durham, Walter T. *Volunteer Forty-Niners: Tennesseans and the California Gold Rush*. Nashville: Vanderbilt University Press, 1997.
Eccleston, Robert, and C. Gregory Crampton. *The Mariposa Indian War, 1850–1851: Diaries of Robert Eccleston: The California Gold Rush, Yosemite, and the High Sierra*. Salt Lake City: University of Utah Press, 1957.
Groh, George W. *Gold Fever: Being a True Account, Both Horrifying and Hilarious, of the Art of Healing (So-Called) during the California Gold Rush*. New York: Morrow, 1966.

Harris, Benjamin Butler. *The Gila Trail: The Texas Argonauts and the California Gold Rush.* Norman: University of Oklahoma Press, 1960.

Harrison Hall, William Henry, and Eric Schneirsohn. *The Private Letters and Diaries of Captain Hall: An Epic of an Argonaut in the California Gold Rush, Oregon Territories, Civil War, and Oil City.* Glendale, CA: London Book Company, 1974.

Harvey, Charles H., and Edmund F. Ball, Douglas E. Clanin. *California Gold Rush: Diary of Charles H. Harvey, February 12–November 12, 1852.* Indianapolis: Indiana Historical Society, 1983.

Heffernan, Nancy Coffey, and Ann Page Stecker. *Sisters of Fortune: Being the True Story of How Three Motherless Sisters Saved Their Home in New England and Raised Their Younger Brother While Their Father Went Fortune Hunting in the California Gold Rush.* Hanover: University Press of New England, 1993.

Hill, Winifred Storrs. *Tarnished Gold: Prejudice during the California Gold Rush.* San Francisco: International Scholars Publications, 1996.

Hogue, Harland E. *Prophets and Paupers: Religion in the California Gold Rush, 1848–1869.* San Francisco: International Scholars Publications, 1996.

Holliday, J. S. *Gold Fever: The Lure and Legacy of the California Gold Rush.* Berkeley: University of California Press, 1998.

Holliday, J. S., and William Swain. *The World Rushed In: The California Gold Rush Experience.* New York: Simon and Schuster, 1981.

Jackson, Donald Dale. *Gold Dust: The California Gold Rush and the Forty-Niners.* Boston: Allen & Unwin, 1980.

Jackson, Joseph Henry. *Anybody's Gold: The Story of California's Mining Towns.* San Francisco: Chronicle Books, 1970.

Johnson, Drew Heath, and Marcia Eymann. *Silver & Gold: Cased Images of the California Gold Rush.* Iowa City: University of Iowa Press for the Oakland Museum of California, 1998.

Johnson, Susan Lee. *Roaring Camp: The Social World of the California Gold Rush.* New York: W.W. Norton, 2000.

Josselyn, Amos Piatt, and J. William Barrett. *The Overland Journal of Amos Piatt Josselyn: Zanesville, Ohio, to the Sacramento Valley, April 2, 1849, to September 11, 1849.* Baltimore: Gateway Press, 1978.

Kahn, Ava Fran. *Jewish Voices of the California Gold Rush: A Documentary History, 1849–1880.* Detroit, MI: Wayne State University Press, 2002.

Klein, Robert F. *Dubuque during the California Gold Rush: When the Midwest Went West.* Charleston, SC: History Press, 2011.

Koeppel, Elliot H. *The California Gold Country or Highway 49 Revisited: Being an Account of the Life & Times of the People and the Mining Camps of the California Gold Rush.* Malakoff, TX: Malakoff & Co. Pub., 1996.

Kurutz, Gary F., W. Thomas Taylor, and Bradley Hutchinson. *The California Gold Rush: A Descriptive Bibliography of Books and Pamphlets Covering the Years 1848–1853.* San Francisco: Book Club of California, 1997.

Levinson, Robert E. *The Jews in the California Gold Rush*. New York: Ktav Publishing House, 1978.

Levy, JoAnn. *They Saw the Elephant: Women in the California Gold Rush*. Hamden, CT: Archon Books, 1990.

MacGuinness, Aims. *Path of Empire: Panama and the California Gold Rush*. Ithaca, NY: Cornell University Press, 2008.

Marr, Asbury, and Hilliard Marr. *Letters Home: 1849 California Gold Rush Letters*. Garland, TX: Underwood Pub., 2000.

McGuinness, Aims. *Path of Empire: Panama and the California Gold Rush*. Ithaca, NY: Cornell University Press, 2008.

McKinstry, Byron Nathan, and Bruce L. McKinstry. *The California Gold Rush Overland Diary of Byron N. McKinstry, 1850–1852*. Glendale, CA: A.H. Clark Co., 1975.

McNeer, May. *The California Gold Rush*. New York: Random House, 1994.

Monaghan, Jay. *Chile, Peru, and the California Gold Rush of 1849*. Berkeley: University of California Press, 1973.

Mossinger, Rosemarie. *Woodleaf Legacy: The Story of a California Gold Rush Town*. Nevada City, CA: Carl Mautz Publishing, 1995.

Nolte, Carl. *Gold Fever: California's Gold Rush: An American Icon*. New York: W.W. Norton, 2000.

Owens, Kenneth N. *Gold Rush Saints: California Mormons and the Great Rush for Riches*. Norman: University of Oklahoma Press, 2005.

Owens, Kenneth N. *Riches for All: The California Gold Rush and the World*. Lincoln: University of Nebraska Press, 2002.

Parke, Charles Ross, and James Edward Davis. *Dreams to Dust: A Diary of the California Gold Rush, 1849–1850*. Lincoln: University of Nebraska Press, 1989.

Parker, Jerry. *Eureka!: The Story of the California Gold Rush*. New York: MetroBooks, 1998.

Pomfret, John E., Charles Henry Ellis, and John N. Stone. *California Gold Rush Voyages, 1848–1849: Three Original Narratives*. San Marino, CA, Huntington Library, 1954.

Principe, Bill, and Jethro C. Brock. *Nantucket to California: The Gold Rush Exodus*. Rockport, ME: Picton Press, 2001.

Rawls, James J., Richard J. Orsi, and Marlene Smith-Baranzini. *A Golden State: Mining and Economic Development in Gold Rush California*. Berkeley: University of California Press, 1999.

Richards, Leonard L. *The California Gold Rush and the Coming of the Civil War*. New York: Alfred A. Knopf, 2007.

Ridout, Lionel Utley. *Renegade, Outcast, and Maverick: Three Episcopal Clergymen in the California Gold Rush*. San Diego: University Press, San Diego State University, 1973.

Riegel, Martin P. *The Ships of the California Gold Rush*. San Clemente, CA: Riegel, 1988.

Ring, Bob, Steven Charles Ring, and Al Ring. *Detour to the California Gold Rush: Eugene Ring's Travels in South America, California, and Mexico 1848–1850*. Tucson, AZ: U.S. Press & Graphics, 2008.

Roberts, Brian. *American Alchemy: The California Gold Rush and Middle-Class Culture*. Chapel Hill: University of North Carolina Press, 2000.

Roberts, Sylvia Alden. *Mining for Freedom: Black History Meets the California Gold Rush*. Bloomington, IN: IUniverse, 2008.

Rohrbough, Malcolm J. *The California Gold Rush and the American Nation*. New York: John Wiley and Sons Ltd, 1998.

Rohrbough, Malcolm J. *Days of Gold: The California Gold Rush and the American Nation*. Berkeley: University of California Press, 1997.

Rohrbough, Malcolm J. *Rush to Gold: The French and the California Gold Rush, 1848–1854*. New Haven, CT: Yale University Press, 2013.

Royce, Sarah. *A Frontier Lady: Recollections of the Gold Rush and Early California*. Lincoln: University of Nebraska Press, 1977.

Sheafer, Silvia Anne. *Gold Rush Women*. Glendale, CA: Journal Publications, 1992.

Starr, Kevin, Richard J. Orsi, and California Historical Society. *Rooted in Barbarous Soil: People, Culture, and Community in Gold Rush California*. Berkeley: University of California Press, 2000.

Stillson, Richard T. *Spreading the Word: A History of Information in the California Gold Rush*. Lincoln: University of Nebraska Press, 2006.

Trafzer, Clifford E., and Joel R. Hyer. *Exterminate Them!: Written Accounts of the Murder, Rape, and Slavery of Native Americans during the California Gold Rush, 1848–1868*. East Lansing: Michigan State University Press, 1999.

Tye Farkas, Lani Ah. *Bury My Bones in America: The Saga of a Chinese Family in California from San Francisco to the Sierra Gold Mines*. Nevada City, CA: Carl Mautz Pub., 1998.

Walker, Dale L. *Eldorado: The California Gold Rush*. New York: Forge, 2003.

Wheeler, Richard S. *Sierra: A Novel of the California Gold Rush*. New York: Forge, 1996.

Windeler, Adolphus, and W. Turrentine Jackson. *The California Gold Rush Diary of a German Sailor*. Berkeley: Howell-North Books, 1969.

INDEX

About the Author

THOMAS MAXWELL-LONG is the coordinator of public history and museum studies and associate professor of history at California State University, San Bernardino, and is the author of five other books, including *Watergate and the Resignation of Richard Nixon* with Harry P. Jeffrey and *Recent America: The United States since 1945* with Dewey Grantham.